bloodbeats: vol.1

bloodbeats: vol.1
demos, remixes & extended versions

ernest hardy

◊REDBONE PRESS
www.redbonepress.com

Blood Beats: Vol. 1
Demos, Remixes & Extended Versions

Published by:
RedBone Press
P.O. Box 15571
Washington, DC 20003

Portions of this book originally appeared in the *LA Weekly*.

10 09 08 07 06   10 9 8 7 6 5 4 3 2 1

First edition

Cover photo copyright © 2006 by Alex Demyanenko
Cover design by E.M. Corbin
Logo design by Mignon Goode

Printed in the United States of America

ISBN-13: 978-0-9656659-8-8
ISBN-10: 0-9656659-8-4

www.redbonepress.com

This book is dedicated to the memories of

Dianna J. Hardy
Ernest C. Hardy Sr.
Irie Lessie Perkins
Rosa Hardy
Robert Hardy Sr.
Leslie Perkins
Richard Perkins

thank yous and acknowledgments

THANK YOU:

Ben Adair, Donnell Alexander, Lorraine Ali, Shawn Amos, Ron Athey, Erin Aubry, Elizabeth Mendez Berry, Nathan Brackett, Dale Brasel, Greg Burk, Steven W. Burt, Sonya Chi, **Alex Demyanenko,** Joe Donnelly, Jack Curtis Dubowsky, Hazel Dawn Dumpert, Ben Ehrenreich, Scott Foundas, Shari Frilot, David Hansor, Hilary Hart, Monica Hernandez, Dylan Hicks, Jim Hubbard, Diane Hurd, Jerome Joseph, Ellen Krout-Hasegawa, Joe Lee, Kristi Lomax, Joe Loya, Paul Malcolm, Jordan Moore, Lisa Moore, Rhonda Murphy, Mimi McCormick, Jim Nicola, Eve Oishi, John Payne, Ben Quinones, Ron Stringer, Kate Sullivan, Ella Taylor, Delores Taylor Walls, Chuck Wilson, Connie Young, Kimberly Yutani.

THE HEROES AND HEROINES:

Dorothy Allison, Pedro Almodóvar, Erykah Badu, James Baldwin, Jean-Michel Basquiat, Andy Bey, Kristen Bjorn, Donald Bogle, Octavia Butler, Jean-Daniel Cadinot, Don Cheadle, Countee Cullen, Manohla Dargis, Angela Davis, Miles Davis, Claire Denis, Electrifyin' Mojo, Nikki Giovanni, Aretha Franklin, Herbie Hancock, Dianna Hardy, Essex Hemphill, Kim Hill, Lauryn Hill, Billie Holiday, Shirley Horn, Lena Horne, Langston Hughes, Frenchy Hodges, Diane Hurd, Zora Neale Hurston, Derek Jarman, Chaka Khan, Martin Luther King, Gladys Knight, Frankie Knuckles, Spike Lee, Audre Lorde, David Morales, Toni Morrison, Meshell NdegeOcello, Huey P. Newton, Prince, Marlon Riggs, Diana Ross, Bayard Rustin, Sarah Schulman, Pamela Sneed, Billy Strayhorn, Sylvester, Greg Tate, Wallace Thurman, Wong Kar Wai, Jeffrey Wright, Malcolm X, Ledisi Young, Howard Zinn.

THE BLOOD FOLK THAT SUSTAIN ME:

Edna Spotser, Robbie Joan Perkins, John and Edna Perkins, Harriett Perkins, Lesley Daniel & Family, Terrence Perkins, Sheldon Perkins & Family, Juanita Poole, Laura Poole & Family, the Rollins Family, the Hardy family.

THE FAMILY THAT CHOSE ME:

Billbrown (*my ace boon coon and beyond-brother*), Dennis Casey (*yo, Duh-NEE...*), Brett Collins (*"Nothing's gonna take you awaaay..."*), Ofelia Cuefas, Vaginal Davis (*"Well, of course I stand in judgment!"*), Jeff Forman (*hey, maaaaaan*), Ngozi Inyama (*poverty aside, are you doing anything fun?*), David Marine (*"a defector from the petty wars..."*), Lainie Nakai (*I got the pow-wah!*), Joshua Nouril (*my Persian son*), Lisa Rosen (*"through the fire..."*), Alfonso F. Ruiz (*mi hermano por la vida*), Jason Van Veen (*tha brotha from anutha mutha*), Jason Vance (*"Pancakes!"*), Marvin K. White (*Lord, THAT chile...*), Antony Yee, John Young.

This book was made possible in part by grants from the Sundance Institute and the A. Ruiz Trust.

contents

bonus disc

sampled slips remixed
(TESTING, TESTING, 1, 2, TESTING)

Hip-hop *is* America. Its only real crime is being so much so. It boils "mainstream" standards and practices down to their essences, then turns up the flame. Violence, materialism, misogyny, homophobia, racialized agony, adolescent views on sex and sexuality... These are the common, bankable themes in mainstream hip-hop because these are the common, bankable, all-American obsessions. They're the underbelly items that have always defined this country's real, daily-life culture. What that means is that top-of-the-line hip-hop and its true *artists* (be they "mainstream" or "underground") soar on the same terms that America's real artists—and everyday folk—have always soared: by being *un*-American, by flying in the face of the fucked-up values and ideals that are wired and corroded in this country's genetic code even as no-lip lip-service is given to notions of equality, justice and fairness. They soar by actually struggling to embody and celebrate life, liberty and the pursuit of happiness, even though those ideals were really only ever meant to be accessible by a privileged few. And niggers were never ever meant to be part of the smart-shoppers crowd. (*Year-end wrap-up;* LA Weekly, *December 1998; see page 87*)

<snip>
Criticism for me has always been rooted in the very personal impulse,
<snip>

You don't need to be a student of sociology or psychology to realize that much of the turmoil that has enveloped the globe over the last few years is simply due to ever intensifying questions of identity: What does it mean to be Christian, Muslim or Jew? To be black, white, Asian or Latino? Gay/lesbian, straight or bi? To be atheist or devout believer, capitalist or socialist? What does it mean to be an American? Lying at the crux of many of these questions is the rhetorical equivalent of a lit match tossed on spilled gasoline: What does it mean to be a man? For over a hundred years now, the movies have played a huge role in answering that last question, in shaping and defining masculinity. Templates created by mainstream, box-office hits are then challenged or subverted (or merely reinforced) by indie, art-house and underground cinematic treatises. Notions of machismo and masculine honor feed and sustain themselves across national borders as inner-city kids in America consume images of martial arts warriors shipped from clear across the globe, as Mexican youth take in the cross-genre film-sampling of Quentin Tarantino for representation of north-of-the-border male cool. It's all part of the never-ending quest to bottle that fragile, intractable, elusive, intimidating, daunting definition of a *man*. (*Flaunt Magazine* DVD column; Men's Issue, Feb. 2005)

> <snip>
> **and the art I have been most viscerally drawn to (and that which has inspired what I think is my strongest writing)**
> <snip>

Long before the Internet and multi-media corporations made it too easy for a movie or pop star to rule the world, long before Madonna and Lil' Kim pushed the envelope of sexual imagery, and eons before Angelina Jolie crafted a fledgling rainbow tribe from impoverished nations, Josephine Baker—the barely literate daughter of a St. Louis washerwoman—did all of the above. Now a symbol of international glamour and the patron saint of expatriated black artists, Josephine Baker made her name in provocative, controversial, risqué theater fare that juggled the avant-garde with tricky, resilient and profitable racial stereotypes. Her filmography only captures some of her far-flung talent. While the three recently released DVD titles—*Siren of the Tropics; Princess Tam Tam and Zou Zou*—are as delightful (check the ecstatic Charleston that Baker dances at the end of *Tropics*) as they are problematic (the same trope—savage native-girl falls in ill-fated love with a white Frenchman—repeats in every film), the real value lies in the DVD bonus materials. There, the icon's adopted son Jean-Claude Baker, actress Lynn

Whitfield (HBO's *The Josephine Baker Story*), *The New York Times* theater critic Margo Jefferson and dance critic/historian Elizabeth Kendall break La Baker into three categories—the woman, the stage performer and movie star, the cultural icon—and offer anecdotal and analytical information that humanizes her while deepening her mythology. (*Flaunt Magazine* DVD column, September 2005)

<snip>
has been that which wrestled with the questions that have plagued me since adolescence, having to do with issues of race and class and sexuality,
<snip>

What I love about Jean-Michel Basquiat's work, even when I don't actually *like* it, is that it is a struggle for new language in the effort to overthrow… everything. But it also hums a slivered craving for validation from that which it claims and seeks to challenge. When your life is not valued, when you are shoved to the margins, the art you create to reflect who you are and what you experience of the world might likely be a howl of protest against the so-called norm; the howl may be violent or deceptively soothing. To those who are not tone deaf, it will be both at once. And those with perfect pitch might also detect the subtle attempt to harmonize with the status quo.

Your life doesn't align with that which is valued and elevated, so why would or should you create along lines and formulas that exist to exclude you? Your creativity manifests along the same lines of your life and experiences. You need new language.

Here's the paradox: Basquiat's work was about exploding formula and convention, about harnessing the energy and vision of the street (low culture) even as he was a serious and learned student of the masters (high culture) with whom he wanted to be counted. His calling was to create art along the same grids he lived his life – chaotic, beautiful, overwhelmed with information and history, full of humor and biting wit. High culture and low, effortlessly intermingled. The historically correct manifestation of niggerdom.

The vitality and energy of so many of the works was staggering. The depth of captured emotion and unfettered intellect, the unstoppable flow of ideas that float off the canvases with so much power that it's almost overwhelming.

Most artistic and cultural "norms" are about gatekeeping as much—if not more—than they are about actual quality. The powerful institutions that house, support, legitimize and critique art and artists are created around ideas and language that cradle some bodies while marginalizing others. On the surface, this makes perfect sense. It's called standards, refined aesthetics. Less cool is the fact that it's also about codifying lives, experiences, culture and comfort zones of the dominant cultural or political class while keeping *others* in their place, forcing them to jump through hoops or chase the dangled carrot of validation.

When you are the one marginalized and you struggle to represent self and experiences, you can either do so by funneling your shit through the vocab and paradigms that have been historically set in place and elevated (and, in doing so, you effectively reinforce the primacy and superiority of the dominant/established order) or you struggle to create new models, thereby not only challenging but even mocking or dismissing the accepted model which likewise dismisses you. You may not create beauty, you may not create lasting "art" but you forge a new tongue, force a new way of looking and interpreting—a new value system. The power of Basquiat's work, its almost palpable life force, is its rail against... everything you thought you knew.

Juxtaposed against and in tandem with the work of Josephine Baker, Basquiat's work underscores the flip-side-of-the-same-coin nature of Negro primitivism and the Negro avant-garde, the discomfiting and the reassuring, the clichéd and the visionary, the raw sexual outlaw and the forward-pushing artist, the instinctual sensualist and the nuanced artist/intellectual... (*Rough and admittedly repetitive notes I scribbled in the margins of the program as I walked through the Los Angeles Museum of Contemporary Art's Basquiat exhibit; August 13, 2005*)

<snip>
having to do with the ways that pop culture reflects and shapes the realities and dreams of the audience, but also how people construct themselves from the cultural

artifacts they are sold (movies, music, TV, radio, music videos.)
<snip>

The metaphorical black body is always splayed and cut open on the cultural coroner's table—nude, insides spilling onto the floor, blood dripping, bowels exposed. All our secrets, the many enclaves of blackness—from the nether regions of 'hood life to the little-examined realities of the Negro elite—are scooped out and placed into jars, to be catalogued and studied. Theorized and sold. And the experiences that are wrung from the organs, the bones, the skin and the flesh become metaphors for other people's experiences, tools for them to expand their own consciousness, models for their salvation. (*Some random shit that floated into my mind as I was assembling this book.*)

<snip>
I'm just trying to figure shit out for self, then share whatever I deduct just in case it might be of interest or value to someone else.
<snip>

We all receive the same lessons, the same information. People have a way of contouring consciousness along their very specific identity outlines and not pushing much beyond the borders. They might realize—if they do the work, if they truly fight the power and don't simply relax their gag reflex—that much of what the cultural-corporate-political apparatus propagates about them is untrue. Yet many seem completely at ease accepting the distortions and misrepresentations of (other) others as being absolute truth. We'd like to believe that the cross-pollination of cultures that hip-hop represents and sparks, and that globalization and unbridled capitalism use as their selling points, will forge new mind-sets, new perspectives. But without doing the hard work of pushing past prejudice, of refraining from the battle of *my imaginary friend in the sky can kick the ass of your imaginary friend in the sky,* of doing more than uncritically embracing fucked-up cultural habits and justifying them as tradition, all the cultural consumption is just this—fleeting blood beats: vol. 1

fashion, disposable music, fucking across color lines and confusing cum with consciousness... (*Some more random shit that came to mind as I was assembling this book.*)

A friend recently sent me an e-mail link to a personals ad on Craig's List. The header and body read:

RACE PLAY – BLACK MAN SEEKS WHITE OR NON-BLACK PARTNER 4 DOM/RACE PLAY

Good looking, healthy, fit, smooth and muscular 33-year-old black man seeks white (preferred) or non-black partner to engage in intense race play. Scenarios include racial slurs, humiliation and dominance. Light bondage okay. Toys and light spanking. Master/slave set-up. Experienced or novice. I want to be controlled and humiliated. Not looking for a lot of back and forth in an email chain. Serious only. If this is not your thing or it offends you, just click the next ad and move on. Not interested in negative commentary. Thanks.

My friend was apoplectic. "What the fuck is this?!" he wrote beneath the link. "What is wrong with my people? This nigga [*Oh, the irony, the **eye-row-knee**!—EH*] gonna actually set up a situation where he LETS some white boy [metaphorically] shit on him? Call him nigger? BEAT his ass? And this nigga is the one asking for this shit? He's the one setting it up? What the FUCK is THIS?"

"Twenty-first century hip-hop?" I offered.

—*Ernest Hardy*
March 22, 2006

"The best advice I ever got was from an old friend of mine,
a Black friend, who said
you have to go the way your blood beats."
—*James Baldwin*

no fear
ME'SHELL NDEGÉOCELLO'S *PEACE* BY PIECES

When Me'Shell NdegéOcello toured behind her 1994 debut album, *Plantation Lullabies,* press reports painted her susceptible to the mood indigo. Critical praise for the show was tempered by footnotes claiming the bassist/singer was an unwavering perfectionist—easy target for the flat note or missed cue. When she played the Roxy here in L.A., she cringed at mistakes that only she heard, rolling her eyes, pursing her lips, furrowing her brow. It was hard to tell how much her disconnect was due to genuine fuck-ups and how much was fueled by the thorny nature of her material.

Plantation is a captivating series of color snapshots reflecting various shades of inner-city blue. It was the hip-hop/R&B fix so many black folks have been jonesing for, though most of them slept on it. Deceptively airy love songs and scathing social commentary darted in and out of each other. Art was imposed on—and meaning found within—the relentless upheaval of black life. Racism, romantic obsession, self-hatred and ghetto escapism were themes that drove the wagon.

Being immersed every night in the tense urban poetry of *Plantation* would scrape anyone's emotions raw, and by the time the tour was over, NdegéOcello (then recovering from drug addiction) was worn down by industry and media politics. The [white] gay press was especially hard on her, taking the bisexual singer to task for singing love songs to men. Although she was nominated for a Grammy, married her girlfriend and made pop-chart headway with a John Mellencamp duet, she was suicidal. A conversion to Islam turned everything around; it focused her life and renewed her dedication to both her partner and her son, Askia.

But a listen to her new album, *Peace Beyond Passion,* proves that NdegéOcello is still far from a tranquil soul. If *Plantation* was a series of staggering photographs, *Peace* is a niggafied art film shot in black and white. Jazz and hip-hop feed the score. It's a gospel album that challenges Christianity's saving power of a "pretty white Jesus." Where *Plantation* noted that white folks "enslave all in God's name," *Peace,* in tackling homophobia, abusive fathers and aloof mothers, owns up to how black folks do, too. It's a set of love songs where need, desire and insecurities are stripped to their grasping essences, then rendered in deep, sensuous grooves that cup a voice that's like black coffee, served both scalding and iced.

Clad in Dickies, a striped shirt and work boots, NdegéOcello sits warily in Chado, a teahouse near the Beverly Center. Linen napkins and heavy silverware lie before her; classical music plays softly in the background. Smaller than she appears in photographs, she's warm but shy. Me'Shell is not a big fan of the press.

Where do you put the frustration of opening up a magazine, reading something attributed to you, and saying...

..."I didn't say that." [*Smiles.*] That's funny. There's a lot of that in there [*nods to a copy of* Out *magazine that lies nearby.*] I'm like, "Your [the *Out* reporter's] tape recorder must be faulty." He hurt my feelings. I thought he was a pretty cool guy. You know, I'm a touchy-feely kinda person and he said I was trying too hard. Has the world become so jaded that showing a little affection means I'm trying too hard? I don't mean to be highbrow, but maybe he wasn't that great a writer. 'Cause I read the article, and he starts it off with "Niggers don't sell." He gave no one anything before that—no context. And he paraphrased me incorrectly.

I told the writer of the *Billboard* piece that, last tour, I was recovering from being on drugs. When I was onstage and playing, I'd have this tremendous high; afterward, I'd be down. I told him it felt just like being a drug addict. He put in there that I got high every night.

In concert a few weeks ago, you said you initially thought *Peace* was less angry than *Plantation,* but now you're not sure. The difference between the two seems like the difference between an angry 30-year-old and an angry 15-year-old. Not that *Plantation* isn't a mature work.

No, I know what you mean. I wrote a lot of *Plantation* when I was 18 to 23. I'm maturing. I'm different. I really feel this is my last Me'Shell record. I don't even want to do this anymore.

Will you make music in some other incarnation?

Yeah. I think I'll join a band or something. Maybe disappear for a while. It's time for Me'Shell's passing away.

I wrote some notes on *Peace* that I want to read to you: "Although the album's title is *Peace Beyond Passion*, the vibe it most consistently evokes is a post-suicidal stillness, a state that might be mistaken for peace by the protagonist and those around her. The pain might be calmed, but it's not gone. The desire to blast herself out of existence might have subsided, but there is still the desire for relief, and release. There's wariness and desperation; there's anger. But there's also the battle-scarred knowledge that those fleeting moments of happiness—a mother's smile, a lover's kiss—are what sustain us. *Peace* outlines the journey toward peace but it's not a peaceful journey; there's no fake happy ending."

[*Smiles and nods.*] Yeah. I mean, that's good.

In a recent interview, you said you thought fame would solve everything for you, but it turned out not to solve anything.

I thought making a record would make everything hunky-dory. I thought I would see myself differently. That was a big ol' joke.

What didn't fame solve for you?

Actually, I didn't get that famous; that was a good lesson for me. But I just realized, I go home, I gotta wash my clothes, I gotta take care of my son, I gotta try to maintain a relationship. I'm still bearing the wounds of [*mock dramatically*]

Why don't my parents love me? That's the reality.

Someone close to you was quoted as saying your mouth was your biggest strength and biggest weakness.

Mm-hm. [Her life-partner] Winnie said that. That's the truth. I'm very volatile. Visceral. I say what's on my mind at the time. And that's not always good.

That brings to mind another quote where you said that if people try to destroy you because of what you say, then that...

...simply proves everything I've been saying. I have no fear. I feel like Allah has painted this path for me, and I have to go down it. There's so much power in releasing fear. I mean, I fear death a little bit but I fear none of this [*nods toward the street*]. I fear absolutely nothing.

The mainstream gay press has gotten used to celebrities kissing its ass. It's a perverse, constant shifting of roles and power in which the white, upper-middle-class queer establishment grovels for validation while bestowing upon said celebrities the mantle of liberal coolness—a mutual jack-off fantasy in which the fluid exchanged is that of rare privilege. Both that process and the queer world that feeds it are irrelevant to a young generation of gay, bi and lesbian folks of color. NdegéOcello, like many of this generation, uses "gay" to mean white, gay male aesthetic and perspective. Openly bisexual, she feels little connection with the gay community.

After *Plantation* came out, the gay press really went after you. Were you surprised by the attack?

Oh, yeah. Gay men kill me. They think I'm homophobic, which is absolutely far-fetched. I said to that guy from *Out*, I was like, y'all can kiss my ass. I thought it was really funny that you had this guy critique my person—not my music—and expect me to be all hunky-dory about this interview. It's like you're at this huge BYOB dinner and everybody brings something different. If you don't want to drink it, that doesn't mean you have to turn up your nose, like, "Oh I can't *believe* she brought that." That's how I feel with gay men and their reaction to me. I like men; I have to raise one. And that writer had a problem with the fact that I sang to men on my album.

In the June 3 *New York* magazine, the cover story is titled "Feminism Rocks." Flipping through the piece, though, it's like roll call at a white girls' sorority: Alanis Morrisette, Courtney Love, PJ Harvey, Tori Amos... There's no mention of Me'Shell, Dionne Farris, Skin [from the U.K. band Skunk Anansie]...

It's 'cause we're not white, bud. Where you been? I'm not an angry white female. That's the bottom line. What's funny is, they won't play a song like [*Peace's* first single] "Leviticus: Faggot," but they'll play Alanis talking about giving a guy head. I'm telling you, if I were white... That's why I'm gonna start jumpin' up and down onstage when I perform. [*Laughs.*] You know how Metallica cut their hair off? I'm gon' grow mine so I can toss it.

I'm not a feminist. I'm more on the humanist vibe. One of the failures of feminism is, they don't know it's not about climbing the corporate ladder. The real world is: I had a baby, the guy's not taking care of it and I'm on welfare. To me, it's about those issues and Medicare and how capitalism is a bitch. It's connected to the larger workings of society but people don't wanna see that.

Let's talk about the image of contemporary black women. Your new album is filled with asides that contain whole stories in themselves, like the one in "Deuteronomy: Niggerman" where you say, "My image of self was that of the divine ho / like the ones portrayed on the white-man-colonized-minded rap shows." Nowadays, it's either ghetto hos or elevated light skin and good hair—closet whiteness.

Yeah, I have a line in a poem I just wrote where I say, "Just like every black revolutionary, I'll marry a white woman." There's nothing wrong with that but I just find it ironic… But then, too many black women are into "I gotta get a brother who got bank." I don't understand when that happened to us.

Black folks have been conned into thinking getting paid is the revolutionary act.

That ain't the revolution. People totally assess themselves by what they have. When did this happen to black folks?

What is your relationship to the black community?

We don't have a *relationship;* I'm a part of it. That's been the hardest part. One time my label said to me, maybe you'd have sold more records to a black audience if you hadn't come out. Well, I was never in. It hurts my feelings that my brothers and sisters think like that. I do black music. I make music to tell my people about a little part of my world. Jimi Hendrix's greatest torment was that his own people didn't like his music. I'll probably die the same way, knowing I'm not embraced by my own. So I'm gonna be as loud and as clear as possible: Brothers and sisters, if you forsake me, I will have no one.

Do you have a safety net in place if they do forsake you?

Yes. Allah. Allah is my safety net.

LA Weekly, August 2, 1996

do thug niggaz go to heaven?
TUPAC SHAKUR, 1971—1996

"What happened that they would forsake their lives just to be hip? To be this pathetic gangster? I love Tupac with all my heart. Every time I'm with him, he's probably the sweetest guy I know – the sweetest guy I ever met in my life. But then I go, Is he just doing this other stuff as a front? I mean, when did all that become so glamorous? I don't get it."

—Me'Shell NdegéOcello,
from an interview I conducted earlier this year.

My one encounter with Tupac Shakur occurred a few years ago. He was walking by himself down Sunset, shortly after one of his first run-ins with the law. As we headed toward one another, he locked his jaw, cocked his head up and to the side, and gave me that patented daggers-in-the-eyes look that black men reserve just for one another. I feigned nonchalance and looked over his shoulder. He kept his eyes trained on me as we brushed past one another. After he passed, I turned around to see where he was headed; his whole demeanor had changed. His head hung forward, his shoulders slumped, and his clothes swallowed him. He must have felt me watching, because he turned around quickly, but forgot to put the mask back on. His face was the one that he once told *Vibe* had gotten him teased mercilessly by his cousins when he was growing up: pretty, almost girlish, and unguarded. He seemed tired. He quickly swung back around and made his way down the street. I was shocked at how small he seemed.

A lot of Tupac's harshest critics dismissed him as a studio gangster, a Hollywood concoction. But that's what made him, arguably, one of the most important figures in hip-hop. (In hip-hop, as with every pop-culture borough, "good" and "important" aren't necessarily the same thing.) Tupac was, at best, an average rapper who willed himself into iconic status. What made him important and forged a bond with so many of his young (especially black male) fans was that he was a signifier trying to figure out what he signified. He knew he lived in a society that still didn't view him as human, that projected its worst fears onto him; he had to decide whether to battle that or to embrace it. Embracing it gets you acknowledged; embracing it gets you paid. But where his detractors sneered at the *pose*, I suspect a lot of his fans identified with it. Even black folks don't wanna know you if you're not playing the part.

The problem is, it's an impossible game to win. You assume the role prescribed and then spend all your energy trying to convince yourself and the world that you're "real." You reach a point where you no longer know what goals, desires and realities are your own and which have simply been dictated to you. That created a tension in Tupac's work, marking him as a phony to some, a symbol of larger struggles and questions to others. It also created a gap, a narrow but crucial area, where the mask slipped away from the real "real" man. Ironically, this is where his best known tracks, the tender "Keep Ya Head Up" and "Dear Mama" spring from. The most fascinating thing about Tupac was watching him juggle the illusion he was trying to sell with the many lives he tried to lead.

Tupac's choices brought him unnecessary tragedy and grief. He ultimately has to take responsibility for the script he wrote with his life. But he should be cut a little slack; it has to be noted that he improvised as he went, awkwardly and clumsily embracing authenticity clichés because he had little proof that his existence would be recognized otherwise. A lot of us watched him "act out" not because we were fans of the music and not because we bought the crude gangsta myth that was being constructed, but because we suspected there was someone more complex, more interesting and even more talented beneath the poses and tattoos. We're saddened not because the world has lost a great rapper (it hasn't), but because the battles and conflicts embodied in Tupac's career and life have ended in a too-familiar hail of gunfire. And the message he leaves behind in his failure to become a conqueror—and not a victim—of the myths of black manhood is depressing beyond words.

LA Weekly, September 20, 1996

devil's helper
TRICKY: BETWEEN A ROCK AND A HARD PLACE

Tricky's muse is a pissed-off, misanthropic hermaphrodite: black skin inked with red and purple hues, kinky hair coiled tightly to the scalp, clenched fists folding—what?—in the palm of her hands, *eau de ganja* wafting off a thin, wiry body. In Tricky's world, testosterone and estrogen are ladled out in equal measure. Feminine strength is a given, as is female rage—and male vulnerability. (Male rage is, of course, oxygen.) But this isn't the threat-free androgyny hawked by Madison Avenue, edges smoothed out for mass consumption. Tricky's divine *homme/femme* lives in the creases, at points of fracture.

Within the man himself, that chaos means someone uncomfortable both in his own skin and the world around him, someone who crosses all sorts of racial, sexual and gender lines while fitting in nowhere, misunderstood even by those who champion him. Beneath the groundbreaking slow beats, the thrashed genres and philosophies, lies a heart that beats to cliché: Tricky, the cynic, is a profoundly disillusioned idealist. He's hardcore because he feels so much.

"I don't like the human race as such," Tricky's been quoted as saying. "We're a bunch of horrible fucking creatures... [Making music] is my way of taking revenge on people without murdering them." That misanthropy, and the wrenching self-loathing that flows from it, are the primal forces behind Tricky's aural assaults, yet they were rarely commented on by critics assessing his 1995 solo debut, *Maxinquaye*. The disc's technical wizardry and surface readings of its bleak, darkly humorous lyrics were offered in proof of the album's undeniable brilliance. Tricky's brooding sexiness was underreported, as was the genderfuck in both his lyrics and image; the sheer sadness that permeates the record was virtually ignored, despite the blue-funk moments such as Martine (Tricky's co-vocalist) citing Paul Laurence Dunbar via Maya Angelou, crooning matter-of-factly, "I know why the caged bird sings/I know why..." The media hype machine dammed up Tricky's dark currents, reduced them to Vedder/Reznor-style Nuggets McAngst. Crowned the king of "trip-hop," Tricky was dubbed one of the saviors of the why-the-fuck-won't-it-just-die-and-stay-dead corpse of rock 'n' roll. But that's an appointment he doesn't want, a misunderstanding that his two side projects, *Nearly God* (Durban Poison/Island) and *Tricky Presents Grassroots* (Payday/FFRR) are meant to clear up.

"Trip-hop is just hip-hop with black people taken out…"
—Crack MC

Rock critics have embraced *Nearly God* a lot more warmly than they have *Grassroots,* and that's understandable. It's more easily read as artsy and experimental, therefore "daring." It don't be havin' so much 'dentifiable nigga in it. The truth, though, is that the two discs are of a piece, complementing and commenting on one another. Recorded in just under three weeks and summarized by Tricky as "like a bunch of demos," *Nearly God* is the more predictable of the two. Its chamber-of-horrors sound, the subtle and graceful melting of industrial/hip-hop/blues/dub/goth strokes into a bubbling vat of neuroses, is a natural offshoot of *Maxinquaye*. Not quite as polished as its predecessor, *Nearly God* is a completely wired "unplugged" album in which all involved strip and submit to Tricky's machinations. (Guests include Björk, Neneh Cherry, Alison Moyet, Cath Coffey of Stereo MCs and Terry Hall of The Specials.) Sick-fuck relationships rife with threats and pleas, accusations and apologies are played out against strings and discordant wheezing noises. On "I Be the Prophet," a mournful cello and upright bass collapse onto one another, ebb and flow against lines first mumbled by Tricky, then sung by Martine: "Would you like to ride on my train / Would you drink from my vein?" Repetitious electronic clanging and submerged strings on "Make a Change" set off Alison Moyet's white girl soul wail, a potent reminder of how she once sparked the cold, technoid grooves of Yaz into flaming blues. "Keep Your Mouth Shut," a duet with Björk, turns chilling when it juxtaposes snatches of "You've Been Flirting Again," from Björk's new album *Debut,* with newly-penned lyrics by Tricky. Björk's vocals float beneath murk in this mix, her sighing "All that she meant was good" met by Tricky's "Better keep your mouth closed, baby

/ keep it close to your chest." And Terry Hall, coolly androgynous on "Poems," intones, "I rue the day that I ever met you / I deeply regret you... getting close to me / I can't wait to deeply neglect you, deeply forget you."

The standout performance, though, comes from Martine, hitching Billie Holiday to Patsy Cline on the staggering "Black Coffee": "I feel so lonely, I haven't slept... / I walk the floor, watch the door and in between drink black coffee / I'm talking to the shadows from 1 to 4... all I do is pour black coffee since the blues caught my eye."

Technology makes it possible for Tricky to erect and steady a frame while wrecking shit inside that frame. He takes familiar images (i.e., sounds) and splatters them, etching his name into someone else's mundane handiwork and transforming it altogether. He doesn't play an instrument, doesn't read music and has no respect for the sacredness of genre. He knows that the only real value rock 'n' roll has at this point is as raw material to be sampled and carved into something relevant (a point driven home on the guitar-feedback-driven *Pre-Millenium Tension,* his proper follow-up to *Maxinquaye* that's due later this year). Ditto R&B.

On the five-track EP *Tricky Presents Grassroots,* he turns to the withered remains of American soul music and the cliché-ridden world of rap, drizzling their conventional textures with his own juices. He takes the generic bravado of the Hillfiguzes' flow on "Heaven, Youth Hell" and sets it in a brooding groove, providing the menace that the rappers' posturing can't. In the sparse "Devil's Helper," measured, prominent bass lines parallel Laveda Davis' smoky vocals, coming down to a duet between the singer and the boulder-heavy bottom. "Do you get an erection / when you look at your own reflection?" asks the honey-voiced Stephanie Cook on the smoldering "Live W/ Yo Self," her sweetly bared fangs obliterating R&B credit-card divas who do fashion layouts for *Vibe.*

In tandem, *Nearly God* and *Grassroots* are a map through the myriad tunnels into Tricky's aesthetic psyche. Both discs react to the perceptions and agendas projected onto him by the rock critics and "alternative music" fans who embraced him initially. The two efforts have to be taken together in order for the refutation to be successful. When the two works are heard as a whole, Tricky pulls off the feat of self-(re)definition that De La Soul has been grappling with ever since "Me Myself and I" made them alterna-negro posterboys.

Tightly controlled studio genius is the bridge between *Nearly God* and *Grassroots,* firmly guiding the listener backward from those apparently dueling ends to the middle ground of common influences, ensuring that musical shifts and hybrids are subtle and gently manipulated, resulting in a kind of logic when seemingly conflicting sources are combined or merely juxtaposed.

The most fascinating of those conflicts, though, aren't necessarily musical; they're in the conjoining of madness and sadness, machismo and vulnerability. They're in the way the female voices whisper, growl and belt against the jagged musical landscape Tricky creates, carrying the weight of his demons and fantasies, while his own mumbling, sneering vocals play Greek chorus. The end result is a whole—and wholly fucked-up— human being drifting in agitation from your speakers.

LA Weekly, October 4, 1996

i, amazon
QUEEN LATIFAH SPEAKS

"Cleo's what you might call an aggressive lesbian," laughs Queen Latifah, speaking by phone from New York. "A big ol' dyke, you know what I mean?"

As played by Latifah, Cleo walks away with *Set It Off.* Swigging from bottles of tequila, crowned with a head of tightly woven cornrows and doing a modified pimp-stroll in sagging overalls, she's the movie's hypnotic bass line in a quartet of archetypal 'hood women. It's Cleo, though, who lingers. Latifah has a staggering screen presence. From the moment we first glimpse her—shades riding low on her nose and cigarette dangling from the corner of her mouth—she's using large and small brush strokes to sketch the character. Cleo's the most unlikely of screen heroines: an unabashedly butch ghetto dyke. "Next time I page you," she tells her gorgeous girl-toy, "you better be calling me back."

Cleo's rage simmers rather than roils; its causes are so specific they've become abstract and, paradoxically, almost intangible: the crowded housing project the friends all live in, the shitty jobs they hold, the bursts of gunfire that open the movie, turn its plot and then end it. It's the daily grind called "just life" that leaves the interrogated proletariat speechless when asked what's their fucking problem. It's the bleak prospects for improvement.

Latifah graces Cleo with layers of subtlety that let both the film's heart and socio-political agenda easily exist within the character. Fans who've followed the rapper-turned-actress-turned-entertainment-mogul since her debut album, *All Hail the Queen*, are familiar with that two-pronged approach. But even those who've grooved to her portrayals of a successful magazine editor on *Living Single* and pissed-off waitress in *Jungle Fever*, as well as to her primary calling as a trailblazing womanist rapper ("Ladies First," "U.N.I.T.Y") will be blown away by her performance. *Set It Off* and some of the actors in it occasionally wobble; Latifah never does.

"Blood, sweat and tears went into this movie," says Latifah. "I definitely wanted to give it my all. I hired an acting coach, and we did a lot, lot, lot of work. The hardest thing was to strip away all traces of femininity while also making sure that you got to see her as a human. I wanted people to connect with her on a basic human level."

That connection is forged by making the character an unapologetic 'hood rat. When the group decides to start robbing banks, it's Cleo who acquires the weapons from ghetto don Black Sam (played by Dr. Dre). She's allowed inside the decidedly male lair because she's proven herself on Black Sam's terms, working for him, stealing cars and taking blows—going through the rituals like one of the boys.

"Yeah," agrees Latifah, "she's tough, she's strong. I didn't play her like a man, 'cause that's not who she is. She's a woman who's proven herself in certain ways." When asked how she prepared for the role, the 26-year-old actress laughs softly. "I just went to a couple of clubs. I watched the boys in the family; I watched the hard girls and how they handled their girlfriends. I studied the way they walked, the way they wore their hair, the mannerisms. I wore men's briefs. I went all-out. I went to an Army/Navy store and bought boots, Dickies jeans, men's Fruit of the Looms with the blue and gold stripes—I went the whole nine."

In playing Cleo, Latifah stirs anew questions about her own sexuality; the question is, has she figured out a response for inquiring minds?

"No, I haven't," she says sweetly. "I really haven't."

LA Weekly, November 15, 1996

nouveau negro valentine
HAVING A JONES FOR *LOVE JONES*

Neither documentary nor rap star vehicle, the true hip-hop film would be some hypnotically surreal shit. It would be a world where comic-book heroes, Afro-American icons and a filmmaker's own biography fuse into opposing, crisscrossing and ultimately harmonious narratives. Tragedy and comedy would be interchangeable. Elements of horror and slapstick would be the rouge in this quasi-documentary. And the soundtrack—that hook, bait and ultimate marketing tool—would alternate tracks of mad beats with long, long stretches of silence. The films now sold as hip-hop flicks have been grotesquely flattened, distorted versions of blackness, 'hood tales revolving around boys with guns. Not just too literal, the films have been too narrow, close neither to the letter nor the spirit of real hip-hop, which is about endless possibilities—open ends that lend themselves to myriad interpretations.

We are already in the age of the post-hip-hop film, without the definitive hip-hop flick having been made.

Love Jones is a post-hip-hop movie, a Nouveau Negro valentine. It drops on the here and now because the world, especially and obviously that of black folks, is starved for more fluid definitions and broader representations of Negritude. Spike Lee may have gotten the ball rolling, but a lot of us expected hip-hop itself to impact Hollywood's depictions of blacks more radically. It failed because the culture was hijacked, the revolutionary potential thwarted. The outer boroughs of the music industry wised up to this fact first (of course), moving on to a pool of artists who were both retro and ground-breaking, artists who drew hungrily from the past in order to reshape blackness and black art for the present. Ironically, by returning to the R&B and black pop sounds of the late '60s and '70s, these artists have tapped into a vibe of familiarity that gives them enormous crossover appeal. *Love Jones* is both beneficiary and reflector of this latest shift in black culture. Paradox: This film is so relentlessly and unapologetically black that it's universal.

Set in a world of black poets, artists and bohemians, *Love*

Jones boasts a soundtrack full of Negroes deemed "alternative" by the media and entertainment industries, whose worldwide pimps continue to view black folk as the ultimate exotica. And make no mistake, the film's soundtrack is crucial. Its lineup—Dionne Farris, Me'Shell NdegéOcello & Marcus Miller, Cassandra Wilson, Groove Theory, Maxwell, Lauryn Hill of The Fugees—has brought an aesthetic and groove to the *Billboard* charts that most of America (black and beyond) will recognize as simply being like life; film studios must hear it as the sound of new market strategies falling into place.

To this end, the movie's opening credits play like a video. Within it, writer-director Theodore Witcher unfurls artsy black-and-white video footage and photos that offer glimpses of Chicago ghetto life, all as Farris croons her new single, "Hopeless." Cut to Nina (Nia Long) and her girl Josie (Lisa Nicole Carson)—definitely not 'hood rats. They're packing a truck full of Nina's stuff because she's just broken up with her boyfriend and as Josie—a girl with Neneh Cherry hair—quips, "a cynic is born." From there, Witcher plunges us into a world of coffeehouses, bookstores and Coltrane-cool characters riffing Sonia Sanchez-sharp dialogue. Shortly after she declares that love is "played out like an 8-track," struggling photographer Nina meets struggling novelist Darius (Larenz Tate) and it's on. The main action is black folks talking about their hopes, dreams, fears and—most powerful of all—their need not just for love, but tenderness. Tain't *nobody* exhalin'. These are conversations that are equal parts earnest philosophizing and bullshit, with even the characters sometimes losing sight of which is which. Games are played, mistakes are made, and hearts are broken then healed. Getting from one point to the other is, at least for the audience, nothing but joy.

If the whole thing sounds like a labored "positive image" corrective, don't panic. It's not. Raunchy and romantic, sweet and erotic, *Love Jones* is filled with shaded-in characters whose egos and insecurities make them as recognizably human as their quick wit and palpable sexiness make them classic romantic-comedy figures. Like the Nouveau Hollywood musicians whose work (and audience numbers) let Hollywood bigwigs know that there were potentially new profits on the horizon, *Love Jones* looks longingly back at the days of craftsmanship in order to move forward. In the music, that longing is signaled by a return to live musicians, singing that's equal parts heart and technique, and reflective lyrics. In the film, the longing means focusing hard and refreshing emphasis on character and dialogue. It also means employing some rather corny conventions: lovers' walks and reconciliations in the rain; Darius chasing after Nina's train; a montage that includes the couple running through the park. Some of these moments work, some don't. But all those over-the-shoulder glances are a search for artistic authenticity, for a kind of purity and integrity that we now locate—and not just out of misplaced nostalgia—in the ways of the past. The approach is shared by both Witcher and his characters: Darius the writer composes not on a computer, but on a bulky vintage typewriter; Darius the former DJ still buys vinyl. He prefers the warmer sound.

One of the film's most interesting devices is its spare use of white folks. They show up only twice, and then briefly, existing mainly to fuck up some Negro's world. It sounds more race nervous than it is. The point is simply that white folks are largely beside the point in these characters' lives; these Negroes are neither Yoda nor wet nurse to white folks' fears, needs and insecurities.

The black worlds of Nina and Darius are incredibly rich. They're nearly—not quite totally—complete in their insularity from whites. Brought to vivid life by supporting actors like Isaiah Washington and Bill Bellamy, the lovers' friends are not only support systems, but emotional retreats—and not just from the fledgling romance. Blackness is the salve when Nina's fired by the bitchy white photographer who is her boss; it's also a tonic when a prospective white employer flips through her portfolio and asks, "Is there any way you can be a bit slicker in your approach? Less raw?" That's a question that goes beyond Nina's book, one whose vibrations will cause many black folks in the audience to nod in recognition of the quandary created by the query. It's also one of the quick but powerful strokes that gives the film its heft.

Love Jones is far from a great movie, but it's a very good one.

Whether it's laying out Josie and Nina's ribald girl talk in a cab; a hilarious and blasphemous argument on the gender of God ("Now, when a man gets a hard-on, you know where the blood comes from, right? His brain and his feet. So, A. he's stupid and B. he can't run. Only a woman God could think up some shit like that"); or even moments of intense conflict, the movie sends a jittery charge from the screen to the audience. It's a jolt of intelligence, wit and sexiness that is—in Darius' words—urgent like a muthafucka.

LA Weekly, March 14, 1997

ice is nice
BJÖRK

M usical styles are like clothes you wear on different days," says Björk, speaking by phone from her publicist's office in New York. "I don't mean the styles are trivial and you can just throw them away, but it's important that on Christmas Day you wear your red velvet outfit. When you go to the beach you wouldn't wear that, would you? And you wouldn't wear a bikini at Christmas. Actually, that's a good idea. Maybe I'll try that sometime."

The subject was remixers, and how the Icelandic singer/songwriter/producer and remixer-in-her-own-right (she retooled A Tribe Called Quest's last single, "Stressed Out") chooses to work with knob turners as disparate as junglist Dillinja and House master David Morales. What's the common ground between Tricky and Brodsky Quartet?

"What they've all got in common," she replies, "is the only thing I'm interested in, which is human nature. Music is supposed to be about humans, you know? I don't like the kind of snobbery which puts music or people in rigid categories. Human nature is much more complex than that."

Fans of Björk groove on her music—and persona—for the unforced contradictions embodied within. Her voice is that of someone firmly grounded in her own reality without taking leave of her senses. Idiosyncratic without being contrived, she's poetic, sensual, earthy, goofy and deep. Her latest release, *Telegram* (Epic), a completely overhauled version of her previous album, *Post*, is all of the above. "I Miss You" is transformed from a feast of drum patterns and percussive sounds into a cool, midtempo hip-hop vibe; "Cover Me" amps its way through a booming drum 'n' bass setting; "Army of Me," whose original foundation was a sample of drums from Led Zeppelin's "When the Levee Breaks," is now an instrumental track, erasing the singer from the picture, but retaining its kick.

Not everything works, though. The sweeping, beautiful build of *Post*'s version of "Hyperballad" is jettisoned for a Brodsky Quartet string morass; it's now coy and cutesy. "Possibly

Maybe," one of Björk's most lyrically evocative songs, contains the lines, "Since we broke up, I'm using lipstick again/I suck my tongue in remembrance of you." Those words capture every nuance of a failed love affair: the oppressiveness, the loss of identity, the mourned great sex, the cost and rewards of starting over, and the erotic charge of memory. Mark Bell's remix feeds Björk's vocals through electronics as an industrial-tinged groove crawls behind her, flattening it all to a rich but comparatively much flatter grind of grayness.

The one color missing from Björk's palette is rock 'n' roll, not only on *Telegram* but on her albums *Debut* and *Post* as well. In fact, the only time she's really acknowledged rock's existence (aside from using it in samples) was on the Skunk Anansie remixes of "Army of Me," which were released abroad on CD-single. Does she feel that rock is an exhausted genre?

"I just think it's a generation thing," she says. "I was bored with it from my parents, who played rock music 24 hours a day in my ears from the day I was born. By the time I was 7, I'd had enough. For life. And I never wanna hear it again.

"There's nothing wrong with rock," she continues. "But for me, music is about freedom of expression and being able to say whatever enters your mind. We have language and daily communication with people where we always have to be logical and functional and all that shit. Music's been the only abstract area—and it's been this way ever since the monkeys decided to become men. It's where you hear five notes and they make you cry, or you hear two notes and they make you laugh your head off. Music's supposed to express things you can't even express with your best mate. So why go to as boring and traditional and predictable a form as rock to do that?"

LA Weekly, March 21, 1997

monsters
ARTHUR DONG AND THE FACES OF HATE

R eligion is a vicious thing," says Jay Johnson, a former
seminary student currently serving a life sentence in
Minnesota. Arrested when he was 24 for the murders
of two gay men, Johnson is one of the seven convicts featured in
Arthur Dong's compelling *Licensed to Kill*, winner of two awards
at this year's Sundance Festival. The documentary, by turns
depressing and infuriating, purposefully graphic, turns a camera
on those who prey on and kill gay men, asking them the simple
question, "Why?"

Over 20 years ago, Dong was attacked by gay-bashers in San
Francisco; he saved himself by jumping onto the hood of an
oncoming car. Haunted by the incident, the filmmaker has spent
the ensuing two decades exploring the roots and fertilizer of
homophobia. What he's found is a hatred often justified on
spurious religious or cultural grounds, but whose depths and
intensity remain unfathomable—and wildly out of proportion
even to fucked-up rationale.

In *Licensed to Kill*, Dong forgoes pop-psych analysis of the
killers, and instead lets them speak for themselves. Cutting back
and forth among his original footage, videotaped confessions,
news reports and film shot at the murder scenes, he orchestrates
a series of disturbing narratives that refuse to be boiled down to
consensus. The faces, class, races and justifications for stilling
queer lives all shift quickly. The hatred, exactly the same yet so
very different, speaks in a tumble of accents.

Sometimes the accent betrays a bitterly dark humor. In his
videotaped confession, filmed as he sat at a table flanked by
detectives, Donald Aldrich boasts freely of his part in a murder.
"I knew how the police felt about homosexuals," he recalls
casually, and that knowledge gave him security. He was certain
that the disdain felt by the police toward queers would mean a
free ride for him, unaware that a newly minted hate-crimes bill
would throw a wrench into his plans.

By simply rolling film, turning on the mike and asking
questions, Dong illuminates his conflicted and confused

subjects. By sitting at a cool remove, no cultured voice-over prodding the viewer, no histrionic music, Dong allows the monsters to humanize themselves. He lets them introduce their own complexity, and it's often strangely moving. Sometimes it's just a mind-fuck.

Aldrich states that he didn't need women for sex, he could go to any of his male friends and be just as well satisfied; when pressed to explain himself, he shuts down. Aldrich also tells the camera that he was molested as a child, which is why he hates gays, who, he claims, are pedophiles-by-definition. (Although the molestation may have really happened, he seems to be pulling the excuse out of the air.) Another subject, William Cross, reveals that he too was raped as a boy and the pain of the memory plays on his face. But when Dong says to Cross that a negative stereotype of gays is that they're child molesters, Cross disagrees with that notion. Dong has shrewdly constructed a conversation between Cross and Aldrich, one in which he lets the two men wrestle with a persistent and damaging myth: that gay men prey on children. One man tries to exploit the myth to his advantage; the other, while claiming the same victimization, dismantles it.

In this powerful 80 minutes of film, though, it's Jay Johnson who stands out. Many of the subjects interviewed by Dong seem to be acting out of a homophobia that's rooted in *self*-loathing. Aldrich slips up and gives that much away. Others, not all, simply emit that vibe. But only Johnson, a biracial, HIV-positive young man full of quiet rage, really owns up to the fact.

"I believe I was a confused person," he says. "I wasn't exactly black or white; I'm half. I don't belong specifically to the black or white community. I have gay preferences, but I don't embrace the gay community. I'm religiously very hostile to them. I'm not white, but my interests were white. [But] I found that racism [in the gay community] was in some senses more pointed." Sweating profusely, Johnson looks into the camera and adds, "It's very hard [when you're] unsuccessful at something you already hate."

LA Weekly, April 18, 1997

thief of hearts
LA PROMESSE

ifteen-year-old Igor (Jeremie Renier) dabs white-out on the rotted parts of his teeth, looking in the bathroom mirror and giggling almost asthmatically as he does. It's only a few seconds of the film, La Promesse, but this glimpse of adolescent silliness reminds us that the character is, after all, still a boy, only on the verge of manhood. His facile attempt at cosmetic dentistry comes as a break from his real chores: forging immigration papers for the human cargo that his father, for a hefty fee, illegally imports into Belgium. Only a few scenes earlier, Igor, dragging glumly on a cigarette and haggling rent with the immigrants who reside in his father's tenement slum, shows absolutely no trace of the child.

Written and directed by the brother duo, Jean-Pierre and Luc Dardenne, La Promesse is set in contemporary, post-industrial Belgium. It's a bleak place, one bustling with an underground network of people who've escaped the horrors of Eastern Europe and Africa only to find themselves stranded in a hostile, cynical new environment. Aboveground are lifelong residents who've seen their factories close and their economy disintegrate, creating not only an angry, embittered citizenry, but a crop of unsavory entrepeneurs. One of them is Igor's father, Roger.

An unemployed former factory worker who's turned to smuggling and exploiting illegal immigrants, he's already molded his son into a no-bullshit, fast-talking partner in crime. But Igor is also an ordinary kid who cruises the streets on his moped, repairs go-carts with his friends, and has an apprenticeship as a mechanic. The character is a blatant if wonderfully fleshed-out symbol of the future, of a fragile moral correctness and of the agonizing cost of doing the right thing. When one of the immigrants has a fatal accident and, with his dying breath, makes Igor promise to take care of the man's wife and infant son, it sparks a crisis of conscience in the boy, forcing him to confront his father's moral culpability. The death also stokes the film's saccharine-free pathos, locating the Dardennes' political allegory in flesh, blood and more than a few tears.

Luc and Jean-Pierre Dardenne grew up in Seraing, Belgium

in the '50s and '60s, when the small industrial suburb was supported by factories that employed tens of thousands of workers and spawned vibrant, left-wing labor activism. But most of the factories are now closed. In the center of town, stores and huge buildings have been left abandoned. Those same structures have become often dangerous housing for the Turkish, Eastern European and African immigrants who have flooded Belgium's borders. Drawing on the political and economic realities of Seraing (where the brothers still live and base their work operations), as well as their history of left politics, the Dardennes have carved out a career for themselves as documentarians and feature filmmakers (*La Promesse* is their third feature), with Belgium's '60s labor movement and resistance against the Nazis being their main subjects.

The brothers' documentary background is in full evidence here. The actors are unmannered and physically realistic—no Nautilus refugees or aerobics queens in sight. The film is filled with measured tension, where silence and an actor's face are often all that fill the screen. Renier and Assita Ouedraogo (as the widow, Assita), neither of whom have much acting experience, are particularly good. And the Dardennes (who co-wrote and co-directed the film) have a fine eye for the unforced detail. There's a shot of Igor zipping by on his moped, oblivious to the figure of Assita carrying a chicken in one hand, a huge package in the other, and her baby boy strapped on her back as she walks through a rocky, desolate field. The scene is brief but potent, indicative of the film's lean approach to acting, directing and dialogue. The characters' stations and situations are sketched with a minimum of fuss.

La Promesse ends on a bittersweet, open-ended note. It's optimistic, but not necessarily uplifting. A hugely compassionate film, it scores its biggest points in juxtaposing Igor's moral coming of age with the pressing helplessness of being an immigrant in an unwelcoming land. *La Promesse* suggests that as the world's borders turn to liquid, how we treat those who swim through is a measure of our decency, perhaps of our humanity. Igor's response marks him as one of the summer's cinematic heroes.

LA Weekly, May 30, 1997

the delta

The zipless fuck that opens *The Delta* is the intersecting of wildly disparate worlds—wealth and poverty, community and isolation, half black and definitely white. It's an overlap that means nothing and everything, sparking fantasies of love and salvation in one boy, fading from memory almost before it's begun for the other. The act itself, fleeting and discreetly shot, is a front-seat blow-job on a deserted street, soundtracked by no more than a handful of words. It's only when the two men—after a subsequent rendezvous—go their separate ways and we're led on a meticulous tour of the places they call home that we, and one of the pair, gauge the full impact of their meeting.

Lincoln (Shayne Gray) is from a well-off white family in Memphis. He has a slim, blonde girlfriend who's from the same tax bracket, and a few friends who clearly are not. Except for the family maid, his world has been fairly well scrubbed down with bleach. Both Lincoln and his girlfriend have the somnambulant quality of the well bred. The couple's white-trash friends, by contrast, are brash and edgy: They eat too much junk food, smoke pot and argue with their parents. But they're all caught in the same web of small-town doldrums. Throughout the episodic film (it spans a weekend) writer-director Ira Sachs, who was born in Memphis, acutely captures the tension of nothingness that surrounds them.

When the group gathers on Friday night to look for distraction, their conversations are both banal and spiked: laughing buddies quickly become irritants, and vice versa. The party they finally settle on has a club-kid spinning techno and House, leading to some low-key grumbling, with one forlorn voice asking, "You got any KC & the Sunshine Band?" Meanwhile, in a back room, the girls talk nonchalantly about racial conflict on their school campus, odd-shaped dicks and glow-in-the-dark condoms, while a baby is balanced on a succession of accommodating laps.

Leaving the party, and his girlfriend, Lincoln goes cruising, attracts a freak, and beats a hasty escape to an adult theater. Once there, he again meets up with John (Thang Chan), his one-off at the movie's beginning. John is attractive but has the weary air of an old whore. He also has her lingo. "You so cute, boy," he tells Lincoln, then asks, "You want to love me?"

The problem is, John is completely sincere. The son of an American G.I who abandoned him and his mother, John grew up ostracized in Vietnam because he was half-black. Though he had a marriage of convenience back home, he lives more truthfully, if not less painfully, as a gay man in the States. He flirts relentlessly but there's a shrill desperation beneath his come-ons. Poverty and alienation have manifested in him a boundless, grating need, and it's a measure of the film's honesty that a character who could have been a one-dimensional poster boy for the marginalized is instead allowed complexity.

The two end up on Lincoln's father's boat, where they take a slow cruise down the Mississippi. It's here that John pours his heart out to Lincoln, who in turn is busy doing a slow retreat. And we don't blame him. John is an oppressive, throbbing wound. The reasons become even more clear when Lincoln abandons John and the film switches entirely to John's point of view.

Sachs sets up his study in contrasts with soft but detailed strokes. Lincoln is shy and sweet but betrays imperiousness in his dealings with John. Melancholy blankets him, and there's room for doubt as to whether or not his late night excursions are truly deepening his psychology or just casting a faint shadow over it. Money, some social standing and the color of his skin have granted Lincoln the privilege of indecision, flightiness and childlike oblivion.

John has no such luxury. Unemployed, with neither country nor real family, and with history pressing on his shoulders, he sweats steeliness and desperation. When his affection is not returned, he leaves Lincoln a memento that's intended to destroy him. As he says after clumsily inflicting a hickey, "If I hurt you, you'll remember me. I want you to remember."

The Delta is a soulful movie. It builds slowly and through careful detail, gliding at an unforced pace. It's a wonderfully sketched look at small-town life, with peeks into psyches, hearts and sexualities that are scarred and stalled, but its tremendous depth isn't immediately apparent. It's a film whose impact hits upon reflection, whose fallout is a pungent commentary on the ways race, class and sexuality feed off one another. The movie is Sach's first feature, but you wouldn't know it from either his tight script or the terrific performances he pulls from his largely non-professional cast.

LA Weekly, August 15, 1997

les enfants terrible
NENETTE ET BONI

Claire Denis' *Nenette et Boni* is set in a Marseilles of immigrants and working class French nationals. It's a place teeming with scam artists and hustlers, where the black market belches up everything from fishing rods to bogus telephone cards—the latter being a dense metaphor masquerading as a running gag. In the foreground of this freeform class struggle are 19-year-old Boniface (Gregoire Colin) and his 14-year-old sister, Antoinette (Alice Houri). Their prickly relationship is already shuttered by longstanding hurts, resentments and accusations.

When the film opens, Boni is living like a squatter in the house left to him by the pair's dead mother; messy and in a severe state of disrepair, it's also home to the boy's scraggly posse. It's with this "home" as her goal that Nenette, cigarette in one hand and a small bag of belongings in another, scales the wall of the Catholic girls home where she's been living. The young actors, Colin and Houri, share a dour shadow around the eyes, and the first time the siblings set sights on one another after a long separation, their eyes blaze a mutual wariness and hostility. Without even a word being passed between the two, we recognize this exchange as one full of history.

Boni supports himself by selling fresh-baked pizza out of a truck given to him by a friend of his much loathed, pathetic father. Seamlessly intercut into his banal workday are the hilarious and raunchy sexual fantasies he has about the baker's wife (a lush Valeria Bruni-Tedeschi). Denis shoots these imagined moments without making any visual distinctions between them and the boy's "reality," not so much claiming an equivalence between his real and dream states as testifying to the vital force of the boy's overheated imagination: These flights of erotic fancy are what gets him through his days. (He chronicles his brash and ribald swagger in a journal that he has tellingly titled "Confessions of a Wimp.")

Nenette is more mysterious, cryptic. Even before we find out that she's pregnant, or are given clues as to the source of her indifference-bordering-on-contempt for the baby, Houri graces her character with a solemn weight, making her seem both preoccupied and terribly grounded.

Nenette and Boni stare at each other across the male/female divide with both fascination and repulsion. She's disgusted by the fantasies she's spied in his journal, and taunts him; he's baffled and outraged by her reaction to her pregnancy. (Both have far more complex emotional lives than they can even articulate to themselves, let alone each other.) Without hammering the point, Denis, who steers the film completely clear of sentimentality while plumbing deep emotional ground, reminds us of the fact that girls mature faster than boys—not always by their choice—and what that costs them. Boni drifts inside his head and the lusty, comedic contents are then spilled for us—and the camera—to see. Nenette's earthbound secrets are kept locked behind her eyes and never completely decoded. The kicker is that Boni sits in uninformed judgment of his sister.

Denis tells this character-driven tale less through plot than through gorgeous, often iconic imagery: the opening shot of Nenette floating in the crystal-blue water of a pool, her eyes closed and body half-submerged, her dark hair wafting out to the side; the camera traveling in slow motion across the bakery's pastry-laden shelves as the baker's wife drags her finger through frosting and sticks it in her mouth while her full breasts hang over the confections; Boni's pet rabbit twitching between the feather-muled feet of the baker's wife; Boni, heartbroken and tear-stained, standing silently in the street as passersby brush and bump against him, his body absorbing the blows and then springing slowly back into position, much like the dough he punches when making pizza. What makes these moments add up to more than just a series of beautifully composed surfaces is the almost subliminal information contained inside them. The first glimpse of Nenette—eyes closed and body drifting, her form carefully covered—telegraphs all the crucial information about her, right up front. Through lighting, music and tight shots, Denis uses visuals to create moods, then uses mood to explore emotion. That last segue comes through her love of faces, her knack for finding astonishing ones and her fondness for close-ups. Whether it's the hard angles of the baker's face (in the visage of Vincent Gallo) turned soft and appealing through the glow of marital contentment, or Colin's offbeat beauty as it colors from vulnerable to furious to adoring, the actors' faces give emotional weight to Denis' visual flair.

In her previous films *Chocolat, I Can't Sleep* and *No Fear, No Die*, narrative twists and turns were fairly easily mapped along fairly traditional plot lines, at least in hindsight. In *Nenette et Boni*, not an awful lot happens in conventional movie terms. Brother and sister, both of whom are moving aimlessly in their young lives, come together reluctantly and combatively. The sensual mother (the baker's wife) of the boy's dreams strolls into frame, recedes, then strolls back again. The siblings' father is given a few economic scenes to establish both his ineffectualness and dubious character. Modern-day Marseilles is sketched in through moments we spend with the immigrants, Boni's McDonald's-eating roommates, and the two leads as they haphazardly move the tale forward. And yet, volumes of soulful conversations are being held throughout the film, relayed through brilliantly conceived and controlled ambience.

Perhaps the most affecting moment in the film is when Boni, after staring at the photo of an ultrasound, a deep chord having suddenly been struck inside him, turns his red eyes toward the camera. The emptiness and lovelessness of his existence hit him like a bolt, leaving him emotionally shell-shocked. It's then that the metaphor of the calling-card scam becomes clear. Like the far-flung exiles who buy the bogus cards, Boni—his route outlined by testosterone-fueled fantasy—is simply trying to reach "family" through whatever convoluted channels he can navigate. But Denis, rigorously unsentimental throughout, hasn't simply been working toward a pat, feel-good ending. Without the slightest hint of political grandstanding or agenda—in fact, with a lot of humor and tenderness—she's captured the coarseness of our times: the places we live, how we treat ourselves and those tied to us by blood or familiarity. She's captured that often hidden but undying part of us that longs for the ritual and hope of family, of connectedness. But she also knows that the reality of those ties can be more bitter than sweet, and it's the film's final image, a tight close-up of Nenette's blank face, that turns that ideal on its head and lingers in ours.

LA Weekly, October 24, 1997

thicker than blood
FAMILY NAME

In the South, delineating bloodlines used to be a feat mastered at a young age. Lavish family reunions and informal get-togethers were just two occasions where memories and facts were trotted out, appendaged and passed down. The process was facilitated by an omnipresent past that hung tight with the present, and by a lively oral tradition that cemented the bonds between then and now. For black folk, this trip through time would eventually unearth a white or "Indian" body—perhaps one that was added a little too eagerly to the mix by the storyteller. But the further back you'd go, the lower the guiding voices would drop; soft murmurs let you know that you'd landed at a place where things were simply understood, not spoken.

Family Name, a thematically frayed documentary that almost bursts with information, attempts to amplify the murmurs by pushing past the false starts, dead ends and seemingly unanswerable questions that one young white man from the South has about race, his family and the legacy of slavery.

Filmmaker Macky Alston says he always felt like an outsider in his own family, a fact he attributes to his homosexuality. It didn't help that both his father and grandfather were preachers. (Alston himself dropped out of seminary after two years and, as a member of ACT UP, later railed against the church.) When he was 5, his father—a staunch civil rights activist—enrolled him in a predominantly black public school in their hometown of Durham, North Carolina. It was while there that Alston *fils* encountered a slew of black kids who had his last name. Years later he learned that his family had once been one of the largest slave owners in the state; from there the pieces began to float into place.

With the blind determination—and dash of self-righteousness—that characterizes the obsessed, the 27-year-old Alston set out in *Family Name* to prove that his ancestors owned the slaves whose descendants are today's black Alstons. With camera in tow, he travels across North Carolina, up to New York, and down to Alabama in his quest for answers. In North Carolina, he finds two Alston family reunions—one black, one white—taking place within the same week and only miles apart, with neither clan aware of the other. When he speaks to the black Alstons, he seems shocked, then disappointed, that they aren't filled with rage. "I guess I expected black Alstons to be angry and white Alstons to feel guilty," he admits. "And I asked questions to provoke those specific responses." In the subtext of that admission lies the possibility that the filmmaker's agenda may have had as much to do with sticking it to his family—for whatever reasons, and using shame over the past and the fact of the black Alstons' existence as his tools—as it did in aligning history in honesty.

In one of the movie's highlights, he unspools the life of Charles "Spinky" Alston, a fair-skinned black artist who, in 1935, was a co-founder of the Harlem Artist Guild. In interviewing Spinky's surviving sister, Rousmaniere Alston, and her half-sister Aida Winters, he gets into an amusing back and forth with the feisty Aida. Eyeing the two pale-skinned women, he asks if they ever passed for white. Rousmaniere admits that she did. Aida asks why she'd want to. "Why not?" asks Macky. "Why?" shoots back Aida, eyes blazing. "You could ride in the front of the bus...," offers Macky feebly.

By this point, Alston knows his family owned the ancestors of Spinky and his sister, along with countless other black folks. Building on that knowledge he becomes interested in establishing blood ties. Tellingly, although the "white" skin of the sisters and others he interviews has him (superficially and unintentionally) question "blackness," it never prompts him to consider—not on film, anyway—if he might not be other than "white."

In another potent revelation, he finds out that one of his forefathers, John Joseph "Chatham" Alston, set neighbors' tongues wagging by having young black slave boys sleep at the foot of his bed as "foot warmers;" the boys also traveled with him. But Macky glides over this sexually charged scenario, the implications of which have produced much of the anxiety surrounding contemporary black masculinity. It's not only the historically sanctioned rape of black women, and the inability of black men to protect them, that has left black manhood scarred, but the unspoken, rarely unacknowledged sexual violations of the black male body—and the black man's inability to protect himself. There are at least a half dozen other fascinating "plot" threads that Alston touches on but lets slip. To be fair, there isn't room to develop them all. Still, with his painstaking research (old photos, recordings and archival footage), he does a stellar job of crafting his three-year search into a dense but entertaining tale; its raggedness is part of its punch. And be sure to stay through the credits for a "twist" worthy of the best Hollywood fiction.

LA Weekly, October 10, 1997

ambersunshower
SEE HER FOR HER BEAUTY

In midsummer of last year, on the night of the day that her solo-debut album, *Walter T.*, was first stocked in record stores, Ambersunshower (full name: Ambersunshower Nadine Miligros Villenuevo Smith Piper) performed before a sparse crowd at the Viper Room. Clad in a calf-length, form-fitting black dress, her hair coiled in a Medusa-like twist of braids, and with guarded eyes, she took the stage sporting a strained smile. In attendance were a handful of music journalists, some folks from her label, a few industry fucks and a smattering of "ordinary" people, one of whom was a fat wigger puffing on a stogie, bellowing loudly to impress his Beverly Hills posse. Fronting a band whose members she'd met only hours earlier, Amber dug deep into the music, a galvanizing dose of what was then being hyped as "alternative soul." (A few weeks later, an article in *Time* magazine would lazily lump her with both Maxwell and Me'Shell NdegéOcello, though the trio have little but melanin in common.) Amber and her backing players fanned a sound that was hip-hop in essence but thick with strokes of folk, blues, glistening pop and untethered soul.

It was deceptively breezy stuff, R&B gunned by a dark undertow. Twisting and contorting her voice, she sang lyrics that glinted with pain, grief and dog-eared catharsis. While the band stretched the album's meticulous, experimental hip-hop-soul grooves into a taut jazz-funk jam—keyboards, bass, drums and guitar all deliquescing into a controlled flow of sound—Amber's voice floated on top, dived below and hung tight in the center. A couple of middle-aged industry guys, standing roughly six feet from the stage, laughed and loudly talked shop as the show unfolded, ignoring gestures and whispers for them to shut up, and more pointedly ignoring Amber. After one of the songs, the fat wigger swaggered to the edge of the stage and motioned for a free T-shirt. Amber's face tightened as her eyes fired daggers, but she stayed cool. At one point, in defense/retreat/self-protect mode, she burrowed so far inside a groove that her eyes rolled back into her head just before the lids folded down, a slow smile of self-pleasure spreading over her face. It was an amazing performance.

On the sidelines, a guy from her label's distributor, Island Records, bopped enthusiastically and snapped his fingers, grinning broadly. "This is great!," he exclaimed. "Even *we* can't fuck this up!"

A woman co-worker slowly looked him up and down and shook her head. "Wanna bet?" she asked drily.

Guess who won the bet.

"That whole situation was really drama in itself," laughs 27-year-old Amber, speaking by phone from her home in New York. It's a space she shares with her husband/producer, Thomas "Tikk Takk" Piper, and their 7-month-old son, Zion. ("I named him that *before* Lauryn had her baby," she laughs.)

"We had just flown in from New York, the monies weren't coming in properly from the label, and the band was a real makeshift thing. They were totally not the cats I was used to working with. We'd just found them! We spent the whole afternoon rehearsing and trying to pull it together. My husband was my MD [musical director], and we were just in a show-must-go-on kinda vibe. But whatever. You know, things happen for a reason."

Walter T. eventually racked up raves from *Rolling Stone*, the *Source*, *USA Today*, *Time* and almost every media outlet that reviewed it. The alterna-soul label stuck early on, but it's a lazy, empty handle. It's a tag that only has meaning if black folk and the world at large surrender to the idea—admittedly put forth by the texts of contemporary pop and "urban" albums/CDs/movies/music videos—that modern black American culture, its architects and residents, are emotionally and intellectually spent, have nothing to say, and don't possess the vocabularies to say anything, anyway. Those artists who defy this hollow wisdom are put in quotation marks, set aside as exceptional—even somewhat freakish. Those artists and fans who subscribe to the view—be they black or otherwise, be they conscious of their subscription or not—are simply adhering to the program, receiving and believing all the cues sent out by a machinery that thwarts and flattens black creativity, and then elevates the stunted results as representative of "real" black lives.

Walter T. kicks off on an accusation. "Did you believe?" asks Amber repeatedly, her voice belting the words with contoured force, "Did you believe?" We've been dropped in the aftermath of a failed love affair, but land smack in the middle of a lover's white-hot pain. "Look around my window," she commands, "and see what you've done." Snagged on her pain, she chants non-sensical words in a loop: "Chicki Chicki I / Chicki Chicki I, I, I, I..." And as a Greek chorus coos in the background, "Too bad 'nother man/too bad one man," the singer replies in defeat, "I lay him down to rest." Dogged by Hallmark cliches, she turns them inside out: "The sun don't shine / the rain it falls / My heart is lost."

Though various keyboard and synth effects gurgle and surge across the backdrop, it's bass, beat and voice that underscore the potency and rippling emotions of the sparse lyrics. We're slowly guided on a tour of the doomed love affair, with flashbacks revealing that even in bliss there was doubt. On "Voices Inside My Head," she asks plaintively, "How could you do this to me? / Why would you do this to me? / 1-2-3 Now, I see what the voices really mean."

Fucks driven by vengeance and revenge fill the album's narrative; themes topple and scramble over one another as a childhood memory dovetails into current injury. On the title track (written in tribute to the singer's late grandfather shortly after he died), the album's heroine guides us to the blueprint for her ideal man. The model wasn't simply drawn from fantasy, but from the grace and gentleness of an elder. And the bridge, "All I know/my soul has been trying to find you," addresses both Amber's personal loss and *Walter T.*'s heroine's search for her heart's companion. Her pain is brought to a boil on the single, "Running Song," a track produced by label mates, P.M. Dawn, and grounded by a throbbing sample from the Loose Ends classic, "Hangin' on a String. The first verse sets the situation—"What am I gonna do now? / Four years passed and still no word/Heard a story about you that said/you went to the moon"—while later we're served the moral: "Had to search for myself / and learn for myself / and be by myself." But like the Jenny Jones guest we all become when unmercifully dumped, she confesses at song's end that: "If you wanted our lovin', I'd come running all the way."

The song's gleam is in the way it perfectly channels the

essence of that classic Loose Ends track ("I waited oh so long for
you to come to me/What did I do wrong?/It's all a mystery to
me...You got me hangin' on a string, now/You never told me
you were waiting, contemplating/with my heart, my love.")
"Running Song" is, in many ways, a cover—but of the
sentiment, not the literal song. And Ambersunshower leaves her
indelible stamp all over it.

"I'd gone to London to meet some people over there," says
Amber, explaining how the track came into being, "and they
[P.M. Dawn] flew out as well, and we just kinda got together.
They gave me the track and I went back to my hotel and wrote
out the lyrics for it. It was very intimidating at first because it's
such a powerful track, but then I kinda said, 'Fuck it.' By listening
to the mood and vibe of the music, it invoked some energy, and
it all came together."

The disc's bleakest moment, "Serengeti Plains," is a trek
back through history, one that locates the original source of
the heartache that's been passed down through generations.
The metaphor extends beyond the specific characters, its
reach speaking to larger aches and divides in American history
and culture.

"For some reason," says Amber, "the deep South, blazing,
came to my mind when I was writing that song. I named it
'Serengeti Plains' because that's the name of the girl who it's
about. Basically, her mother is the mistress of a plantation,
married to the owner. Her mother slept with a slave and that's
how she was born. She's got dark, chocolate skin and indigo
eyes. And [when she gets older] Serengeti falls in love with the
plantation owner. I guess it's sort of like a black spiritual that
encompasses the whole song. [Amber sings a line from the
song]: *"If you took the time to see / you'd know / Hearts like that
don't come around every day, and so..."* It's kinda like a spiritual
voice talking to the plantation owner. [She sings another line]:
*"Serengeti Plains, exchanged for corn and tea / she watches as her
mother pleads..."* See, he's in love with her too, but he's selling her
[because she's] his wife's daughter. She's the real innocent in the
situation. She's just in love with him. And that's what the song is
about. *(Laughs)* You know, you start writing and you gotta keep
the desperation in there. It's a real desperate song. When the

stakes are really high, you get a better moment, a better song."

When *Walter T.* was re-released a few months ago (Amber's label, Gee Street, worked out a distribution deal with Richard Bramson's new label, V2, and the folks there were so impressed with the album that they wanted to give it a second life), a generic House remix of "Running Song" had been tacked on. In the process, the whole arc of the album had been fucked with. Originally, the album ended with "Desoto," which came right on the heels of "Serengeti Plains," and the juxtaposition was bracing.

In "Desoto," the heroine and her new guy are "Chillin' in the back of my ride / and he don't mind." The car, a jalopy, is a metaphor for the way she sees herself. Having been burned in love (and, by inference, life in general), she's ragged and insecure, with sadness stalking her. But the guy she's singing about "... sees me for my beauty / He says beauty is me." There's a tentative smile in the singer's voice as she sings the line, a weight that allows for how wonderful the feeling is, but she doesn't quite trust it. There's an element of shock that anyone has found beauty in her, that anyone sees her as beautiful at all: "We're laughing and we're being / He can see what no man sees / Loving simple more than a gesture / He says beauty is me." As the horns swell ecstatically and the chorus breezes along, she finally lets herself feel the love and happiness that's been so hard to find, so long coming. "Come on in," she sings joyfully. "Come on in."

Amber's less than thrilled with the anti-climactic remix of "Running Song" that now undermines the album's thoughtful ending.

"The album was complete as it was," she says in frustration. "But, you know, record companies... That's all I can say on that. I said I didn't want to do a remix. I don't want to do them period. I felt that remixes were a knock on the original version, like you couldn't be bothered to get it right the first time. And I don't think that's the case with my album."

Los Angeles, 1997

penal colony
THE KEEPER

Writer-director Joe Brewster earned a degree in psychiatry and worked in the prison library at the Brooklyn House of Detention in New York before fulfilling his childhood fantasy of becoming a filmmaker. He brings all that to bear in his unsettling and striking film debut, *The Keeper.* It's a work both delicate and forceful in its goals: showing the ties between internalized racism and the fear and loathing of one's own people; mapping how the violence and rage that dogs the black community springs from that self-loathing, with class schisms feeding the flames; and finally, gingerly outlining how the burgeoning prison industry thrives on and perpetuates the divisions. What makes the film so affecting is how Brewster personalizes these issues around the locus of shame. Shame in all its permutations, from familial to cultural, is what guns *The Keeper's* engine.

Thirty-six-year-old Paul Lamont (Giancarlo Esposito) is a black corrections officer at the Brooklyn King's County House of Detention. He works in the facility's law library while prepping himself for law school. His also-black co-workers, openly contemptuous of their charges, chide the soft-spoken Lamont for being a "college boy," mocking his efforts to reach out to the prisoners. One guard longs for the good old days when "prisoner's rights" was an oxymoron, and when "All you did was feed 'em." Another tells him that the cons "drive college boys like you crazy trying to figure out how to save them." After a distraught, wrongfully imprisoned Haitian inmate, Jean Baptiste (Isaach De Bankolé), attempts to hang himself, Lamont pays the man's bail and reluctantly—and against his wife's angry protests—takes him in.

Baptiste's arrival in the Lamont home unleashes all sorts of demons, and not just within that home. Lamont, who is half-Haitian, has flashbacks centered on his deceased father, a dark-skinned, French-speaking man whom Lamont shied away from even as a child and whose Miami-based relatives he still ignores. Guilt (and anger at its manifestation) starts to eat away at his rigid self-image; it's an emotional twist that's compounded by having his wife, Angela (Regina Taylor), thaw from outright disdain to chumminess in her dealings with Baptiste. Lamont's mounting, increasingly incoherent frustrations find an outlet in his interactions with the prisoners. When he finally explodes on one, his co-workers note approvingly that he's "got nuts after all."

As a director, Brewster is noticeably wet behind the ears. The fact that *The Keeper* is a no-budget affair explains the flatness of a lot of imagery, but doesn't shield the fact that he often doesn't know how to work his cameraman to maximum effect; his rudimentary skills aren't up to the sophistication of his ideas. There's a scene in a Haitian dance club that's meant to be frenzied, sexy, hypnotic. The actors are clearly doing their parts to bring it all to life. But the moment never leaps off the screen, its power thwarted by an uninspired eye and unimaginative editing. There are other instances, though, when the static camera is absolutely perfect, as when it captures a pensive Baptiste sitting on the edge of the sofa while Paul and Angela argue about him in the next room.

Where Brewster's gifts glow, and outstrip many of his more technically proficient filmmaking peers, is in both his writing and his way with actors. The script, lean and direct, is politically and psychologically astute. Brewster knows that a self- or race - loathing black man isn't necessarily perming his hair or fucking white women, not even fleeing to the suburbs. He also knows the many insidious ways American culture fans and profits from that hatred, and he has it play out in every arena of his characters' lives. He wouldn't be nearly as effective in making his points if he weren't also adept at orchestrating the onscreen talent. Esposito (who co-produced) playing another of his patented tightly wound black men here, unveils the tragedy and misery beneath that taut façade. Regina Taylor is rock solid, as usual. And Isaach De Bankolé, a movie star who can really act, nearly strolls away with every scene he's in.

The Keeper was given limited release last year, and though it's played the festival circuit, seems to have baffled most mainstream critics. It's not an easy film, but it's not a difficult one either. It just depends on a willingness to *see* black people onscreen, full of complexity, contradictions and the refusal to pander.

LA Weekly, January 16, 1998

last rites
MOTHER AND SON

A few weeks ago, at the end of a Nuart theater press screening of Alexander Sokurov's *Mother and Son*, one of the theater's employees asked what I'd thought of the movie. Before I could answer, he quipped, "It was like watching paint dry." He won't be alone in that assessment. A Russian film that's about death, history, isolation and making amends, it's demanding viewing. To call it measured is to be coy with understatement. But within its painstakingly crafted world, one that's caught somewhere between a dream and a lush painting, is a fount of beauty and emotion.

A dying mother is tended by her adult son during the last day of her life, and at times their blood-inscribed roles are reversed. At other times, he cradles her as tenderly as a lover while her body quiets itself from seizure. They even share the same dream. Long stretches of silence serve to accent their intimacy; foreground and background blur into a single plane as the two figures curve into one another, their faces and bodies tilted and stretched then held still by the camera. Just when you're convinced you really are watching a filmed painting, there's movement or conversation. Yuri Arabov's sparse script strikes just the right balance between dialogue that's deceptively mundane and almost self-consciously lyrical. But none of it is extraneous.

Near the end of the film, the mother tells her son that on the day he was born, the weather was clear and cold. Everyone in their village said it meant the boy would be clever but heartless.

"That's right," he smiles softly. "I'm a 'head' person. Otherwise my heart would break."

Only, it's obvious from his delicate interactions with his mother, and the shadows of grief that pass over his face, that he's not ruled solely by his head. That mother/son exchange—and the falseness of the villagers' prophecy—also work, unintentionally, as a defense of the movie itself. On top of being labelled boring by its harshest detractors, *Mother and Son* has also been called a purely neck-up exercise. While it's true that Sokurov makes you hyperaware of scope, composition, camera movement and angles, and his considered use of sound, the knowledge registers emotionally, not just cerebrally.

A dark cloud slowly spreads across the screen like a bloodstain, then just hangs there; the son silently picks his mother up and carries her down a winding path, with the dull, nondescript fabrics of their clothing acting like a camoflauge, seamlessly blending the characters into the forest and fields; as the son stops to balance the dead weight of his mother, storm clouds gather overhead and the screen is filled with autumnal colors, the only disruption being a white plume of smoke billowing out of a distant train; the home the two reside in is huge, bleak and crumbling, with its windows boarded up; an elongated throat fills the screen in tight close-up, barely recognizable as what it is, then constricts tightly in grief, issuing forth a wail of pain.

Mother and Son's overall look is overcast, smudged and blurry; the feel of death and decay, as well as profound loneliness, throbs through its images.

Some critics have suggested that the film is about the fall of Mother Russia, and it undoubtedly works on that level. The background we're given on the characters through their conversations is hastily and murkily sketched in, intentionally rendering them somewhat vague even as their poignant summations of life and their impending separation are concise and specific. That, coupled with the sum total of images, desolate if gorgeous backdrops, and sense of approaching loss easily serves as political commentary. But what makes the film brilliant is the way Sokurov renders personal drama and political wreckage one and the same.

Shortly before she dies, the mother says to her boy, "Your life was hard at times. But hard is not always bad."

To which he simply responds, "You and I. We love each other."

LA Weekly, February 20, 1998

pitted against the lizard
BEATTY TALKS *BULWORTH*, BAPTISTS, BOO AND THE BULLSHIT OF THE BOTTOM LINE

Warren Beatty, 61, is sitting in his room at the Four Seasons Hotel in Beverly Hills, cradling a phone to his ear and discussing the critical response to his latest film, *Bulworth*. "Listen," he says into the receiver, "the reviews have just come in from around the country, and they're the best reviews of my life. If people would rather go see a seven-billion-pound lizard [*Godzilla*], what can you do? That's what it's come to." He looks across the table at me, shrugs and laughs. He laughs a lot during the interview. The Beatty who's notoriously lock-jawed with the press, the one who lets questions hang unanswered for excruciating stretches of time, is nowhere to be found. Instead, he's funny, quick and almost freakishly charming. It's easy to see how he earned his rep as the mad seducer: He listens intently, leans in, looks you in the eyes, asks thoughtful questions, then nods and gestures for you to keep talking. He's got big-dick confidence. He's also playfully competitive. "There's gonna be a lot written about *Bulworth*," he says before hanging up the phone. "There won't be a lot written about the lizard."

This is why *Bulworth*, an anomaly at the multiplex, warrants serious attention: It's a film of ideas and ideals. That those ideals center around the issues of race and class, that the film—at its center—is a hardcore, intelligent, unapologetic and very funny leftist tract is why it's both dazzling and refreshing. It's a movie that, despite some wobbly moments, works on about a dozen levels: a brutal send-up of left-wing politics as well as a heartfelt lament for the fall of the same; a satire of political and personal corruption; a gleeful clanging of racial and cultural stereotypes against one another until the sounds that fall out ring forth truths; a series of speeches so purposefully over-the-top in their didacticism that they're as hilarious as they are truthful; a celebration of cultural blending that doubles as a giddy presentation of the caricature known as the white nigger. The foundation of the film, though, is the question posed by 'hood rat, Nina (Halle Berry), to Sen. Bulworth (Beatty) near the film's end. "You're insecure because you're white?" she asks incredulously. The answer, of course, is yes, and Beatty spells out how that particular insecurity has played out on—and continues to shape—our cultural, political and personal playing fields. What follows are excerpts from an interview that took place on the day *Bulworth* went into wide release across the country—pitted against the lizard.

Although the film has gotten some amazing reviews, a lot of those that haven't been so positive have either explicitly or subtly asked why a rich, famous white man would make this film...

I'm not rich.

You're richer than most. You're in the top 20% of the nation's wealthy.

Much higher than that.

Then you're rich.

(laughs) Okay.

So, there's been this undercurrent in those reviews that, for you to make this film, you're either a hypocrite, a poseur...

I'm a traitor to my class.

But why? There are people who don't even belong to that class who labor very hard to maintain its privileges. Who are you to do otherwise?

(long pause) Well, deep down I'm not rich. I'm from a Southern family... Bulworth says it in the movie when he says [ordinary] white people have more in common with [ordinary] black people than they do with rich people. It's the failure to

realize this that has spawned an entire century's separation of the races. In truth, I was lucky. I had a set of parents who had strong ideas about fairness. My father was in public education; so was my mother. There's something in my past that's very democratic, something back there that's Christian—Southern Baptist. I think it's just something I grew up with.

The *Village Voice* recently ran a couple of articles about *Bulworth* that really took the movie to task for its use of stereotype and paternalistic politics. How do you respond to those charges?

I think when you do anything of this nature... Going to the movies has become such a lull that if you can do something that breaks the mold a little, it can at least start people talking. People say all the time that they don't mind being attacked—and I've said it too, even though I don't mean it—but I really don't mind being attacked if it comes from people who feel that the subject wasn't covered fairly. I mean, you do the best you can. You try to get people's attention through whatever means you find necessary. I'm just glad that the objections transcend the boring objections to how you use the form. The [critics] get into the subject; they deal with race and class and money in politics—which has a tremendous bearing on race.

Is the film set in California, as opposed to Washington, precisely because it is about the pull of race and class and money on politics? Because California, much more than D.C. or New York, is really grappling with those issues in a way that seems to be setting the path for the rest of the country.

Things come to a boil in this country from West to East. Not only West to East, but I've grown to think it's Southwest to Northeast. It's called money. Infotainment. Media. Things get hot here then move back to what used to be the industrial center. Part of it is our initiative system, which has its good points, but also a lot of bad ones. But the other thing is the huge population of this state. When something is voted into place in

California, that's a huge number of people who are affected. That's a wonderful testing ground for politicians.

A lot of critics and movie buffs bemoan the current state of film, and everyone knows that money is at the root of the mediocrity. But there also seems to be less of a willingness on the part of audiences to be disturbed by a film, to be unsettled. Do you think that's because of some shift in public taste that's divorced from film industry machinations, or is it that the decline of Hollywood artistry has shaped the tastes?

Well, I think we make a big mistake if we compare the music business of today—the music business; that's an interesting slip—the movie business of today to the movie business of 25 years ago. It's a different business. It's the difference between a guy who ran a pretty good steak place 25 years ago and now heads a McDonald's franchise. You make a lot more money from the burgers than steaks. And most of the attention in the cultural pages of newspapers—not yours—is paid to what's grossing the most money. It's a chart ranking the weekend's top movies. That didn't exist 25 years ago. I think the audience is still there to see films that don't go to the middle, but it's hard to see them if you're busy looking at a mass of a million people going toward something. That hundred thousand going toward something else tends to get overlooked.

I've seen *Bulworth* twice, and each time you could feel some audience members slowly pulling away from the film. You could tell that they felt betrayed. The trailer almost made the film seem as if it was going to be another angry-white-guy's anti-PC rant. That the film is so politically to the left when the ads suggested something so politically to the right has, I think, left a lot of people feeling betrayed. The last time I saw it, an older white guy hissed throughout the last half.

Yeah. The intention of the trailer was to convey the idea that the means of expression and the mode of expression would be societally impermissible. Surely you cannot say motherfucker or cocksucker in a movie trailer, 'cause you can't get it played. So, then I had to go for things that were unacceptable, but then you had to ask yourself why are they unacceptable. *Malt liquor and chicken wings; They always put the big Jews on my schedule.* Somehow, the combination of words is unacceptable. They're not what is politically correct. You don't go forward without a certain amount of trepidation. I mean, I'm an inhibited WASP from the state of Virginia. I don't drop my pants easily, um, in public. So, yeah, a lot of thought went into that trailer.

It was interesting watching your recent interview on "This Week With Sam Donaldson and Cokie Roberts"— it was like watching outtakes from *Bulworth*. The questions were so inane, and when Cokie Roberts drew herself up in her best pinched schoolmistress air, chastising you for making a film that would undermine the public's faith in the government, it was really great comedy.

(laughing) Yeah, yeah. Well, when you analyze Cokie—who's a very nice woman, works hard, does a good job—she doesn't realize the fact that she's working for Disney, her brother is one of the most important lobbyists in Washington, her mother was a congresswoman, her father was a congressman, and her mother is now ambassador to the Vatican... She means well. It's very difficult to be in that position and look at the statistics in a different way when we're fed a positive spin on so much that shouldn't be spun positively. I didn't want to be rude; I was down there promoting a movie, and I wanted to be good-natured about it. But we spoke afterward and she really, in a good-natured way, said, "It makes me nervous when people do things that make the public have less faith in the government." And I said, yeah, me too.

There were three instances when I thought *Bulworth* really faltered, and I wanted to talk about those. The first is the conversion of the drug dealer. Even on comedic and satiric terms, that seemed forced, unbelievable.

It was a little neat, huh? Well, it's a style. Because, really, how could anybody make all those transitions in a day and a half? Everybody gets wise a little easily. Let's just say it was not done frivolously or in an unexamined way. My feeling was always that we were doing a musical, and musicals have certain formulas, certain marks that have to be hit. Like in a Noel Coward play. This is a different cultural milieu, but that's what we were going for. It was pretty meticulous, whether it failed or succeeded.

The second was when Bulworth rescued the black kids from the white cops. That seemed to drift over into pure white-savior territory.

Yeah. You know, sometimes you just do things even though they're expected. It's like, at a given point, the fat lady sings. I mean, another way of saying what you're saying is, isn't that a cheap joke? And it probably is.

The last thing is when Nina says to Bulworth, "You my nigga." Because that's a term of endearment—and a controversial one—that black folks use with one another. When she says it to him, it's bestowing so many layers of validation on him, and that's what makes it a real eyebrow-raiser—again, even within the confines of satire. I mean, on one level, she's simply saying, you're my boo...

Boo? I don't know the expression.

Roughly, it's like sweetheart. But, when Nina says it to him...

Where's it come from? Boo. Does it come from booty?

No. It's something you could say to a friend or child as well as lover.

My boo. I like that. I like it so much, I'm gonna use it tonight. It sounds sorta French. *Ma boo.* My boo. I like that.

But even more than a sweetheart thing, your nigga is someone who's got your back, someone who's been through the fire with or for you, and it's very much rooted in shared trials, shared blackness—it's an affirmation grounded in blackness. When Nina calls the senator that, it's just the ultimate white-boy fantasy—to be granted that title on top of his own skin privileges.

Yeaaahhh... You know, that's an interesting point because I took this picture up to Oakland for a screening, and when it got to the point where I had this long kiss with Halle, three of the brothers who were sitting up front—big, strong, good-looking guys—got up and started heading for the exit. Then they heard *bang!* from the screen and they turned around and went back to their seats.

On one level, we're forced to admit that we may never know the answers between the sexes, between the generations, between the races. But I would put the races pretty far down on that list. I mean, her saying that to him is a leap, but it's just a movie; it's not a cure for cancer.

The casting of Halle Berry as Nina was a very interesting move. *Bulworth* already works on so many levels—including the notion of the identity-glitch—and her casting adds another layer. Berry—who is biracial—is perceived, unfairly I think, by a lot of black folks as a black-white girl, and a lot of her recent acting choices seem consciously geared toward challenging that perception. With all those factors in mind, using her to play a girl from the 'hood takes on a certain resonance. Were you aware of that extra weight when you cast her?

Definitely. But you look at Halle Berry and you see the future of America. There is no choice. That's where it's gonna go. Halle Berry is a fact of life. There was never a moment's doubt in my mind once I met her. I'd thought of other people, people who could have brought a lot of interesting qualities, but Halle is not going to be denied. She's a person who's getting her perspective on this mantle that's been thrust upon her, and I think she's gonna handle it very well. But she is the future of America. She's the essence of it.

One last question. In the movie, every group you spoke in front of—the black congregation, the gathering of Hollywood Jews—you chastised, you offended. Yet, when you were to speak before a white, Presbyterian church, the character flees before saying anything at all to them. Why is that? Is it because, if you had to pick one group to direct the whole film toward, they would be it?

Yeah, if you were to address the film to one group, that would be the group. That's the group I come from. To me, their visible amount of repression and inhibition, the level of Puritanism, the thickness of their vanilla armor is very funny to me. Talk about stereotypes. These are stereotypical vanilla, soulless people—the Massachusetts Bay Colony all in one gathering. *That's* what he was running away from. That's what I'd run away from.

LA Weekly, March 28, 1998

under the influence
HIGH ART

L ucy Berliner and her friends live in mummified bliss, spending their days snorting heroin, having intimate, time-indifferent get-togethers, and eating in trendy cafes. They move in a druggie's staggered haze, not in a hurry to do anything or get anywhere. Their lifestyle is funded, financially, by Lucy's trust fund and spiritually by her uncompromised talent. The clique revolves around her and she, a lauded but cult-figure photographer, has immortalized them in her work. A glamorously seedy aesthetic (both artistic and personal) has been forged by this symbiotic relationship—a relationship where who's using whom is not only in a constant state of flux, but is ultimately unimportant. When an ambitious young assistant editor from a hipster photo rag stumbles into their world, the lenswoman is intrigued and aroused by the girl—even by her dry academic tongue. "I haven't been deconstructed in a long time," says Lucy wryly.

In writer-director Lisa Cholodenko's very fine film debut, *High Art*, issues of art and commerce are fanned through the more primal channels of eros and sexuality. The nature of exploitation—professional, personal, the ways the two mingle—is the film's subject. More specifically, Cholodenko is interested in exploring exploitation when the lines are blurred between motives, emotions and societally compartmentalized aspects of one's being. The film's intellectual and emotional powers register acutely because Cholodenko is insightful and compassionate without moralizing, without losing her balance and letting any character drift into pure villainy or victimhood.

When Lucy (Ally Sheedy) first encounters Syd (Radha Mitchell), they're each in relationships, Lucy with Greta (Patricia Clarkson), and Syd with her boyfriend, James (Gabriel Mann). Both couplings provide the comfort of the doldrums. What really links the women, though, is their connection to the art world. Beneath her cool, almost shy demeanor, Syd is desperate to be part of that world, to have real power within it. The enormously talented Lucy is in self-imposed exile from the same. Their mutual seduction pivots on knowing how much of themselves to dole out in order to get what they want and how willing they are to flow with their honest feelings about one another.

It could have been rather dour cinema. Instead, it's funny, touching. Though never slow, the film moves at a measured pace, giving you time to absorb the characters. Witty writing helps; so does Cholodenko's fondness for close-ups, her willingness to let the actors' faces tell the story. Lucy's photos (actually snapped by San Francisco-based photographer, JoJo Whilden) are somewhat reminiscent of Larry Clark but, more to the point, Nan Goldin (whose life seems to have loosely inspired the movie). Chunks of the film, in fact, channel Goldin's distinctively funky aesthetic. For all that, it's the across-the-board acting (and the assured mixture of acting styles and tones) that really carry the film.

Sheedy's performance is pitch-perfect. She lets fierce intelligence and integrity beam from her chemically dimmed headlights. We never doubt for a second that Lucy, a trust-fund baby living a clichéd artist's existence, is also a radical, even subversive entity, giving the art world (whose unctuousness is expertly captured and lanced by Cholodenko) the finger by claiming her art as her own. Mitchell is appropriately hard to read, simultaneously cold and opportunistic, and uncertain of herself and her own actions. Clarkston, as a perpetually doped up German actress (a former Fassbinder favorite), has Greta turn her emotional/artistic/geographical displacement into a grand performance, one that blends comedic and tragic aplomb into a single stroke. She nearly steals the film. Even the secondary characters shine (especially Tammy Grimes as Lucy's Holocaust-surviving mother, spitting out inquiries about "the German" that her daughter's taken up with and pronouncing, as though peeling back a curse, that Lucy is "gifted and passive.")

By the film's end, although Cholodenko has never lost her focus—in fact, precisely because she hasn't—the audience is caught in a blur of uncertainty as to who's doing what and why. We know that genuine emotions are at work; it's just not clear to what end and under whose control. We've come to realize that Lucy's self-destructiveness and self-protection instincts are deeply intertwined, and that sorting them out is to dive into an impossible murk. The one certainty we're granted is that Cholodenko has crafted a fantastic film.

LA Weekly, June 12, 1998

to hav and hav not
HAV PLENTY

Last year, when *Soul Food* and *Eve's Bayou* opened within weeks of one another, conversation in my largely Afro-American and Latino barbershop spun squarely on the two films, with comparisons favoring the decidedly mediocre *Soul Food*. Explaining his preference for *Food* (and echoing the sentiments of many in the room), one of the young barbers in the room remarked, "When I looked at *Eve's Bayou*, I just saw *people*... but when I saw *Soul Food*, I saw *black* people." He smiled and exhaled as though Terry McMillan had indexed his every fantasy. But his statement, one of the most depressing, Bizarro-world confessions/cultural critiques imaginable, revealed the dilemma faced by every serious contemporary black filmmaker: How to get not just the larger world, but *black* folk to engage images of blackness that are not cartoons? How to get "us" to see us as "just people" and see the triumph in *that*?

It'll be interesting to see what the barbershop crowd makes of writer-director Christopher Scott Cherot's *Hav Plenty*. (Actually, they won't see it, but let's pretend.) Like *Love Jones*, another small gem that Negroes napped on during its theatrical release (it really found its audience on video), *Plenty* is a romantic comedy in classic Hollywood fashion: Struggling guy writer infiltrates the world of the snooty rich girl he loves, and his wisecracking presence alternately charms and appalls her, her friends and her family. Like *Love Jones*, still, the specificity of the cultural milieu narrows the broadness of the formula, ladling unmistakably black flavor into the mix. In this case, that means taking well-aimed potshots at the current state of black music, its practitioners and its content. It means giving the female lead, Havilland Savage (Chenoa Maxwell), a distinctly Jack & Jill air. (Jack & Jill being the hyper-exclusive social club for the sons and daughters of moneyed Negroes with light skin and good hair.) It also means putting black bohemia onscreen in the tattered threads that the gilded *Love Jones* strenuously avoided.

When *Hav Plenty* opens, Lee Plenty (Cherot), who's been living out of his car, is house-sitting for Havilland in New York while she visits her mom in D.C. It's the New Year's holiday. At the last minute, she invites him down for the weekend and he accepts. What follows is a bank of flirtations, miscommunications and thwarted love connections. Hav is avoiding her two-timing fiancé, Michael (Hill Harper), a slick and successful R&B singer; her younger sister, Leigh (Robinne Lee) is a newlywed on the brink of divorce; her best friend, Caroline (Tammi Katherine Jones), is a horny diva who speaks in butchered French; and mom is an off-screen presence whose voice fills the house like God's. Aside from a few moments of slapstick, the whole thing is dialogue—Whit Stillman's rewrite of *Philadelphia Story* by way of Spike Lee.

It's a crudely made film, and at times its $49.95 price tag all but waves from the screen. But Cherot, as both writer and director, has a good-spiritedness that never wavers, that smoothes over some of the rockier acting moments. In other hands, Havilland would have been a one-note bitch (I suspect a lot of folks will read her as such, anyway), but Cherot allows her moments of humor and reflectiveness that flesh her out. He's also sharp enough to let us glimpse the snobbishness beneath Lee's laid-back struggling artist/boho demeanor and sarcastic quips—Lee's undoubtedly the hero of the film, but he's not above looking at some folks from down his nose.

What's really wonderful about *Hav Plenty* are the bolts of realness that ground the film: the rug that's pulled from under us at film's end, when we should be standing firmly on happily-ever-after; the smart but not too exclusive insider-joke of the film-within-a-film that comes at *Plenty*'s end (cast with a handful of young black Hollywood luminaries); the fact that Lee wore the same clothes for three days running, in authentic broke-ass artist style. What I really loved, though, were the close-ups on Cherot's own face, as Lee. His unvarnished pimples and blemishes told much about the character's poverty and priorities. They did the same for Cherot, as writer and director, cluing us that here's a man who knows that the real stories are in the details.

LA Weekly, June 19, 1998

flying high
DO YOU REMEMBER DISCO HEAT?

A skinny black man with pencil-width dreads stands on the periphery of a packed dance floor, eyes closed and head bobbing in rhythm with the music. His white shirt (matted with sweat to his back, sleeves rolled to just above the elbows) is unbuttoned and flapping to the sides, leaving Hershey-Kiss nipples to flash the crowd. Dark, loose-fitting pants flare out from his legs, one of which is pumping furiously; the other anchors him in place as he bounces up and down on the ball of his foot. The deejay's serving the old Ecstasy, Passion & Pain disco hymn, "Touch and Go," and like Precious said, it's the definition of a track: Barbara Roy's real diva vocals, lisping high hat, a tune of love done wrong. Horns, tight percussion work and sweetly sung "*boo boo boo's*" underscore the song's emotional drama. As the vocals drop away and the deejay sits deep in the cut, the dancer clasps his hands to the sides of his head—fingers interlocked on top—and almost imperceptibly sways his shoulders and hips; unless you look closely, he appears to be frozen in place. He keeps his eyes shut tight.

The boy is having an Audrey Rose moment. He's been snatched back to the arms of the legendary Paradise Garage and the late Larry Levan. An entire era is crashing down on him. Next on the turntable is the sweet, goofy and gorgeous, "To Each His Own," by the aptly named Faith, Hope & Charity, who chant-sing the lyrics: "The best of business in the line of business is to mind your business / If you got no business then make it your business to leave other people's business alone / To each his own; that's my philosophy... I don't know what's right for you, and you don't know what's right for me..." It's all the boy can do not to weep.

There was a time when the tempo was pitched somewhere between 'ardkore madness and ambient sleepiness, when the grooves—pure but multi-dimensional R&B—hugged everyone and everything from Hamilton Bohannon's "Foot Stompin' Music" (a deep pocket jam that makes most contemporary "acid jazz" seem wan and anemic by comparison) to Jerry Knight's "Overnight Sensation." The latter was one of those tunes that, in its day, was admittedly generic and unabashedly derivative, yet still had a little *sumthin' extra* that made it click in the mind; think of Next's current hit, "Too Close," a track that's exactly like every other bit of Negro boy-group product that's out right now, only... somehow not. In between there was space for Linda Clifford's classic, thumping overhaul of the standard, "If My Friends Could See Me Now."

All those songs and over thirty others are gathered on *Super Rare Disco, Vols. 1 and 2* (Robbins Entertainment). It's a collection that puts a lot of myths to shame. Lost beneath nostalgia's glare of spandex, sequins and black-girl cleavage are the overwhelming contributions of black male singers (and not just Sylvester) to the disco genre; it wasn't all bubble-gum, kitsch and endless loops of "Shame" and "Got to Be Real." In these two discs alone, there's Jimmy Ruffin's Al Green-ish "Tell Me What You Want," the magnificent Trammps' "Hold Back the Night" as well as their soul-drenched cover of Judy Garland's "Zing Went the Strings of My Heart," and Mike & Bill's "Somebody's Gotta Go (Sho Ain't Me)." Jerry Knight, the Main Ingredient, Eddie Kendricks, and even Gil Scott-Heron are just a few of the other brothers who also clocked time on the dance floor. Digging these titles up, brushing them off and putting them under the disco banner they originally occupied reconfigures the memory of what disco was, both musically and culturally.

That these tracks, shoo-ins for old-school funk and R&B retrospectives, were once disco mainstays will surprise many. That a lot of the scene's black male energy was anything but swish will shock keepers of the stereotype flame.

What's neither shocking nor surprising is that the barometers of contemporary dance music, which have been blasted wide open only if you foolishly believe the hype, have collapsed along lines that still manage to exclude Funky Black Maleness, especially that which doesn't sashay or shantay. But that doesn't mean FBM isn't still being pumped, isn't still one of the most crucial arteries in the heart of the music.

"Don't you wanna go back, back to paradise?...," croons Byron Stingily on "Back to Paradise." The second track on his recent CD, *The Purist* (Nervous), it functions as both tribute to and lament for the Paradise Garage. The album is a mission statement; "Back to Paradise" is the album mantra. Starting with the disc's title, Stingily throws down a gauntlet. Naming his collection *The Purist*, and then backing the gesture with an album of defiantly soulful House music, is the radical fuck-you gesture that Prodigy will never pull off. There's no speed-garage, nu garage or Big-beat nonsense, no concessions to ham-fisted genre fusions that desperately scream out the marketing goal of reaching a "white youth demographic." There's no infusion of "punk" attitude to make the music accessible to suburban lads. This is music whose lineage is unmistakably hot, stank Harlem rent parties from the '20s, sepia soul shouters and blues crooners spread over decades, and prophesizing sissies crowded into dark and sweaty New York discos and Chicago warehouses circa the late '70s and early '80s. "Do you remember, do you remember?..." asks Stingily repeatedly, his trademark falsetto veering dangerously out of control—that's what happens when bittersweet memories, shadowy grief and snatched joy all try to huddle within a single note.

Stingily and his producers/collaborators (such stalwarts of American-style, inner-city House as Masters at Work, Frankie Knuckles, David Morales, Basement Boys, Paul Simpson, et al) dip into the past to invigorate the present. "Get Up" (best dance single of '97) nicked and tweaked the chorus and energy from Sylvester's "Dance (Disco Heat)" to create its stomping anthem; the cover of Sylvester's "You Make Me Feel (Mighty Real)" deftly incorporates fragments of "Devotion," the signature tune of Stingily's former House group, the iconic Ten City. One acquaintance, when hearing the Basement Boys-helmed "It's Over" for the first time, exclaimed, "Larry [Levan] woulda rocked that shit!" But *Purist* isn't simply an elegy for what's gone before. It necessarily fills a void.

From the lush and romantic opening track, "Flying High," to the Morales produced "Don't Fall in Love" (a cold-hearted but fierce player's anthem), to the churchified new single, "Testify," Stingily & Co. operate under the belief that House is lifestyle music: You pump it while getting dressed to go clubbing, while cruising in your buddy's car, clowning on the dance floor, getting a serious groove on, flirting madly, or chilling by yourself. A good House groove is applicable to a variety of situations; a great one encompasses enough colors to fit any given emotional moment.

The Purist isn't flawless; if anything, its weakness is that it's too much of a good thing. In working with over a dozen producers, Stingily left the door open for an unspoken competition. Everyone tried to come up with an anthem, and listening to the set from beginning to end can be wearisome. Almost as a self-correcting measure, the album creates floating lulls that vary from listen to listen, depending on your own endurance level: a track that at one time is the perfect groove will, at another time, seem the very definition of monotonous overkill. Best to break the album up into bite-size portions as helpfully suggested on the back sleeve: early evening; crowd pleasers; garage set; after hours; Sunday morning.

By returning to antiquated notions of soulfulness, to complexity of emotions, melody and sexuality, Stingily and his crew offer to change—if not save—your life. Those were the promises held out by disco (the real stuff, not the cheese), and those were the promises kept by Larry Levan and the Paradise Garage.

LA Weekly, July 3, 1998

behind the mask
A MAN NAMED RACHID

J ack's Studio is one of the many airy lofts and soundstages that've been carved out of a towering old building on West 25th Street in New York. The elevator ride takes forever and the elderly operator takes his time sliding open the creaking door and lattice once we reach our floor. The occupants pour out of the lift, buzzing as they make their way down a long white hall; band flyers and posters of supermodels are plastered on the walls. Tonight, Jack's Studio is a huge white space crammed with wicker chairs that cluster around tables draped in thick black cloth. Candles flame in the center of the tables, right next to large bowls of cashews and goldfish crackers. Overstuffed chairs, sofas and ottomans are pressed against the walls and enormous pillars. Waiters dressed all in black push sweet-potato-and-shrimp pastries, as well as that old standby, skewered chicken. An elevated stage juts from against the far back wall, whose windows open onto an amazing night skyline. Incense and phoniness waft through the room, which is slowly filling up with media and music-biz types. A big-shot Negress magazine editor holds court in a corner, looking like a crackhead Tina Brown, sucking up and exhaling air-kisses: "Sweetie, *wassup?*"

Rachid Bell, whose demo was an insider's hot item two years ago, and whose advance CD was feverishly taped and passed around earlier this year by music industry folk, is having his official launch tonight, even though he's been playing around the city for a while now. Sitting at my table is a guy who works in music publishing at ASCAP, and who tells me that he now uses Rachid as the model for potential signees. "I see kids every day who are trying to break into this business," he says, "and I ask them, is this what you really want? Do you want to be an artist, to work hard? Or do you just want to be famous? If you just want to be famous, do something else. Shoot the President or something." He says he sees Rachid perform at every opportunity, even though the singer-songwriter's not signed to his company. "He's an artist. Plain and simple. Do you know how rare that is nowadays?" When I ask him what Rachid is like live, a gorgeous half-black/half-Asian sissé sitting across from me blurts out, "A flaming queen."

"Yeah," laughs a dreadlocked sister at the table, "but I hear they're working really hard to bring that under control."

The lights dim and everyone in the now crowded room scrambles for the best vantage point, applauding wildly as Rachid steps to the mike. *"What mask shall I don today, what role shall I play today? / Who will I fool today, tell me which fool will fall prey,"* he sings sweetly, mournfully over sparse accompaniment— keyboards, soft bass, angelic backing vocals from his two singers—just before his drummer kicks in with modified but pummeling drum 'n' bass beats. The song is "Charade," opening track on the singer's astonishingly sure-footed debut album, *Prototype* (Universal). On that disc, the song sets you up for all that follows, both musically and lyrically. A tune about epiphanies, self-doubt and identity fissures, it smoothly melds R&B, drum 'n' bass, hip-hop and Indian vocal textures. All elements come together around a vocal performance that has Rachid *singin' his ass off.* As the kickoff to a live performance, it's an inspired choice. The tense emotional gamut of the song, stoked by the singer's dramatic reading, works the crowd into a screaming, clapping mass.

Unfortunately, the momentum doesn't last. With a houseful of acquaintances to cheer him on, Rachid stalls the show repeatedly with hellos and shout-outs. He starts to lose the folks in the back, whose chatter rises up over the rest of his set. As a performer, he's good but still forming, having yet to figure out how to turn clichés into idiosyncrasies. He swirls his mike overhead like Robert Plant, swivels his hips like Elvis, and emotes like Stevie Nicks; all his references are clearly rock icons. But there are hints as to what he may become with some seasoning. At one point, immersed deep in song, he turns slightly sideways to the mike, and as he wails, his arms go straight and rigid at his sides, his hands clenched into fists. He jerks his head at an odd angle toward the audience and gives a madman's intense glare, never missing a note. It's an unguarded, unself-conscious moment of natural showmanship, of instinctive excess that somehow slipped out and stole the moment.

"Did you see that shit!" exclaims the guy from ASCAP.

"He's serving us *Carrie!*"

Still, he doesn't completely get the audience back until his last song, "Prodigal Pete." A rich, detailed lyric tells the story of a boy who's run away from home to be a star but has to turn tricks in order to survive. In letters home, he assures his family that he's doing great, that he won't let them down. Tonight, Rachid seems to rip the words straight from his gut: *"Get on the bed, that's what they said / You've got to give head to get ahead / The more they spit, the more I shine / Dear mom and dad I'm doing just fine..."*

The room falls absolutely silent as he sings, then goes insane when he finishes up and exits the stage.

"How was that compared to his past shows?" I ask the woman at my table. In my head, I'm committing this concert to memory: Rachid dressed all in black, including a leather jacket that he sheds after the first number, save for his white shoes. Cornrows that stretch into shoulder-length braids that are then plaited into two shoulder-brushing pigtails. He's all fluttery fingers and watery wrists, pursed lips and a wagging finger. He has the emotional and physical fluidity that we continue to reflexively, reductively associate with the feminine. Even so, he often seemed to be holding himself back. In the future, he'll be an amazing live act if he finds the courage to just let go, to become the madman inscribed in his work, someone completely undone by his passions, dreams, desires and nightmares.

"He was still flaming," said the woman, "but he's gotten reined in a bit. But you know what? He shouldn't fight it 'cause this middling thing ain't working. He should just go all out and be a freak."

"Yeah," added the biracial queen, "you cannot control the freak in you."

The next day, sitting in his publicist's office, sipping fresh juice and eating grapes, Rachid is nothing like you'd expect. Several battered personas navigate the listener through *Prototype*: a heartbroken but defiant lover, a tortured teen who fantasizes the death of his abusive mother, a faded and homeless old movie star, a young man still pained by the absence of a father when he was growing up. The album has an emotional nakedness that brings to mind Marvin Gaye and a brashness that's reminiscent of early Prince. Like a small handful of other contemporary Negro singer-songwriters (Me'Shell, D'Angelo, Erykah), Rachid has dropped a debut that's seminal, announcing with this first effort that he's the real deal. There's nothing battered or defeated about him.

Popping grapes into his mouth and speaking in a clipped manner, there's a haughtiness about him. Staring into his face, you can see the foreshadowing of an old, demanding legend who will not suffer fools gladly. But for now, he's also very funny, his cockiness dusted with wit. He's clearly been training to be a star all his life. When the huge distance between him and his songs' tormented characters is brought up, he answers with studied colorlessness.

"Yeah, I'm aware of the disparity," he nods. "It's about projection, really. It's about whatever people are bringing to my music from their own luggage. Sometimes that's really separate from me, sometimes it's bang-on. I've heard so many different interpretations, so many different people's images of me." He pauses and looks me dead in the eye. "There are a few constants, though, that I'm sure you might want to remark upon."

In truth, whether Rachid's ever sucked a dick or not (or even wanted to) is irrelevant, although confirmation of faggotry might serve as the DNA sample that explains some of the anguish and beauty at the album's core. Art transcends both the specifics of the artist's life and his or her artistic intentions. It sometimes speaks greater truths than the artist is aware are being spoken, truths that might be removed from the artist's own life. Rachid is correct when he says that it's about projection. At least partially, art is what the audience brings to it. It takes on as many meanings as there are audience members. If it really succeeds, it renders its maker invisible, if not insignificant. That's a definition which has been all but lost in popular music. Boundless confession, pop-psych bullshit, and clumsy cribbing from personal lives is what now constitutes "artistic" content, and its chief function (aside from bolstering celebrity that is then confused with artistry) is to deflect criticism with the weak defense, "But it's *real*."

The specificity of the lyrics, the nuanced layers of the music, and the often harrowing emotion in Rachid's singing forge an intimacy between the listener and Rachid—or more accurately, between the listener and the characters in Rachid's songs—that can be wrenching. One reason *Prototype* is the only serious candidate, thus far, for album of the year is that it creates so many openings for a variety of listeners to find themselves.

Ironically, even as his album serves up genuine substance, not needing to be peddled on the back of controversy or pimped autobiography, Rachid says he actually welcomes the inquiries into his sexual orientation.

"I understand why questions of my sexuality are going to be raised," he says. "I feel like some of the motivation behind the questions is just based on ignorance, the need to stereotype a guy because he doesn't fit the macho archetype. I also find it racist when people expect me to wear my cap to the back and swagger, to wear certain clothes, to look a certain way, to speak a certain way. I'm perfectly aware that when people make these comments, it's because they're stereotyping men, they're stereotyping men of color. But I'm here to deconstruct those things. So, I'm glad that if I'm met—*when* I'm met, because I will be—with all that speculation, the fact of what I'm doing and who I am will shatter those perceptions to a certain degree. And if I'm successful, as I intend to be, that will be my contribution to pop culture—to challenge notions of what it is to be a man, to be a black man, to be masculine.

"I mean, there are really macho, Wu-Tangish gay men, and then there are the stereotypes. There are really fey straight men like [Suede's] Brett Anderson, and then there are regular Joes. I think it's really ignorant when you see actors on TV or in films playing 'the gay guy,' and its always so stereotypical. I just think that's an injustice as well. I love the fact that I was not self-conscious in making the record, that I could write the lyric, 'You've got to give head to get ahead,' because I'm in no heterosexual panic. And I think that, as a man who likes women, what I'm doing will be very powerful. Don't you agree with me?"

Rachid was born 24 years ago to Nasim and Khalis Bayyan (formerly, Ronald Bell). His father was the main producer in the group, Kool & the Gang. His uncle was Robert "Kool" Bell. Bayyan spent most of Rachid's childhood on the road. His parents divorced when Rachid was a teenager, with mom raising him and his two sisters in a New Jersey suburb. He briefly attended Pitzer College in L.A. before transferring to NYU, then Sarah Lawrence, where he studied French, English lit, and theater arts. Throughout his college years, he was working on his music, at one point being courted by Geffen until he was finally told that they "weren't trying to hear non-whites singing songs like mine." He finally signed to Universal Records in the fall of '95, after doing much soul-searching to be sure a career in music was what he really wanted.

"I have had a problem a lot of my life accepting who I am as an artist," he admits, "because I am completely anti-essentialist. I am against clichés. And it is a cliché to be black and an entertainer. Or a sportsman. So, my whole movement at one point in my life was toward trying to do something more academic—because I can do that as well. But I have to follow my heart. This is what I've been put here to do. This is my calling."

Prototype is bookended by "Charade" and "Back to the Room." The former easily lends itself to a number of readings that overlap in the end, from being the lament of a closeted gay man, to exploring the underbelly of Black machismo, to simply outlining the pressures of being a man, period. It's the sound of a nervous breakthrough, of the moment in an epiphany when you're most vulnerable because you're in transition, shedding what you thought you knew and gaining new insights. The lyrics go back and forth between fear and extreme confidence, but Rashid's vocals are on edge throughout, adding serrated edges to the lines, "Just before the curtain rises, afraid they'll see through my disguises/stage fright at the curtain call, makes me fear my mask will fall."

"Back to the Room," however, brings the identity crunch full circle ("They want to try me, call me a sissy / they try to rough me up, see if I'm man enough... I'm not black enough, I'm not white enough..."), with guitar feedback collapsing into swirling strings, then giving way to strummed guitar that explodes all over again into feedback fury. As if the room and "womb" analogy weren't strong enough, a Prince-like chorus chants, "Oh, mother / oh, mother, dear..." while the antagonist tries to crawl back to the room where "I would be pure, I would feel safe / and I would swim and sleep all day." It's the crash of a breakdown.

In between, standout tracks include the gorgeous, piano-driven "The One to Destroy Me," a ballad about finally opening yourself up and exposing all your fears and weaknesses to a lover, finally learning to trust, only to be abandoned when you're most in need; the Prince-like utopian dream of "Zoe's World," a place whose inhabitants have been able to shrug off the *isms* and bigotries of this world ("Colors unseen, yet they exist....); "Evil," a stark and moving psychological study of child abuse and its consequences, told from the child's perspective ("I wait for you to die so that I may celebrate / To free the man inside you tried to castrate...) with the startling imagery of a teenaged boy putting on his mother's wedding dress, jumping into a river and trying to drown her out of him; the aforementioned "Prodigal Pete," and the haunting "And the Angel Comes," based in part on teachings from the Koran, and in part on Ionescos's *Le roi se meurt (Exit the King)*.

"I was inspired by Islam on 'And the Angel...,'" says the singer-songwriter, "with regard to the account that's in the Koran of what happens when you die. The angel of death comes to get you, and either he shakes you violently and leaves you there till judgment day—that's how you know you haven't done well, here—or he wakes you gingerly and carries you to the waiting point. Islam is not the most comforting thing if you don't do well on earth. You're fucked. But if you do well, there's so much beauty to be had in the afterlife.

"Ionesco's *Le roi se meurt* is a really beautiful play about a king who's dying and is afraid. All of a sudden, his wife metamorphosizes into this angel and carries him away through these shadows, cobwebs, and wolves, through all these really dangerous things in the darkness. She's leading him to God, basically, and he becomes much more confident and comfortable with the whole thing. He finds solace in death at that moment. I synthesized those two texts and wrote from the position of someone who is obsessed with death, someone who is hell-bent on dying and has romanticized death as this beautiful thing. I was really pleased with the outcome because I think the lyrics really transport you to a different place. I think it's an ominous place but it's also comforting. That's the metaphor running through the whole record, in a way."

Other songs based on Proust, inspired by old Hollywood films and sparked by Rachid's background in experimental theater lead one early reviewer to label *Prototype* "pretentious and portentous."When that review is brought up, Rachid clasps his hands in front of him on the table, stretches his mouth into a tight smile, and grunts. "I feel that the standards of what's expected from black artists—R&B and otherwise—have been lowered," he says evenly. "Whenever something comes along that doesn't fit that lowered expectation, it's perceived as excessive. I read the review that critic gave the artist before me and she was really gung-ho about that person, then she got to me and I was like, 'Well, if *that's* what she's praising, then my work is gonna go completely over her head.' And that's fine, because her expectations are completely different. I wonder if she were reviewing my album and it was by a white artist, though, if she'd have that reaction.

"My lyrics are completely from a rock 'n' roll and literary perspective, they're punk spirited; my music is from drum 'n' bass, trip-hop, hip-hop, ambient, illbient, art-rock and classical. Vocally I was trained in both classical and gospel. With all that in mind, people are gonna consider me a soul singer. That's fine with me because I sing with passion." He smiles. "And gymnastics. I'm breathing new life into the [pop music] art form, and it's not based on race. It's based on talent. I'm completely forging my own way and I'm comforted by the fact that I'm not a cliché. I may be black and I may be an entertainer, but it's nothing like you'd expect and it's nothing you've ever seen before. And if I'm successful, it'll be like nothing that comes after. I'm fine with that."

LA Weekly, June 26, 1998

too deep
ARETHA-CHAKA-LAURYN

Three of Aretha Franklin's most sublime recordings rarely get mentioned when critics compile her finest moments; they get lost in the shuffle of her brilliance. "Baby, Baby, Baby" ('67), "Prove It" ('67) and "My Song" ('68) uncork the heartache that throbs from sunup till sundown and all through the night. They're songs that, if you listen to them while in the frame of mind they unerringly capture, can land you doubled over in a chair or curled up on a sofa, head tucked in your hands: the dumped lover's yoga. Everything about the three cuts is on-point—the arrangements, the production, the musicianship. But it's the union of lyrics (simple but poetic, directly from the heart) and that voice (technically flawless, soaked with pain, lovely) that push the tracks to transcend genre and achieve timelessness. When Aretha cries out, *"I'm bewildered, I'm lonely and I'm loveless / without you to hold my hand,"* on "Baby," all you can do is go *amen.*

'Re single-handedly created the soul diva. It didn't exist before her. There were, of course, female titans who drafted the blueprint that Aretha would eventually singe and then redraw—women like Etta James, Ruth Brown and Dinah Washington. But in the '60s, it was Aretha who liberated soul music's ache and joy from both narrow definitions of "race music" and stultifying crossover dreams (including her own). In the process she redefined not only "pop" but also what it meant and took to "cross over" in the first place. She unchained the gospel impulse from the choir stand and brought it to the streets. In doing so, she underscored the revolutionary thrust in '60s R&B, giving voice and body to both the psychic unease and defiant hopefulness of the cultural moment.

When the '70s rolled around, Chaka Khan took it to a whole 'nother level.

Chaka, whose politics were shaped by her early involvement with the Chicago branch of the Black Panthers, has never made a secret of the fact that her ambition was to be a jazz singer, a "real" singer. To that end, she uses her voice like a horn. While Aretha's influence is undeniable (more in terms of shaping marketplace amenability to Chaka's next-level style than in regards to Chaka's sound or aesthetic), so is Coltrane's, so is Miles'. In fact, those last two are the primary influences. At the same time, it was Khan's immersion in the sinewy grooves of '70s funk rockers Rufus that taught her how to vamp, how to pocket and how to bottle the sound of a slow screw against the wall. The wonder of her voice is not just that she can effortlessly segue from a gritty, earthy growl to a breathy come-on, from a crystalline wail to a sultry riff, but how often these varied qualities play out simultaneously. Throughout her career, but especially since leaving the group, Rufus, she—working with producers that include Aretha's old helmsman, Arif Mardin—has showcased these strengths by layering tracks with countermelodies, duets with herself and her own backing vocals. What Chaka brought to the game was a jazz musician's discipline, technical finesse and musical ear, as well as the life force that is at the heart of classic soul singing. Like Billie and Aretha, Chaka's influence is so pervasive as to be immeasurable.

On her new album, *Come 2 My House* (produced by The Artist/Prince for his NPG label), Ms. Khan's voice is as astonishing as ever. "Betcha I" has the 45-year-old singer in as fiery and funky form as when she was the halter-topped, feathers-in-the-hair, bell-bottomed front woman for Rufus. The first single, "Spoon," has a grown woman's playful sultriness, annihilating the wan female sexuality that now pervades R&B. (Sparkle? *Mya?*) Likewise, the rock-tinged "I'll Never Be Another Fool" (*"I'll never open my legs again to a man who's insecure / I'll never open my legs again unless I'm really sure…"*) is the oath of a woman battle-scarred but undefeated. And on the tropical flavored title track, Chaka's whispered invitations and heavy breathing are warmups to a show-stopping blast at song's end, where she goes toe-to-toe with white hot horns.

But it's the lovely, autobiographical "This Crazy Life of Mine" that gives the record its center. *"This is a story of mind, soul and heart,"* she sings gently, and the burnished tones in her voice are pure tonic. Reminiscent of her hit "Love Me Still," from the *Clockers* soundtrack, the track punches with the power of unadorned singing, complete with pitch, musicality, heart—and lyrics that are actually about something.

For all the wonder that is Khan, though, *Come 2 My House* is only partially satisfying. Truth is, the Artist/Prince's creative well settled at a low mark a long time ago. He gets points for clearing away clutter, for showcasing Chaka's voice with due respect, and for hearing and shaping it as a powerful musical *instrument* in its own right. Piano and horn licks sprout up and flourish throughout the disc, and Chaka has entire conversations with them, sprinkling in some cool scatting. But the production is embarrassingly dated, epitomized by the grating thwack of an '80s drum machine that runs coldly throughout the record, casting a chilliness over what should be a triumphant comeback.

The penultimate song on *Come 2 My House* is a cover of the Larry Graham-penned "Hair": *"People ask me everywhere / Is that really all your hair? / I just tell them, if it ain't / Then it sure don't mean that now I can't."* For Chaka fans the song works as both inside joke and too-deep social commentary. Chaka was the first to turn her wigs and weaves into an Afrocentric statement, tossing a big, bushy Afro-mane with black girl prerogative. Nowadays, though, that prerogative is exercised in the fling of ass-brushing euro-weaves and blonde extensions. Is there anyone left who doesn't want to be a Barbie hip-hop ho?

I*t's silly when girls sell their soul because it's in / Look at where you be in, hair weaves like Europeans / Fake nails done by Koreans,"* sings Lauryn Hill on "Doo Wop (That Thing)," the first single from her solo debut, *The Miseducation of Lauryn Hill.* This is the hip-hop anthem and personal manifesto that Latifah's been trying to birth for three albums now. It's the populist political tract Souljah couldn't pull off in a technicolor dream. It's damn near brilliant.

Miseducation has beats that are hard and funky, it blends girl-group harmonies with ghetto raps, fierce patois with slinky R&B, and its warm, live instrumentation (including a turn by Carlos Santana) uses samples like condiments. It folds political ideology into personal theater (and vice versa) but without the consumerist, adolescent bent that defines the ghetto-fabulous aesthetic and Trump-style politics that rule hip-hop right now. Lauryn's dropping knowledge, unafraid to be pedantic and using her own personal missteps and broken-heart insights as primary text. There are no "gotta lotta Prada" rhymes because Lauryn knows that Big Willie stylin' ain't what three centuries of Negro blood's been shed for.

With *Miseducation...*, Hill (the heart and soul of The Fugees, no matter how ubiquitous Wyclef becomes) functions in much the way Franklin did in the late '60s. She reminds us that hip-hop's struggle and identity battles are about something deeper and more fragile than pursuit of the benjamins. There's a map drawn to show the connection between bedroom politics, affairs of the heart, and the devastating consequences of rampant consumerism / capitalism. So, a line about artists selling out, spoken in the lyrically and thematically dense "Lost Ones," doubles as a warning to a floundering lover: *"It's funny how money change a situation / miscommunication leads to complication / My emancipation don't fit your equation..."* And "Superstar" has the withering hook: *"Come on baby, light my fire / Everything you drop is so tired / music is supposed to inspire / How come we ain't getting no higher?"*

Hill's flow is hard but feminine, a contradiction that hip-hop is still wrestling with but that she sidesteps by simply being both. Her singing alto is marbled with thick, fat ribbons of sensuality and warmth. It's filled with street wisdom and compassion. Like Chaka, she doubles her vocals, does her own backgrounds, pulls key phrases out and repeats them for maximum effect. Others have done it since Chaka, of course, but few have been able to put their own signature twists on it as powerfully as Hill has. Even the rap cliché of "yo" is reinvigorated by the way she cascades it at the opening of "Ex Factor." While the sum effect of the assorted musical elements is body blows tucked inside political commentary, it also means that Hill's love songs (whether addressed to her young son Zion, to a wayward man, or to the object of growing desire) are old school in the best sense: There's not a phony moment in them.

Her duets (the eroto-spiritual, lovin' till the break-uh-dawn "Nothing Even Matters" with D'Angelo; the homegirls break-it-down session "I Used to Love Him" with Mary J. Blige) have integrity because the guest artists complement Hill's own vision; they're not used to fill in outrageous gaps, as with most current R&B and hip-hop cameos. (Listening to mainstream rap and soul music radio stations, or watching black music videos, you're sometimes left to wonder if Negroes can even complete a thought on their own without calling for an assist.) Confessional declarations—"To Zion"; "When It Hurts So Bad"; "Can't Take My Eyes Off of You"—have the power of late night whispers pulled from somewhere beyond self-consciousness.

Compare, for instance, Hill's "To Zion" with Will Smith's cornball "The Two of Us." Smith raps, *"It's a full-time job to be a good dad / You got so much more stuff than I had…"* By contrast, Hill (currently pregnant with her second child) tells of waiting outside her boy's door while he sleeps, of being spiritually re-wired and reborn by her maternal role. Her repeated, ecstatic shouts of "My joy!" at the song's end roll off her tongue with gospel fervor. To be fair to Smith, his conflation of material wealth with good parenting speaks to the ways in which men are evaluated as fathers and *men*—for their ability to provide *things*. Similarly, Lauryn speaks from the position of the culturally fetishized mother, the mom of our collective dreams, fantasies and candy-coated mythology: She lives and breathes for her kids, would kill or die for them.

While Bob Marley is a clear role model (if not almost scary obsession) for Hill, Stevie Wonder is also a palpable influence. That's most obvious on the funky "Every Ghetto, Every City" which is two parts "I Wish" (which is actually referenced in the song) for every one part "Living for the City." It's also a potent reminder that the hip-hop scribed autobiography, filled with minute, personal details, is still one of pop culture's most viscerally thrilling joyrides.

Still, nothing on the album is as powerful as "Ex-Factor." The hook alone is devastating: *"Cry for me, cry for me / You said you'd die for me / Give to me, give to me / Why won't you live for me…"* And there it is, the crushing grind of being with someone who claims they'd take a bullet for you—and would clearly rather do so than extend everyday consideration, would almost rather swallow lead than give the gifts of decency and kindness. It's a lover's paradox that brokers no comfort as you try to navigate the gaps between declaration and deed, between what you give and what you get back. "Tell me who I have to be," she implores, "to get some reciprocity."

If *The Miseducation of Lauryn Hill* is read as one woman's story, she's someone who comes off as being on surer footing leading a protest, organizing a picket line, or rallying the troops than she is in sustaining her love life. That's a tragic way to live and speaks powerfully to the unchanged, difficult lot of the thinking woman, the political female, the woman-child as artist—particularly a black woman with race consciousness. But it makes for hella-fine art. The cool thing about *Miseducation* is that, if nothing else, it's the sound of tragedies being shouted down, sometimes with a whisper. Aretha, for whom Lauryn produced the single, "A Rose Is Still a Rose," earlier this year (the best thing the Lady Soul's done in a decade) should be proud.

One thing keeps this album from being a masterpiece: Those played out between-song interludes/skits that, on first listening, are merely okay but by the time you're spinning the CD for the second or third time, are annoying as hell. Maybe future pressings will delete them.

It would be a shame if *Miseducation* were simply categorized as " a female MC" joint because Hill has dropped an album that at moments ranks as one of hip-hop's all-time best, period. It's also a shoo-in for classic R&B status. And it'll earn deserved props for being a stellar pop effort. Hill has unchained contemporary soul music's ache and joy from stultifying crossover dreams. Most importantly, she's giving voice to our psychic unease while she and we search for something more substantial than the Hilfiger-sponsored, money-grasping hopefulness of this particular cultural moment.

LA Weekly, September 11, 1998

ziggy stardust memories
TODD HAYNES' HEADY FILM

V*elvet Goldmine* is a celebration of the '70s, and of the fact that for a fleeting moment there was a seamless blend of lo-fi sci-fi with the gay underground, of the vibrant sexual avant-garde with feather boa glamour and mascara. It was a moment in which rock 'n' roll was pushed hard into the realm of identity politics, in which subtext and text flipped back and forth constantly, and gender roles were demolished. Sexuality was liquid, and queer still had meaning beyond simple faggotry. And the soundtrack—David Bowie, Roxy Music, Lou Reed, Iggy Pop, the New York Dolls, Marc Bolan—was glam.

Directed and written by Todd Haynes, the film—a brainy boy's love letter to that cultural flashpoint—galvanizes us partly because it jolts us into asking, "Could things have ever really been that amazingly free? Could there have been a moment in which the feeling of anything-goes possibility was captured and sold in a glittering, perfumed bottle—and yet still felt like something other than mere product?" There's a dazed hum vibrating in *Velvet Goldmine*, a sense of spiritual hangover specifically located in scenes set in the '80s, a measured lament that answers, yes, there was such a moment. And it's gone.

It begins with a spaceship dropping the infant Oscar Wilde off on a doorstep in 1854 Dublin, a small, ornate broach pinned to his blanket. The film then cuts to him as a young boy in school, with the teacher asking him what he wants to be when he grows up. "I want to be a pop idol," responds Oscar, positioning himself as the founding father of glam. With his dandy aesthetic, his flair for the well-tuned epigram, his manner of cloaking staggering subversiveness in a style-over-matter approach to art and life, his self-destructive bent tucked inside his arrogance, and given the scent of doom and romance that continues to waft from his mythology, Wilde wrote the manual on how to be a rock star. His influence is all over *Velvet Goldmine*. And, like a Wilde play, the film offers up a cast of characters who spout finely polished lines, celebrate artificiality and use lies to get at the truth.

The story proper is told through the eyes of multiple characters, but it's narrated by twenty-something Arthur Stuart (Christian Bale), a British expatriate living in 1984 America and working for a big-city newspaper. He's been assigned to do a story on the long-vanished British glam superstar Bryan Slade (Jonathan Rhys Meyers), who 10 years earlier staged an elaborate publicity stunt to kill off his rock persona, Maxwell Demon, only to have the ploy backfire. The enervated Stuart (Bale's face is a mask of blanked-out despair) sets off on a quest that has the potential for delivering Stuart to himself as much as for recovering the man who was once his idol, a figure very much inspired by David Bowie.

The film takes the shape of a knotty *Citizen Kane* sci-fi musical faux-documentary thriller, one in which the recollections of Slade's first manager, his first wife, Mandy (Toni Collette), a debauched American idol named Curt Wild (Ewan McGregor), and the reporter himself compete for space. When the reporter's journey begins, he finds Mandy—an American girl who crash-landed in London in the late '60s and fashioned herself into a darling of the nightlife—is now a boozy wreck. She recalls that when she first met Slade, she thought she'd found a kindred free spirit. She encouraged Slade's slow shaping of his androgynous persona, her payoff being drugs, money, orgies… and unceremonious dismissal. Mandy gets some of the best lines in the film ("It's funny how beautiful people look when they're walking out the door") including an exchange with Slade that perfectly replicates a conversation from Wilde's own life. Wilde and his friend James Whistler, the painter, were once at a party when Wilde, overhearing a comment made by another guest, remarked, "How I wish I'd said that." To which Whistler replied, "You will, Oscar, you will."

Wild, stitched together from the mythologies of Lou Reed and Iggy Pop, is a walking tragedy—talented, fuckable, doomed—a muse ripe for the picking. McGregor exudes both fury and impossibly sad romanticism, making even dopey lines ("The world has changed 'cause you're made of ivory and gold—the curves of your lips rewrite history") go down sweetly. Rhys Myers' Slade, in contrast, is all cool surfaces. Genuine emotion is the very thing that bores, frightens, intrigues and—

in many ways—destroys him. The actor fully inhabits both the sexless alien of the concert stage and the alternately confident and cracking human being who lives, just as flamboyantly, offstage.

When the two men finally meet and Slade propositions Wild, he does so as both fan and Svengali, innocent and mastermind. A spark of recognition flies between them, flaring into sexual energy that they feed off as they transcend musical styles and cultural differences to become lovers, and partners in creation. Wild's primal, American blue-collar energy helps transform Slade's fledgling Brit folk-chanteuse into a dazzlingly theatrical, sexually daring creation; it gives him courage as an artist and a man.

What Haynes is after in *Goldmine* is less a historical film about glam than an elegy for a time of stylish revolt, stripped of didactic politics and dolled up in ambiguity. What interests him is what interested him from his earlier films *Poison*, *Safe*, and *Dolly Gets Spanked*: the complexity and construction of sexuality; notions of authenticity (where so many white-boy rock 'n' rollers strap on black culture's bluesmen in pursuit of that elusive ideal, Haynes tips his hat to the lipsticked Queen of Rock 'n' Roll, Little Richard); the origins of art and desire; and the heroism of those who refuse to make the banal distinction between fantasy and reality.

It's a heady film.

In the end, though, if *Velvet Goldmine* is about anything, it's about the power of pop culture to transform our lives. It's about the circular nature of the relationship between fan and star, about the projection of fantasies and desires, and how that energy is what feeds celebrity in the first place. *Velvet Goldmine* remembers a time when the exchange promised—or threatened—to change the world.

There's a scene in the film, set in a nondescript living room in early '70s London, in which the teenage Arthur sits watching television with his parents when Maxwell Demon begins to perform. "That's me!" shouts the boy, gesticulating wildly toward the TV. "That's me!" The camera moves close to the set as Demon commits an act of transgression that, had the boy been watching by himself, would have served as a kind of spiritual fellowship between idol and fan. But watching with his parents, Stuart—whose teen angst and alienation seem to leak from his pores—is trapped between horror and ecstasy. He'd only wanted to explain himself a bit, to bring identifiable form to his fumbling existence—not have desires that dare not speak their names clarified before folks who'll never understand.

Velvet Goldmine travels fluidly back and forth across time and space, shuffling genres and styles, offering nods in the direction of avant-garde traditions as well as to classic Hollywood convention. (Haynes even throws in an homage to his own cult film *Superstar: The Karen Carpenter Story*.) It's an absorbing, sexy, weighty work—and digesting it is akin to digesting a delicious 12-course meal. That's due in large part to the fact that Haynes still makes movies like a precocious first-timer who's afraid he won't get another chance: He shoots the film as if he has to cram in every idea he's ever had, commit to film every image he's ever imagined. As with Oscar Wilde, he's studied across disciplines and brings all he's learned to bear on his art. Unlike Wilde, though, he hasn't yet learned to synthesize it all. At least not here, in a project that—for all its clear and steely intellect—is transparently driven by its creator's fierce and almost unwieldy passion for his subject. Still, what Haynes has undeniably accomplished is a movie with pure glam-star attitude. Where so many current films nervously hop into theaters begging you to love them, *Velvet Goldmine* saunters in—self-aware, self-involved and rightly convinced that it's the most dazzling creature around.

LA Weekly, November 6, 1998

home of the brave
P.M. DAWN

Future hip-hop/pop/R&B archeologists will be a lot kinder to P.M. Dawn than are folks in the here and now. Future Negro musicians will cite them as a touchstone, speak in hushed and baffled tones about the lack of love given them by the black folk of the duo's day—in much the same way that it's hard for many of us now to imagine Jimi Hendrix's constant struggle for recognition from his own. Or the pain that struggle caused him.

Exiles from hip-hop who keep stretching and furthering the genre from outside the media- and market-drawn margins (where the dissimilar but similarly afflicted likes of Basehead, Lazy K, Hieroglyphics, and Aceyalone keep them company), P.M. Dawn are now more hip-hop in (tortured) spirit than execution. Following a creative path dictated, at least in part, by defiance of the poison-tipped disses of "real headz," and by following the flow of his own aesthetic juices, Prince Be— architect of P.M. Dawn's vision, sound, agenda—has quietly positioned himself as a pop music MVP, one of its endangered-species true artists. Chuck D. and Joni Mitchell can teach him how to keep his head up in the face of diminishing sales and popular indifference.

When P.M. Dawn (Prince Be and his brother, J.C./The Eternal) dropped their debut single, 1991's "Set Adrift on Memory Bliss," they scored a huge pop crossover hit, but earned the scorn of hip-hop purists who heard the hyper-white-boy sample from Spandau Ballet's "True" as the sound of selling out, as the Cheez Whiz soundtrack to hip-hop's bastardization. But some of the same hip-hop gestapo who howled so loudly in protest of that track now sit and spin on Puffy's dick as he clumsily lifts unadulterated samples from the likes of Gloria Estefan. And if P.M. Dawn had sampled the *Annie* soundtrack for a hook, you can bet they wouldn't have made the covers of almost every major hip-hop magazine, draped in praise for their daring and innovation.

It didn't help matters, though, that the duo were garbed in

hippie-gear (making even the Native Tongue collective look hardcore by comparison) or that the lyrics on their album, *Of the Heart, Of the Soul, and Of the Cross: The Utopian Experience*, were an unabashed celebration of the spiritual over the material, of abstractly poetic love songs over dick-waving bravado. Or that Prince Be's voice and flow carried forth everything black men are not supposed to possess: vulnerabilty, woundedness, the grief of betrayal. And at a time when *realness* was fast becoming a narrowly cast, vigilantly policed, highly marketable item, Prince Be had the audacity to rap, "Reality used to be a friend of mine... reality tried to house me / but a house has doors."

With *Of the Heart* tracks like the sublime "Paper Doll," Be proved himself both fan and master of the revitalized Brit soul movement of the early '90s (even the beats for "Set Adrift..." were more Soul II Soul than New York classic); on "Shake" he boiled a thick House groove down to its barest bones, stripping the raw thumping down to beats that were undoubtedly hip-hop, and then leading the chant, "Everybody thank Todd Terry," long before most folks outside deep House environs had any idea who Todd Terry was.

The backlash that followed—KRS-1 taking time out from his Stop the Violence campaign to angrily storm a concert stage where P.M. Dawn were performing and diss them in front of the crowd; constant digs from other hip-hop artists; even wiggers (exercising the plantation privilege that accrues like frequent flyer miles with every purchase on Daddy's credit card) feeling free to question Prince Be's blackness—took its toll, but Be answered his foes in the pained and furious "Plastic," the lead single from the duo's near-flawless sophomore disc, 1993's *The Bliss Album...? (Vibrations of Love and Anger and the Ponderance of Life and Existence)*: "Now I'm accused of spiking the punch," he spat, "and now I'm a scapegoat for fakin' the funk." Wrapping it all up, Be took aim at the *hard niggas* who dogged him: "What's hard at first but melts in the heat? / They call that plastic, ya'll..." The homophobic taunts hurled his way were met with "More Than Likely," a glistening, beautiful duet with Boy George. Be was still knocking the strictures of realness—"I left reality early due to the lack of love..."—but also displaying a gift for pulling off gorgeous melodies: "I'd Die Without You," "Looking

Through Patient Eyes," "The Ways of the Wind." Topping it all off was a cover of the Beatles' "Norwegian Wood."

On their latest album, *Dearest Christian, I'm So Very Sorry for Bringing You Here. Love, Dad* (in the interim was 1995's *Jesus Wept*, an experiment in burning all hip-hop bridges), the brothers harmonize a hard-knock life full of profound and soul-crushing beat-downs. Racism, poverty and everyday violence aren't even spoken of: It's their side effects (and the way they have of reinventing themselves, mutating and being passed from generation to generation) that interest the duo, but without lyrical didacticism. What makes Prince Be such a powerful pop figure is his willingness to risk ridicule for airing his estrangement from community, for putting on the table the pain of existing in a world without connection or bond, and not dressing it up in swagger, indifference or (to use a much overused word) nihilism. Community—for most folks—is the knowledge that if you fell backwards, you'd be caught. Prince Be's heartache is the knowledge that no one has his back. For a black man—raised and indoctrinated with the political and cultural sanctity of that kinship, surrounded by it but not part of it, exempt from its perks and security—it's like looking in the mirror and having no image.

Inspired by the birth of Prince Be's son, *Dearest Christian...* is an internal overhaul, a spiritual rampage through the attic, the basement and all the closets. Musically, it's a lush and free-wheeling montage that sounds like nothing else out right now. Prince Be's love of '60s pop-rock (he's long had a jones for both the Beatles and the Beach Boys) is all over the disc, but so is the bright soul bounce of Billy Preston ("Art Deco Halos") and the kind of epic soul production that Isaac Hayes and Barry White once cornered: sweeping strings and soul crushing melodies; with piano and acoustic guitars high up in the mix. Hand claps and finger snaps run throughout. An air of longing and isolation mingles with a defiant, fought-for hopefulness. Tracks alternate in tone, flipping from the bedroom ardor of Maxwell (with far deeper lyrics) to the chilled loneliness of... Prince Be.

Lyrically, the album runs the gamut from wrenching confessional to prayer to goofy idealism in the face of madness. Throughout are the doubts Prince Be has about inflicting this world upon his child ("I had no right bringing you here / knowing what I know, feeling the way I feel..."), and the upshot is an unexpected one: You get the feeling that Prince Be will be a great dad precisely because he's smart enough to know that conception is child abuse, and he's already taking steps to make amends. The disc's final track, "Untitled," is a suite composed of three different passages, inspired by the abuse Prince Be suffered at the hands of his mother when he was a boy. In it, the angry words of his wife / girlfriend start to mirror those once shouted by his mother, until the two women blur in his mind: "And she'd say to me / I hate you so much, Why can't you go away? I wish you never were / And she'd say to me / I hate you so much, you're nothing to me..."

Ironically, having all but abandoned rapping on this album, Prince Be delivers one of the year's best raps on the track, "Yang: As Private I's." If there's one snatch of lyrics that sums up the album, Prince Be, and the millennial angst of more than one modern-day Negro, this is it:

I'm tryin' real hard not to be exactly the way I am
the next time I come here all I'm bringing to this atmosphere
is the will not to do it again
understand, I got neon King Kong standin' on my back
can't stop to turn around / broke my sacroiliac
tryin' to keep sealed where this brother's really at
to tell the new millennium "Yo, what da deally black"
You look cute in your stars and stripes / she said are you coming
tonight
Hell no, that's why whoever loves me will have to be my killer
'cause here I'm just a slave tryin' to be the nigga...

LA Weekly, December 25, 1998

other side of the game
ERYKAH BADU UNLOCKS THE PARADOX

It's a mystery why it's a mystery that Janet Jackson's new album, *The Velvet Rope*, and its head-nodding, intoxicating first single, "Got Till It's Gone," stumbled out of the gate and has yet to stop falling. The answer hides in plain sight in the video for the single. Selling blackness is permissible in the mainstream marketplace; celebrating it is not. Few folks know the difference. (You can bet Janet does, now.) The most fully realized music video of the year—the only other contender being Missy Elliot's Hype Williams-directed clip for "Rain (Supa Dupa Fly)"—"Got" not only works the artfulness and artsiness that lie at the heart of everyday blackness (stroking black skin, black bodies, black style) but envisions a world of African cool, eroticism and playfulness that is electrifying in its forthrightness.

Stripped of makeup and sporting a nappy Pippi Longstocking 'do, dancing free-form to the sparse but insistent beat, and ceding the screen to a succession of broad noses and thick lips, Janet's most radical gesture is the one that may have cost her most: White folks are almost nonexistent in this utopia. Joni Mitchell, whose sampled voice from her classic "Big Yellow Taxi" provides the song's catchy hook, is glimpsed briefly, framed by the borders of a small television that's set in the background. But Jackson and director Mark Romanek go harder than that. The only other non-black presence is that of a white woman shown in a snippet from an ethnographic/anthropological film; she's grinning into the camera as she fingers an African's kinky hair. The video ends with a beer bottle being smashed against a sign that reads "Europeans Only." White folks may well have read the musical short as the "Welcome" mat being pulled up. They responded by buying Mariah Carey in droves.

But Negroes freaked, too. Not having the conditioned visual hooks of designer duds, horse-hair weaves or synchronized hip-hop head-bobs, Negroes couldn't or wouldn't process the images or the sounds, and continued stocking up on Allure.

A few months ago, while doing a run-through of her new one-woman show at Luna Park, cultural attaché Sandra

Bernhard was doing a riff on celebrity—commenting dryly on Courtney Love's new "heart-shaped chin and computer-generated forehead"; doing a wicked impression of Naomi Campbell at Gianni Versace's funeral ("What does this mean for *me*?")—when a white woman called out from the back, "Erykah Badu!" (Translation: "O! Great white priestess, tell us what the drum-beat means. Why are the jigaboos so excited by this dusky woman?")

"Er-er... Erykah Badu? Erykah Badu?" stuttered Bernhard, uncharacteristically flustered. "Honey, no. No. I can't take anyone seriously who spells Erykah with a Y!" (Translation: "Fucked if I know. I didn't get the memo on that one.") The audience burst into applause.

One reason the jigaboos are so excited by Badu is that she's figured out a way to celebrate everyday blackness, to locate the artfulness and artsiness within it. She's unlocked the paradox of haughty-but-accessible glamour contained within African prints and jewelry, figured out how to make a head-wrap as desirable as a weave, and brought it to mainstream consciousness without compromise or censure. (Though there has already been considerable backlash from black folks who see her as a fraud.)

Badu cribs specificity from hip-hop lyrics and brings it back to R&B, dragging along beats, metaphor and poetic verse in the process, tackling the same topics as her "pure hip-hop" sisters, but with depth and complexity. "Otherside of the Game" never once mentions Versace or LaCroix, but acknowledges the seductive material rewards of being a hustler's woman—as well as recognizing his lack of choice, the fact that love-not-loot is what really grounds the relationship, and the fears about the looming fallout ("What we gonna do when they come for you?") The hip-hop she evokes is that from a few cycles back, when politics and Five Percenter beliefs grounded the genre, so it's a familiar thrill to have her sell "Peace after revolution."

Where the singer's debut album, *Baduizm* (Kedar/Universal), released earlier this year, announced the birth of an icon, her recently released live album, *Erykah Badu Live*, heralds the arrival of a genuine artist. (It takes ovaries of steel to release a live album only nine months after you drop your studio debut set, especially when the live collection is primarily comprised of the same material as its predecessor.) Following a year in which media hype crowned Badu everything from the Queen of Alterna-soul to a hip-hop Sade, it would be easy to view the new disc as a cynical cashing in. It's not. It documents growth and risk taking, presenting a warmer, more layered woman.

The vocal timbre that drew comparisons to Billie Holiday is still the hook, but there's also a bit of Ross in there (and not just in the sometimes sleepy vocals; the next time the video for "Tyrone" comes on, check out the way she works the eyes then cops Ross' trademarked outstretched arms ending). There's also some Nancy Wilson in the mix, as well as the spirit of '70s R&B demi-goddesses like Marlena Shaw, whose "Go Away Little Boy" is a blueprint for "Tyrone."

The singer's stage performances reveal a voice more pliant and more powerful than is even hinted at on *Baduizm*. She belts effortlessly through both "Otherside of the Game" and Chaka Khan and Rufus' "Stay." Onto her breakthrough single, "On & On," she appendages a fierce rap ("I just so happen to be / tough with a capital T / cain't no weak-ass trick MC / keep up with me") while her band—who, on the rest of the album, check everyone from Miles to Stevie—smoothly replicates the Jeff Lorber sample and groove that flamed Lil' Kim's "Crush on You." "Boogie Nights," "All Night Long," and "Funkin' for Jamaica" are all strung together into a lower-back-loosening attack. Feeding off the crowd's energy, Badu is both playful and self-aware, introducing "Tyrone" with the lines, "I'ma test this out on ya'll. Now, keep in mind that I'm an artist and I'm sensitive about my shit."

Nowhere is her newfound power more in evidence than on "Tyrone," already a much-bootlegged favorite by the time ...*Live* dropped. A kiss-off dipped in acid ("Now, every time I ask you for some cash / You tell me naw but then turn right around and ask me for some ass... I think you better call Tyrone / and tell him come on help you get yo' shit..."), this withering break-up song is a ready-made soul classic, bound to become not only Badu's signature but a reference point for a whole bunch of folks.

In the '60s, Nikki Giovanni wrote that the arrival of Aretha Franklin sent Diana Ross running for an Afro wig and Dionne

Warwick scurrying off to Hollywood. Not to follow played-out paradigms of "good" or "real" Negro vs. "bad" or "fake," but Badu may well have the same unsettling effect. We've already seen how her influence fucked up Janet's world.

LA Weekly, December 26, 1998

hip-hop 1998
THE YEAR IN REVIEW

Hip-hop *is* America. Its only real crime is being so much so. It boils "mainstream" standards and practices down to their essences, then turns up the flame. Violence, materialism, misogyny, homophobia, racialized agony, adolescent views on sex and sexuality... These are the common, bankable themes in mainstream hip-hop because they're the common, bankable, all-American obsessions. They're the underbelly items that have always defined this country's real, daily-life culture. What that means is that top-of-the-line hip-hop and its true *artists* (be they "mainstream" or "underground") soar on the same terms that America's real artists—and everyday folk—have always soared: by being *un*-American, by flying in the face of the fucked-up values and ideals wired and corroded in this country's genetic code. Ironically and paradoxically, that makes them the *true* Americans as they demand that more than lip service be given to notions of fairness and equality while themselves struggling to embody and celebrate life, liberty and pursuit of happiness—even though those ideals were really only ever meant to be accessible by a privileged few. And niggers were never meant to be part of the smart-shoppers crowd.

1998 was a banner year for hip-hop in terms of sales and chart rankings. But folks who read those signs to interpret the artistry or future of hip-hop will only offer up false prophecies. One of the most wrongly interpreted signifiers of hip-hop '98 was also one of its biggest controversies: the high-profile attacks launched on black writers and editors by rap artists. The mainstream media pursed its collective lips in a lot of *I'm shocked! Shocked I tell you! ...but what-do-you-expect* posturing, while the hip-hop media said as little as possible about it, at least on the front pages. Speaking with a handful of writers who are stranded in New York, the common and not-too-surprising sentiment expressed to me was: Consider who got beat down and you'll know why they got beat down. Or, as one writer put it a little more bluntly, "Not to condone violence, but..." (Yes, Negroes have about as much solidarity in the ranks of journalism as they do in every other strata of Negro life in America.)

Unexamined in the controversy, whose harsh realities have been a fact of life for years among black and Latino writers covering hip-hop, are the issues of class that roil the culture, with hip-hop being, yet again, a mirror reflecting that which plays out in both black and mainstream [white] Americas. Those realities are simply relayed in their rawest form throughout hip-hop culture.

Hip-hop has been colonized by bourgeois Negroes, with the media being a major entry point of infection. Prep-school jigaboos (and worse, *wannabe* prep-school jigaboos) make up a large number of those wielding power in hip-hop media, holding down coveted staff writer positions, filling the ranks of editors, shaping the questions, agendas and aesthetics of the culture. Only the white media plantation owners have more (i.e., the real) power.

The prep-school brigade brings with them the belief (revealed in the way they cover hip-hop) that ofay mediocrity—in journalism, the arts, ethics—is the platinum standard, the ultimate goal to which to aspire. The "all about the benjamins" mentality of the past few years could not have blown up as large as it did without their endorsement; it is their mantra. It's also where common, if unstable, ground has been found between many hip-hop artists and the educated fools writing about them. They break bread over shared obsessions with status and its signifiers: money, power and (simplistically defined) respect.

Corporate-urban magazines like *Vibe* churn out press releases wit' attitude that are then hawked as critical thinking. Writers are far too concerned with furthering their personal mythology and superstardom by glomming onto celebrities (thug, pseudo-thug and otherwise) and writing ass-kissing puff pieces. Editors fret about getting invites to Puffy's parties or securing reservations at his restaurant, and don't want to run anything that might jeopardize their in-crowd standing. In the meantime, glistening bourgeois dreams and up-from-the-ghetto-but-keeping-it-real fantasies have far more in common than either dreamer's camp seems to consciously realize; their unconscious selves vibe to the energy of kindred spirits. Both poles need to be seriously challenged, not used to prop one another up.

Part of the flare-up that's resulted in writers getting smacked the fuck up is a result of street realness (or, more often and more accurately, its synthetic replicant) conflicting with the phoniness of soldiers from the Negro bourgeoisie: It's a battle of the poses. And it speaks to age-old tensions between real and fake, good and bad Negroes.

A lot of hip-hop artists come to the corporate game straight from the streets, armed with a different set of rules, different codes of honor, and a lot of them have said and done inexcusably fucked-up things when they feel they've been dissed by a writer or publication. But just as many come from comfortable if not solidly middle-class backgrounds that they mask in order to come off like real thug niggas. The threat of violence, however, is very real.

At the same time, however, hip-hop media has dug itself a hole that it's partly responsible for. The prep-school jigaboos writing about hip-hop have fronted for a long time, working out their own class and authenticity issues by giving artists carte blanche in public forums and media outlets, hoping to prove themselves down with the 'hood and its thriving-but-rigid notions of blackness while simultaneously pimping those notions in order to get paid, to land gigs at glossy white, upscale publications and media outlets.

Too many hip-hop publications, operating under a money-driven perversion of the "uplift the race" sentiment, have been complicit in fostering the belief that they only exist to lacquer and disseminate the PR gush created by record companies, rappers and their publicists. They've played the part of the bitch, and now it's coming back to bite them on the ass on those rare occasions they actually show some balls and *say* something. Rap artists and their micro-managing publicists have been allowed to set the terms for coverage, threatening to deny future access or product if their terms aren't met. (This, of course, is common practice throughout the entertainment industry; hip-hop has no monopoly on this brand of gangsterism.) The term "playa hata"—employed to shut down any critical thought or analysis—has been pumped up into a battle cry by both mediocre rap artists and the mediocre writers covering them; it ought to be banned. *Ghetto fabulous* has devolved into yet another validation of the status quo, only smeared in blackface.

An element only recently being examined in the controversy is the role of race. Middle-aged wiggers screaming "Yo!," and smarmy white-boy rock critics covering hip-hop only because its what sells, with neither group knowing anything of the music's connection to *black life*—and not even pretending to care—are all immune to the violence. Sycophancy and/or skin tone are their health insurance. Negroes would never roll up into the offices of *Spin*, *Rolling Stone* or *Details* and break a chair across some white boy's back or spew him with threats. It's strange, the mutated but still pungent forms of racism, self-loathing and deference to massa that even alleged street niggas carry within them—and carve or beat onto the bodies of other black folk. I'll believe in the much vaunted triumph of multi-culturalism when white-boy music critics start getting bitch-slapped on a regular basis. It'll never happen. Niggers are too thoroughly domesticated.

In truth, the polygamous marriage of the Negro entertainment media, corporate America, and the recording industry have created a new frontier, a fresh Wild West, and America has always conquered its frontiers by brute force, violence and no consideration for who gets hurt in the process. Controlling the media through intimidation goes on in Washington and Hollywood all day, every day. It has throughout history; that's the American way. The fact that some hip-hop artists are following that tradition is simply proof of hip-hop's very Americaness.

It's no accident that the best hip-hop albums of the year (some of the best albums, period)—Outkast, Brand Nubian, Lauryn Hill, Black Star—had their brilliance defined by putting black power, black-on-black *love* at the heart of their artistic agendas; that means forgoing America. That means trying to conquer America. That means making America be what it claims it already is. They're albums limned with the knowledge that capitalism—and the violence it spawns in order to secure money, power and status—will not mediate the inter and intra racial conflicts that besiege us, nor will it soothe the class divides. The violence against human beings is inarguably inexcusable and has to stop, but the wanna-sellout writers and editors over at *Vibe*, *Blaze*, etc. are too busy turning Angela Davis' life and progressive, visionary politics into a fashion layout to see the part they've played in the very madness that has enveloped them.

Year-in-music wrap-up. LA Weekly, December 1998

homegrrlz
RECLAIMING TLC

The low ceiling traps the crowd's collective body heat and evaporating sweat close to the dance floor. There's little room to move, and every breath drawn is a thick one. But the Black/Asian/Latino gathering of funkdafied boys doesn't seem to notice; the sex hanging heavily in the air distracts them with issues more pressing than humidity or overtaxed lungs. It's a self-imposed Colored Only zone of ruffneck/*cholo* beauty, and the glacial speed at which ghetto-cruising takes place is chilling all corners.

Though the head-grazing rafters create a less than ideal indoor climate, it works wonders for the Lodge's acoustics. (The sound system is actually kinda shitty.) When DJ Ben, in one of his finer moments, stretches out the keyboard intro to Da Brat's "Ghetto Love," it's like hearing a raindrop shattering, then being looped endlessly. The house grows restless as seconds tick away, but Ben's in his own zone, impervious to the whistles, claps and shouts of impatience. After a while, the crowd falls into near silence; heads nod slowly in unison. At exactly the right moment, Ben drops in T-Boz' signature blue-flame vocals: "I had some problems, and no one could seem to solve them..." The room goes wild.

It would be two more years before T-Boz and her own group, TLC, would drop a record of their own. Tangled in lawsuits, snagged in bankruptcy court, the trio—poster children for the raw industry deal—could have penned the old Debarge lyrics that T-Boz, in her Brat track cameo, had made her own. Having redefined the girl-group—part Ronettes, pure hip-hop, the Supremes after the projects went bad—TLC had to sit out nearly five litigious years while pretenders to their throne (Spice Girls, Britney Spears, an endless barrage of anonymous black-girl groups) bit their style. Hard. But none came close to capturing or projecting the group's delicate but sturdy mixture of femininity, street bravado and homegrrrl power.

Anyone who's forgotten just how potent—singular—that recipe is need only check out the video for the single, "No

Scrubs," which debuted into heavy rotation on both MTV and
BET a month ago. Set on a replica of the spaceship from
Michael and Janet's overblown but classic "Scream" video, TLC's
minimalist-extravagant clip is sly parody, glossy comeback and
confident reclaiming of position. While Chilli works the wind-
machine and oversized swing like a veteran of the Live! Nude!
Girls! circuit (all gyrating hips and come hither looks), Lisa
"Left-Eye" Lopes (the Ol' Dirty Bastard / Florence Ballard of
the group; she even bears a faint resemblance to the late
Supreme) clocks in with techno kung-fu moves and eyes that
are alternately defiant and warm, then some unnerving
combination of the two. T-Boz, meanwhile, melds jerky, robotic
dancing with iconic Michael Jackson moves, throwing in steps
lifted straight from the "Scream" video; her neon hair and
elaborate eye makeup mark her as Japanese cyberpunk to Left-
Eye's warrior geisha and Chilli's classic femme.

Throughout the short, Chilli plays black folks' longstanding
good hair/long hair fetish with a straight face. When she
casually flips her flowing mane to accent the line "'Cause I'm
lookin' like class," the gesture coupled with the phrase is a thick
dissertation on the misplaced meaning and value that black folk
still place on cascading locks. Can't deny that it's sexy as fuck,
though. Left-Eye takes that same hair obsession and pushes it to
an extreme, with falls and wigs shaped into sci-fi Oriental
pigtail sculpture. (She pulled similar duties on MTV's defunct
hip-hop "Gong Show," *The Cut*, where her wigs grew more
outlandish every day.) Intercut are shots of a non-mechanized
T-Boz, clad in white mini-skirt & halter and matching boots,
shimmying inside a high tech go-go cage, then playing the
black-leather tomboy turning cartwheels in the background.
Industry buzz before the record's release was that the girls
weren't feeling each other, but what makes the video pop from
your screen is the obvious pleasure they're taking in
performing, being in each other's company.

When TLC dropped their debut album, *Oooooooh... on the
TLC Tip*, in 1992, they looked years younger than they were but
projected a world-weariness and street-savvy beyond even their
actual ages. Without playing the ho card, they were unabashedly
sexual ("Ain't to Proud to Beg") but also cautious, nursing raw

emotional wounds from assorted past betrayals ("What About Your Friends"). Those two identity poles—sensualist and survivor—also grounded their sophomore album, 1994's *CrazySexyCool*, and flare throughout their latest release, *Fan Mail*.

From the beginning, the group had an energy that's hard to nail down. There's something tomboyish, even androgynous about it, although it's unquestionably feminine. It's tough, but full of humor. A little sad, but resilient. Ghetto and multi-culti. Their lyrics, while confessional, tap into universal frustrations, staying rooted in both a distinctly female consciousness and radio-hook catchiness. They're survivors the way we all fantasize ourselves to be, having shrugged off victimhood but unashamed of the scars or how we got them, strong and sexy in the knowledge we've acquired, still able to laugh if unwilling to forget. Real, in all its configurations. Their lyrics convey this, but so do their voices: Chilli's sweet but strong R&B stylings; Left-Eye's nasal, steely flow; T-Boz' husky rasp. That's why the homo-boys at the Lodge reacted with such thrilled force to the sound of T-Boz' voice; they recognized it as being theirs—at least the one they aspire to.

Watching the new video, and listening to the album, *Fan Mail*, what becomes clear is that TLC's trump card is that they've been able to hold on to their humanity while being fed through the brutal machinery of the music industry, if not life itself. The joyless, military precision that marks the choreography of most contemporary R&B, pop and hip-hop videos (not to mention the music itself) is turned on its head in the Hype Williams-directed clip for "No Scrubs"; there's an oh-so-slight sloppiness to the dancing, a milli-second variance from one to the other in their timing as they all spin or clap or land on the beat. It's not quite synchronized, though it clearly could be and it's obvious that the jaggedness is intentional, that the cold environ of the space ship (which could be read as a stand-in for the music industry, perhaps) is meant to be offset by human variables. It's ultimately the laughter, smiles and good-natured jostling between friends that makes the clip linger in memory, not the pricey *2001* set-up.

The album isn't as successfully realized as the video, with too many bland ballads ("I Miss You So Much," "Come on Down") and generic up-tempo tracks ("If They Knew"), and not enough Left-Eye. (She's likely hoarding her goods for her long-stalled solo project.) Yet there's a telling narrative thread, unforced but powerful, that's strung through the disc. The track "No Scrubs" uses the materialistic language and desires of the ghetto gold-digger to chastise brothers with no dreams or ambition. Contrary to popular (literal) interpretation, the song is actually about male character, or lack of it, not a man's ducats. (Think of the tune as spinning full-blown out of Lauryn's line in "Doo Wop": ...*still in his mama's basement.*) The following track, though, "I'm Good at Being Bad," is the gangsta bitch/ho unleashed in all her ravenous fury. She's straight up when she says she wants a man who's massively endowed and more massively financed. TLC snarl and spit their way through the Jam & Lewis produced track, ridiculing mushy sentiment in favor of the cold hard realities of a cash-fueled relationship. But the song, "Unpretty," just a few stops down on the track list, is a cold dose of reality. It's where they realize the connection between the beauty standards they've been sold, the material things they've been conditioned to want, the kind of "real nigga" they've been programmed to chase, and the gnawing sense of emptiness they feel inside. "You can buy your hair if it won't grow / you can fix your nose if he says so / you can buy all the makeup that MAC can make," they sing, followed by the lines, "Never insecure until I met you / Now, I'm in stupid..."

No, their lyrics aren't exactly subversive or groundbreaking. And their voices are only spectacular in that they're instantly identifiable in a sea of interchangeable pop and R&B singers. TLC stand out from the crowd because they register, period. Their unbroken spirit, even as they telegraph the pain and frustration they've endured as women and as artists, is the key to their success. It's in the way they spin heady pop opium out of the bullshit of daily life, while still keeping a gritty foundation. But their biggest secret may be that, unlike so many heralded contemporary female performers, they haven't made the mistake of thinking that pussy only has power when it's used as a surrogate dick. Having the uncommon sense not to fall into that too common trap makes them damn near radical.

LA Weekly, May 7, 1999

les nubians
BLACK AND WHITE IN COLOR

It's in the voices: the phrasing, intonation, blended tones. The fact that the songs are parlayed in French makes them exotic but not alien; it's merely the stretching of different skin over a familiar/familial body. The conversations exist beyond the lyrics, and the chords struck are ones we already know: the struggle of assembling self when the mirrors are cracked and distorted—a fun house minus the fun; the clawing dragons of poverty, racism and invisibility; trying to figure out who you'll suckle tonight, your lover or your muse; drawing words of wisdom and inspiration from heroes who fought the good fight—and often lost so much that even the victory of survival might seem, at times, hollow.

Les Nubians, sisters Helene and Celia Faussart (24 and 20, respectively) make music whose sounds and influences purposefully span the African Diaspora, drawing from sources like Miriam Makeba, Soul II Soul, Fela Kuti, Sade, Public Enemy, Ella Fitzgerald, Youssou N'Dour and Abbey Lincoln. It's an impressive list, filled with the same names dropped by a lot of self-consciously conscious young black artists. The difference is, the duo's debut album, *Princesses Nubiennes*, doesn't reek of calculation so much as it vibrates finely honed artistic and political focus. This is music that, when it's coming out of your speakers, really seems to be pouring out of you. The grooves are seductive and lilting—jazzy, soulful, full of bass and beats. (You can definitely fuck to it.) What the sisters have lifted from their idols, though, has less to do with styles of singing, production or musicianship than with spirit.

Sitting poolside at the Mondrian, nibbling on gargantuan slices of fruit-topped chocolate cake, listening to and singing along with the African pop music that another hotel guest is coincidentally blasting from his box, the sisters Faussart are gorgeous and funny, smart and unaffected. Helene's short twists sprout all over her head; Celia's long braids are, today, elegantly swept up into a bun. Speaking in coolly accented English, they complement one another easily.

When I open the interview by reading from my notes (now shaped into the opening paragraph of this article) Helene immediately responds.

Helene: I really enjoy your perception of our album because it's absolutely what we intended to do. I mean, we always have been touched by singers who have, not really beautiful voice. I don't care about a beautiful voice but I care about feelings and emotion. Pain, as you said, and beauty. And so, most of our influences are about that, emotions and feelings. Not especially *this* style of music or *that* kind of music, but really, you know [what's] inside, deep inside. When we did this album, we really didn't want to do something that exists already. I mean, we acted like filters, you know, we had so many musical influences, and we were like, okay we want to do a music that really looks like us.

Celia: Even if it's not really you, because pain and love and all those things are not new. They're just human.

Universal.

Celia: Universal, yes. And I think this album is really representative of us because as Afropean people, we have a real African consciousness. That means that we grew up with African influences—and that means the Diaspora as well, not only Africa, the continent. I mean we listen to a lot of Afro American music...

Helene: Afro Cuban...

Celia: Music of South America, Caribbean, all the music of the Diaspora, we grew up with it. And we tried to really integrate all the music and the culture of the Diaspora. What I realized when we arrived here [in America], when we went to a lot of clubs, for example, is that they played a lot of R&B songs, a lot of hip-hop, but not really raggamuffin, salsa, reggae music, not a lot of Afro Caribbean music or South American music, and not even African modern music...

Helene: Because there *is* African modern music...

Celia: And I was really surprised about it. You feel it...

Helene: Like something is missing.

Celia: We're used to a bit of everything.

Helene: A bit of everything, yes.

You found the range of African music missing in America. This is a broad question, so I'll try to set it up properly. In the last few years, a lot of French films that have made their way over to America have used hip-hop or House music to comment on the lives of the characters, and the irony has been that these are both musics that come out of black life, black culture, but you rarely actually see a black character on the screen. The music is used to illuminate the lives and stories of white folk. In part, that's probably due to the kinds of films that are able to travel across the ocean to represent France, so we may not be getting those films that use black music to illuminate black life, but it's also that black music has always been used to score or provide the soundtrack for white people's issues and drama. *(Helene smiles and nods.)* What is life like in modern France for black people, the everyday folk as well as the artists? Is there a strong Afropean political base, arts community? Is there a sense of community at all? Those may seem like naïve questions but I think that black Americans have a somewhat overly romanticized notion of what France is like for blacks over there. I think we have a tendency to think that *our* experience in France is *the* black experience in France. And the mythologies of people like Josephine Baker and James Baldwin add their own gloss.

Celia: There are a lot of black people in France, but we cannot talk about an African community, really. Because people are not really together. We don't really have a great place in society. We're fighting for our place in society. We're fighting for more exposure and more work, good work, to have permission. French people—and black people and French people—are talking about that, are expressing this situation and all that. It's very hard for us to find an exposure without being stereotyped. My generation is acting in a new way than our parents did because our parents used to believe they would go back to Africa, and for us it's not really true. Helene and I have a special case because we grew up in Africa. And maybe we could go there one day. But for people who were born in France, black people who were born in France and educated in France, they have to find a place, to find interests... ways not to be integrated in society, because the politics in France is integration. If you're from another country, you have to become French and become integrated. You have to become French in every way. And this is very hard—

Helene: You have to cut your roots.

Celia: And all differences. This is very hard.

Helene: Forget about your ways, your African ways. Forget about your hairstyles. Forget about...

Celia: For example, if you have dreadlocks, you won't find work. And for some girls, sometimes wearing braids, it's hard for you to find work. It's unbelievable. These kinds of things happen now in France. Or even, for Muslim people, they cannot go to school because they are wearing the traditional clothing, to cover the hair. You cannot. It's forbidden. At school and even at jobs. There were different stories in the news recently in France about school directors that expelled the students who covered their hair. Incredible. What is weird for us, though, is that as you said, a lot of African American people used to go to France to be accepted, to live, to be creative. But it would be easier for them because they are African *American*, than it is for us because we are *African, Afropean*.

Helene: For us, it's hard, hard, hard.

Celia: There are a lot of minorities in France, and black people are the last people. A lot of people are suffering from racism more than us but we as black people, politically, we are nothing. Only a few black people own their own business. Only a few. And we have to do everything, all the dirty work. I can say that our generation and the generation that is before, people who are in their thirties, we are trying to build what will be our future and our children's future, because there is no place for us.

Helene: The thing is that in France we don't have the same system as here. Here in America, there is a community system. In France, you don't really have a community system. You have middle class, upper class and lower class. And in the lower class, everyone is mixed. We all go to school together, we grew up together, we're living in the same projects. You have Italians, Arabs, Africans; we're all immigrants, people from Eastern Europe. We are all suffering the same thing. All the minorities are suffering the same thing, together.

Well, that's pretty much a universal truth, that poverty is the great unifier.

Helene: It's the great unifier. You are right.

In the press notes, one of you had a great quote that, as the world becomes more intermingled, it becomes very important to know your own culture, your own history in order to exist in that world...

Helene: It does, it does. Of course, you have to know yourself, your culture. That way, you will be more able to talk with someone who is not of your culture. You are comfortable with who you are and you don't feel threatened.

Celia: And to share.

Helene: And to share. That's really what we intend to do.

It's not a racist thing where we're saying all black people have to unify and segregate themselves. No.

Celia: We have to unify among ourselves to strengthen ourselves, and go into the world at the same time. Even if we have different cultures, we have one culture in common: Africa. You know, the Afropean have their own skills and abilities; the African-American people have their own skills and abilities. We have to unify all those skills so we can be stronger for the next millennium. But not in a way to segregate. It's to be strong, to have a better presence.

Helene: I know some [white] people, and I think there are many like them, and time will tell that they are lost because they act as if they were black people, or some black people act as if they were white people, but time will show that it's not true. Just be yourself. Don't try to be someone else.

Helene: I know this mixed couple, an African guy and a white woman, and as soon as they got together, the woman changed. She dressed differently, she grew braids, and I was like, "Who are you? What are you trying to show people? These changes are proof of nothing." That's not the way to show that you understand African culture. No, I'm sorry. You can just be yourself. And this woman…

Celia: She can wear African clothes if she wants, but not as a mimic, not as a copy.

Helene: When you would see her with her husband, she would speak French with an African accent but when she would be with her white girlfriends, she'd just speak in a French accent. What's that? I don't need an African accent to understand.

Celia: I don't like people who copy other cultures just like fashion; I don't like clones. But there are white people in France who are doing hip-hop, and they are sincere. It is their culture, and that is very different. It's the posing I don't like.

A lot of critics in America are lashing out at what they call identity politics in art. I think it's just an intellectual excuse for bigotry... All art is identity politics.

Helene: Yes, I really think they act like that because they feel guilty.

Celia: That is our main problem in France, that kind of reaction from critics.

Helene: In France, we did interviews with journalists and when they asked us what kind of music we are doing and when we answer we are doing black music, they were like *(She gives an exaggerated gasp)*, "Why do you say that? You are racists! How can you say that?"

Celia: No, we are not racists.

Helene: Doesn't black music exist anymore? Can we talk about it without this stuff about universal music?

Celia: Please!

Helene: Give to Caesar what is Caesar's. Black music is black music. It comes with its history and identity. You can't say anything against that.

Celia: And Asian music is Asian music. It has different tones, a different scale and that affects the way you hear it. Asian music has a lot of high frequencies. We love bass and we love rhythm, and all that. When we talk about this stuff as Afropeans, it's brand new and they feel like we're trying to attack them.

Helene: We're called black extremists.

Celia: Please!

Helene: I think that if they act like that it's because somewhere they feel guilty, you know. They are resenting, thinking we are building a rebellion. I mean, please. They become, like, paranoid. It's not fair. They think we are rebelling...

Celia: We *are* rebelling. We are rebelling against system, against...

Helene: Well, yes, of course, we are rebelling against the system, but...

Celia: I didn't say "the" system. Against system. Against a mind-set.

Helene: Yes, against the system. But not especially against an individual or group...

Celia: Exactly.

Helene: We have bad and good everywhere. In our community we have some worse guys, some of the worst people.

Celia: It's not against you because you are white; it's just a mentality. For example, on "Désolée," the last song on the album, we are talking about African presidents and we are saying stop your oppression. We are not only talking about whites, saying *you are bad* and *you did this* and *you did that*. No. We are talking about... [*They're distracted by a familiar African song that starts to play on the boom box across the pool, and they stop to sing along.*]

How did your parents help you form what seem to be such healthy identities and such strong senses of yourself? Being biracial, of both white European and black African parents, it could have left you adrift or full of doubt as to who you are or where you belong, but that doesn't seem to be the case at all.

Celia: I think it's because our parents raised us in knowing each culture very well. And our father, who is French Caucasian, used to say, "Don't forget you are black. Every time you forget..."

Helene: The world will remind you.

Celia: Yes, they will remind you that you are black, you are still black. He knew that to be true even though his blood was flowing in us. I believe they were very clever to do that. Because we don't feel lost. I feel grateful for that. We have to fight stupid white people and we have to fight...

Helene: Against black stupid people. We are saying that because we've had white people call us nigger, say that because we were black, we were dirt. And then black people would say our mother was a bitch, a traitor. But I have to say that the African community accepts the mixed children much more than the white part of the family. But that is logical because we are black.

Celia: We are black. It is the predominate color that we have. [*Both laugh.*]

Helene: We really feel European, too. We are French women. I mean, Afropean. We know French culture, French history. I can sit with any white guy and talk about him, about his history, because I know him. I am like him, even if he thinks we are different. We are not.

That's one of the bonds that links African or African-descended people who are flung around the world. We have to have a dual knowledge of ourselves and our own culture and community as well as whatever the dominant culture is. Even if we have really helped build that dominant culture. You have to be bilingual, if you will, even if you only really speak one literal language. And I think that is one of the things that is communicated in black art, black music. That's why those of us who expose ourselves to it and let ourselves be educated to it will feel the music from Cuba, South America, Africa, or the music of say, Soul II Soul, coming from England...

Helene: Of course, of course. European people and white people—they have to know that they are losing their culture, because they think they know their history but they don't. We know them more than they know us; we know the fullness of their history. Asian people know more about white people than white people know about Asia. Us, as black people, we know more about white people than they will ever know about us. Latino people know more about white people... White people, they know about who? Not even themselves. Not really, not honestly. And we are starting to see some young white people who have figured this out; they know what's going on. White people can sense that they are losing something.

Celia: Yes, soon they will be the minority.

Helene: They are the minority already.

Celia: See, when you think you are better, you are losing. It was Hegel who said that there were two people at the beginning of the world, fighting for life, fighting unto death. And one said, "No, please," begging. So one becomes master and the other becomes slave. So, the slave is working, working; he has work as a value. And the master is just going, "Luxury!" And one day, the slave uprises, he becomes the master and the master becomes the slave. I think that's the way it is going. Because, for five centuries European people—French, Portuguese, Dutch, English... It's unbelievable. It's all the same.

One of the reasons there is so much conflict in the world right now is because the dominant eurocentric culture—which includes America—has realized that their real power has come to an end. It's like a star that dies, but its light continues to hit the earth for millions of years. We are all basking in the light of a dead star. The effects and consequences of the colonialism and racism of the last five centuries will be felt for a very, very long time. But what's going on in the world now is a race to maintain the belief in that star's everlasting

light and a lot of horrors are being inflicted on the world to make people still believe. But that star is dead.

Celia: Exactly.

Helene: Exactly. That's the way it is. That's just the way it is. The third world? The next millennium will be the millennium of the third world. For sure, for sure. That's just how it is. That's why they create conflict around the world over gold, land...

Every relationship has roles, what are your roles in your relationship?

Helene: I used to say that I'm the earth and Celia is the sky.

Celia: Or she's the bone and I'm flesh. She's the architect and I'm the painter. I don't know, something like that. Because she makes all decisions quickly. She knows about structure, about who's trustworthy or not. She likes doing things. She will just do it. Sometimes I have the ideas but I will... [*Pause.*] It's not that I don't believe in it, but I will hang back, and she will say, "Let's do it." I stay back a little. I watch her back.

Helene: Oh, I don't watch your back?

Celia: No, no. Of course, you do. But sometimes while you are charging ahead I will be walking behind and I can pull you back to show you something you may have missed. [*They smile.*]

LA Weekly, May 21, 1999

the secret sharer
FOLLOWING

It's a common way for writers to pass the time: Spot a face in the crowd and draft a story to go with it. Sketch in the person's background. Create an occupation for them. Map out their day's itinerary. The whole process can unfold in the time it takes to bite, chew and swallow the corner of a sandwich. Bill, the lead character in Christopher Nolan's smartly gnarled, '90's noir flick, *Following*, takes the game a step further. A struggling writer by trade, he picks random strangers to follow throughout the day, piecing their individual stories together from whatever he observes. It's a kind of inverse intimacy: safe, superficial, one-sided. Hostility floats on the margins. There's no risk of his voyeuristic narratives being contradicted since he alone determines the weight and meaning of all that he sees. In sum, he's the writer as both God and vampire, consuming, contextualizing and interpreting without the corrupting effects of the watched one's feedback.

The veneer of benignity is stripped away when Bill (Jeremy Theobald) meets Cobb (Alex Haw), a nattily dressed man who Bill shadows into a diner, only to have the tables turned. Cobb, it turns out, spends his days breaking into people's homes—not for the bounty, but to upset the rhythms of their existence. Although he makes off with valuables, his main goal lies in "interrupting someone's life, [to] make them see what they took for granted." To that end, when he breaks into a couple's apartment, he leaves behind a pair of women's panties, chuckling that the man will have a lot of explaining to do. He justifies the havoc he's wreaking by saying it will make the couple examine their life together more closely. Cobb pulls Bill into his world of break-ins, fencing and discerning, much like a guru tutoring a disciple. He schools him in the fine art of what to take, what to leave behind, and, most importantly, how to read the lives of those whose homes they invade.

In one of the film's most inspired set-ups, Cobb allows Bill to scout a home for the two to burgle. Once inside, it becomes clear—though Cobb seems not to notice—that the flat is Bill's.

As Cobb sniffs dismissively at the meager offerings, it's obvious that his protégée is serving up artifacts of his own life, in effect asking his teacher, "Who am I? What is my life worth?" As he offers up his music collection for inspection, saying that *it* must surely be a sign of good taste, Cobb simply shrugs, "To each his own."

Once Bill is completely under Cobb's sway, the film veers unconventionally into conventional noir territory. A femme fatale (Lucy Russell) with a vicious gangster boyfriend enters the picture, begging for help in making her escape from the thug. As her relationship with Bill evolves, it slowly becomes clear to the viewer that almost nothing we've seen has been purely by chance, with a series of plot-twists and double-dealings tumbling over one another. Wholly unexpected connections between characters are revealed, and the alignment of every relationship shifts constantly. What's especially impressive is how powerfully, though unobtrusively, the psychological framework lain in the film's first act resonates throughout the rest of the movie. Everything from Bill's isolation and his lack of self-awareness to Cobb's too-polished persona is deftly, purposefully woven through the prickly narrative.

Shot in black and white, with lots of shadows and close-ups, the British film flashes back, forward, then ahead again. A voice-over carefully doles out information. Nolan, in his feature debut, demonstrates a facility not only with dialogue, character, directing his actors and formal concerns, but in the ability to have them all serve each other and the whole. *Following* is a dense (though not cluttered), tautly directed, well-acted movie that—in a brisk 70 minutes—packs more smarts and movie-making savvy than a host of this summer's effects-laden popcorn epics.

LA Weekly, June 4, 1999

like a virgin
EDGE OF SEVENTEEN

Todd Haynes' *Velvet Goldmine* was an intellectual's fevered love letter to his youth, to the era—the glam '70s—that shaped his politics, aesthetic and world-view. It was an art-house celebration of queerness (not just, or necessarily, *gayness*) as construct; the actual sweat and messiness of sex were telegraphed in long shots, lusty glances and fade-outs. *Edge of Seventeen*, a blue-collar companion piece to *Velvet*, is in many ways a braver, riskier film. It moves up a decade to the kitsch-curdled '80s, stripping away all the easy jokes to retrieve a much-maligned cultural moment. It was a period, ironically, that drew heavily from glam's subversive gender politics while issuing a crop of pop stars whose techno-pop tunes aimed squarely for the mainstream. MTV was broadcasting gender-bending images of suit-clad women and femme men, and the music (while mostly disposable) also spoke to loneliness, isolation and the trembling uncertainty of sexual identity.

When the movie opens, 17-year-old Eric (Chris Stafford)—Annie Lennox fanatic, aspiring musician, the oldest of three children in his family—is about to start the first day of his summer job as a food-server at the local amusement park. "You do know I work at a restaurant," he says to his mom as she hands him the bologna & ketchup on white bread sandwich she's made for his lunch. His best friend, Maggie (Tina Holmes), clad in matching brown-plaid polyester uniform, is also starting work at the park. The two sing along to Toni Basil's "Mickey" as they drive in. Standing in a huddle, listening to their crew chief, Angie (dyke comedienne and jazz singer Lea Delaria) blast through the inane demands of their jobs, the laughing Eric and Maggie have no idea how life-altering this insignificant job will really be.

While the butch and boisterous Angie quickly takes on the role of confidant and surrogate mother figure, the real catalyst for Eric's sexual awakening is his blonde, generically attractive co-worker, Rod. A student at Ohio State, Rod relentlessly flirts with and teases Eric, batting his eyelids and rolling out come hither looks. "You'd make the coolest boyfriend," he coos to the stunned Eric. After successfully seducing the boy, Rod ignores him and a confused Eric slides down a painful spiral of self-realization. (One of the film's minor-key jokes is having Rod be a huge fan of the man-eating Material Girl while Eric worships the moodily poetic Lennox.) For every victory—something as simple as pulling off a spiky new haircut—there looms a potentially crushing obstacle. Navigating his way through and toward his burgeoning underdog status, Eric frequently falls under that crush, unwittingly pulling others with him.

Working from a tender, insightful script by Todd Stephens, director David Moreton has fashioned a film that has a wonderfully accurate sense of time and place: The music, clothing and even the way Eric dances are lifted intact from the '80s. The depiction of small-town Ohio is dead-on in the details, sans condescension or cloying irony. Most important, though, is the movie's knowledge of human nature, particularly regarding the nexus of women, gay men and shared or frayed emotional bonds.

Too many recent queer films actually bolster the homophobic theory of gay men as infantilized and/or woman-hating creatures. The women in these movies are either 1) wholly supportive, unwaveringly understanding beings who either have no lives of their own or who quickly abandon those lives to tend to the gay boy, all the while spitting wisecracks and flashing protective talons, or 2) too easily caricatured homophobic bitches. The former is an exhausted, wounded homo fantasy and femme/mommy fetish. The latter depiction, usually ladling out vengeful petulance on the part of the screenwriter and/or director, is often used to stoke facile catharsis in filmmaker and audiences alike with the bitchy female's eventual crowd-pleasing comeuppance. Both are irksome depictions.

Edge is wiser to the truth. After being betrayed by Eric's duplicity one time too often, Maggie angrily exits his life. Her painful grappling with Eric's sexuality and the necessary realignment of her own expectations and dreams isn't about hating him or being homophobic, but is about heartbreak and disillusionment, about her feelings and needs being given equal weight and value to his. And there's no more wrenching moment in the film than when Eric, having finally come out to his mother, tearfully begs her, "Mom, please look at me," and she can't. These women are not merely props for Eric's personal growth; they're characters with their own complicated internal workings and external lives.

Despite its raw, sometimes emotionally brutal depiction of the coming-out process, *Edge* is a far cry from being a roll call of queer misery. But Stephens and Moreton know that if Eric's triumphs are to mean anything, there needs to be an honest telling of the costs. Through Angie, Eric finds a family of old-school queers and trannies. If their lives are a little too booze-soaked, a little bleaker in the subtext than we'd like, with the characters being more stock than fresh, they give to Eric the gift of family. While the acting by the entire cast is wonderful, Stafford's lead performance is the standout. Watching him shift by subtle degrees—not just in the character's overall evolution, but in the way he has to constantly readjust his bearings while conveying the slightest physical and emotional details of his character's double life—is to witness a very fine bit of acting.

LA Weekly, June 11, 1999

darkness audible
AN INTERVIEW WITH ME'SHELL NDEGÉOCELLO

Y ou ever had love so good... it make you wanna buy a house?" Me'Shell NdegéOcello asks the sold-out crowd at the Roxy. Her face, crinkled in mock bewilderment, glows across the tiny stage. The band, vamping an ass-grabbing groove, has just segued out of a song about loss and regret into a musical non sequitur of sexual abandon. It's about transformation: grief to glory. NdegéOcello purses her lips, furrows her brow and makes a Friday night basement party *awww-shit-now* face. She walks over to the stand where her bass is leaning, and as she reaches for it the audience goes nuts. Strapped on, it juts up past her head, dwarfing her. But with a brush of three notes—a liquid, sinewy stroke of understated funk—she's in complete command of both her instrument and the stage.

Tonight the faithful have their devotion justified. NdegéOcello—singer, Afro-boho icon, bassist supreme—is premiering music from her sublime new album, *Bitter.* The new tracks are nakedly introspective, sad and beautiful. Live, however, most of them have been overhauled into muscular catharses. The audience, buzzed off her love high, roars back affirmation.

S he's small, almost fragile. Her recorded voice is bigger than she is. Tattoos decorate her arms and neck, and her close-shaved hair means that her large eyes become the center of your focus. Those eyes are often dark and brooding in photographs, but today they're direct and full of laughter.

It's a few weeks before the concert, and NdegéOcello (still her professional handle, though legally she's changed her name to Bashir Shakur) is barreling through Laurel Canyon in midday traffic, on her way to a hastily scheduled appointment with her chiropractor. "I was in a car accident a few months ago," she says, "and it was really minor, so I didn't go have myself checked out by a doctor. Well, I fell a couple of days ago, and I think I may have aggravated something from the accident. It was a light fall, but when I woke up this morning I couldn't lift my arm. That's a little scary when you're a bass player," she says dryly.

She's come a long way since her days as a student bass player, vibing in D.C. go-go clubs while studying jazz at Duke Ellington School of the Arts and Howard University. Since her debut album, 1993's classic soul/funk/hip-hop opus *Plantation Lullabies*, she's steadily and sometimes painfully secured her status as that most endangered of pop-culture entities: the serious black musician. At a time when hip-hop and R&B sales claim a good hunk of the music-buying public's dollar, and when MTV has figured out how to turn its early disdain of black folk into a lucrative pimping of blackness, American black music sounds like death. At least most of it does. Exceptions—the Roots, Outkast, Cassandra Wilson, Lauryn, Erykah, Black Star—scream life-affirming defiance, but they're up against an ever-growing wall of soul-crushing banality. No sector of pop culture is as bluntly obsessed with maintaining, glorifying and protecting the status quo as is contemporary black music. "I'm a businessman / I ain't tryin' to be lyrical," boasts rapper Cam'ron on his latest single, "Let Me Know," summing up the state of the music in one depressing line. The overriding themes in both rap and R&B are the acquisition of money, power and status, and, in a truly perverse twist, the victimization of celebrities (see: Puffy's dimwitted remake of Public Enemy's "Public Enemy #1").

NdegéOcello connects viscerally with her fans in large part because she hasn't been seduced by the fool's gold of marketplace liberation. A black, bisexual working mother whose art is rooted in unapologetic political testifying and unflinching romanticism, she's after something both rare and powerful: freedom within the margins. It's an increasingly difficult trick to pull off. It means giving serious examination to your actual relationship to power and your desired relationship to it, to your actual vs. desired relationships to socially and culturally defined notions of the norm. It means being brave enough to follow your own voice, and to define your dreams in terms other than corporate.

NdegéOcello's lyrics on both *Lullabies* and 1996's *Peace Beyond Passion* dissect wrestling matches with her fears and her dreams, with the forces of racism, poverty, capitalism, junkiehood, homophobia, suicidal despair, loneliness... with the search for love and acceptance beneath it all. Distinctly late-20th-century-urban in flavor—full of funk-driven bass, born of old-school hip-hop and older-school rhythm & blues—the two albums have had an influence far beyond their lukewarm sales figures or underwhelming mainstream recognition. Though the comparisons are a sore point with NdegéOcello, she paved the way for the likes of Lauryn Hill and Erykah Badu.

Her true peers, however, are Chocolate Genius, Tricky, Kool Keith—visionaries blind to boundaries, and whose careers are hurt by their refusal, or inability, to play the game. She's become a heroine for the poets, musicians and street intellectuals who struggle to integrate their art with their everyday life, arching toward the divine while honoring the commonplace. But perhaps her music's greatest strength has been in its preservation and presentation of the nuanced protagonist in black music, not some industry-generated, flossing jigaboo, but a living, breathing, struggling "self" contained within the grooves.

NdegéOcello considers this summation, then refines it a bit.

"Well, thank you," she nods, "thank you for that. It's really hard, you know, because I love rhythm & blues. I love it. But there's so little of it I can listen to now. Because it's absent not only of a protagonist, but of any real story, any real sincerity. I was arguing the other day with someone who didn't like Eminem. Well, I love Eminem. I think he's dope for so many reasons. He's got that Slick Rick, talking-to-himself thing going—maybe you need to be really deep into hip-hop to hear it—and he's completely keeping it real. He's totally happening. His similes and metaphors are amazing. I mean, maybe they are crass, but . . ." She pauses, then continues from a different angle.

"Everybody trips because he's white, but his pocket is better than half the rappers out there. But the real thing is, you hear his story in everything: his voice, his lyrics, his attitude. He's telling you what it is to be poor and white in this country, to have no education and no job prospects. See, it's not just about race anymore, it's about class, too, and he's a prime example of what we do to people when we don't educate them. There's a real sense of him being profoundly depressed beneath all that anger. It's like, his soul is so large. I definitely feel that he's speaking from the heart. I love him for that."

Pulling into the parking lot of the chiropractor's office, NdegéOcello blows her horn and waves out the window. "That's my girlfriend," she says, nodding toward a pretty black woman getting out of a car parked a few spaces away. As we're introduced, it becomes clear why her face had been so familiar—she's Rebecca Walker, the writer and feminist social critic.

Walker's session is over first. She flexes her back and slowly rolls her neck as she writes out a check at the receptionist's desk. Beneath her spaghetti-strapped T-shirt, her muscles ripple beautifully. Walker first met NdegéOcello when she was soliciting submissions for her book, *To Be Real: Telling the Truth and Changing the Face of Feminism* (1995), though it's only recently that they've become, in NdegéOcello's words, "inseparable." They're currently living with NdegéOcello's 10-year-old son, Askia, just outside Mendocino, while they look for a house in Berkeley.

While their life together clearly marks a new chapter in NdegéOcello's life, it also fits her pattern of wanderlust. Bashir Shakur née Me'Shell NdegéOcello née Michelle Johnson was born in Berlin in 1969 to a military father and housewife mother, grew up in Washington, moved to New York, and then to L.A. "Don't try to psychoanalyze me," she laughs, "I just like to move. I feel better in motion. After four or five years, I get restless." When asked about the recent name change, she says, "There were several reasons, some religious. But, you know, I was coming to a place where whatever Me'shell NdegéOcello meant to me, it had just become this other thing, for other people. It just no longer reflects who I am or what my goals are."

And what does the new name mean? "Bashir means 'a sender of good news' in Arabic," she explains. "In Hebrew, it means 'one in the song.' I didn't actually know that. I was hanging out, smoking cigarettes in this café in New York, and this beautiful man sat down and just started talking—he was, like, an Orthodox Jewish man—and he was like, 'Can I bum one of your cigarettes?' We just started talking, and he asked me my name. When I told him, he told me what it meant. And then, Shakur just means 'most thankful.' That's the place I'm trying to eventually get to."

Waiting in the chiropractor's lobby, I ask Walker if she could possibly slip out of the role of girlfriend and into that of culture critic in order to locate NdegéOcello's place in contemporary pop culture in general, and black pop culture specifically.

"Mmm," she begins slowly. "I think that in the realm of pop culture right now, whether that's black pop culture or white pop culture, she represents both a vanguard and a dying breed. You know, we're on the road so we watch a lot of TV, and all these performers are talking about how they recognize that music is a business first and foremost. A lot of black performers are saying that right now—Missy Elliot, Puff Daddy—and it's just this kind of 'We're so cool that we figured out that music is a business, and you've got to take care of your business.' Which is true to some extent, but at the same time, when you're so caught up in the business, checking SoundScan every five minutes to see how many units you've sold, I think you do lose touch with what you're trying to do creatively.

"I think a lot of these younger artists really feel like they can do both, but I think that's naïve. It's naïve to think you can be worried about trying to make money, money, money, and still be saying something that is empowering to people, that is challenging the status quo, which would rather have your people—black people—in bondage."

Equally insidious is the smug, even contemptuous, dismissal of the idea of music, or any art, as a deeper means of communication, as a conduit for profound personal and societal transformation. To hold on to that belief, to act on it, is to be labeled clueless—or crazy.

"I completely agree," says Walker. "To care about that, to be true to yourself and your soul and try to connect at a deep emotional, psychological, spiritual level with an audience, and to try to create art that's about transformation—*that* is somehow naïve, now. Being obsessed with the bottom line is portrayed as being sophisticated. It's so emblematic of how twisted and backward and reactionary our culture has become. And how cynical. I think a lot of musicians today just feel like, fuck message, forget about using music as a tool. Forget about those deeper levels of what art has been about in many cultures, and certainly within black culture. And I just think that's a tragedy. That's why I love her and her music, and I'm so glad she's doing it."

Walker checks her watch and realizes she has to run. "Tell Bashir I'll meet her back at the hotel," she says before taking off. A short while later an apologetic, and noticeably more relaxed, NdegéOcello appears.

On the way back into Hollywood, NdegéOcello is reminded that just a few years ago she was being lambasted by a lot of female rock critics for not identifying herself as a feminist. Her response at the time was a shrug and a reply of "Whatever." Has her relationship with Walker resulted in her coming out as a feminist?

"No," she says, shaking her head. "That's what we fight..." she smiles slightly and pauses. "I mean, no. What she was trying to explain in her book is that feminism comes in many different shapes and sizes. Of course, there are some things I have a feminist view to. There are some things I just don't agree with feminism about. I'm more..." She exhales deeply. "My politics deal with other things. We argue about that. I just don't like that word."

It's ironic that, with her art so rooted in the rituals of naming and claiming self, so many of the controversies that have blown up around NdegéOcello have had to do with her determination to do that naming on her own terms. The mainstream gay press has harshly criticized her for singing love songs to men and refusing to identify herself as "queer"; many in the music industry have blamed her decision to be open about her bisexuality for her failure to achieve mainstream success; black radio, video outlets and magazines either shortchange or ignore her altogether. (*Vibe* named *Bitter* album of the year, but put the ever-blonder Jennifer Lopez on the cover.)

"As far as the queer thing," she says, "it just bothers me, period, that white gay males define how a lot of homosexuals or lesbians see themselves. Queer? I'm not feeling that. I can't really embrace that. I can't embrace lesbian, either. I hate the way the word sounds; it's not an attractive word. It's hard being bisexual, omnisexual, multisexual, whatever you want to call it, when people have their agenda and expect you to *just* represent *their* agenda."

As she's talking, she's dialing her car phone to check her messages, and accidentally gets her father in D.C. Askia is staying there for the summer, hanging out with his grandparents and spending time with his father. Mother and son have a playful exchange before she hangs up.

"You know what's hard?" she asks, twisting her face into a comedic grimace. "When your parents treat your child better than they treated you. Whoo! I mean, how does that happen?" She laughs deeply. "Seriously, what is that about?" She shakes her head.

What impact does her career have on her relationship with her son, and vice versa?

"Having a child made me really deal with the dark sarcasm I had, with my being depressed all the time," she replies thoughtfully. "Do I want to shortchange my child out of having joy just because I don't have it? [Motherhood] helped me so much, because it allowed me to find ways to make myself feel better, to still understand the world as a place of suffering, but not wallow in it. To find joy and appreciate what I have. Children are born with their own optimism. They have a clarity and a simplicity that we can only wish for. Everything is so new and beautiful to them, and I'm really trying to find a way to stop [for my son] whatever it is that causes them to lose it, which usually happens around the ages of 13, 14.

"I'm reading this book called *Real Boys*, which is an excellent book. You gotta put that in your article. The author's last name is Pollack. It's just an incredible God-danged ol' book. It deals with how men are taught not to be affectionate, not to express their feelings, and it teaches you how to confront them with their feelings, and when to pull back. It's an amazing book."

Asked if her sexuality has yet been a problem for her son, maybe with his classmates, she quips, "He goes to a really progressive school, so I'm not the only one." Then, turning serious, she adds, "I don't think it's been an issue. I'm sure when he gets to high school it'll be difficult, but so far it hasn't been."

She smiles softly. "I love children. I want more. Rebecca and I plan to have children, maybe next year. I'm hoping we have a daughter."

A t some point the conversation turns to the topic of race. Race in America, race in Africa, race in the music industry. NdegéOcello's detractors have often accused her of being racist, militantly anti-white. That's because they're tone-deaf to the complexities of her music. They're blind to the ways that race plays out in modern-day America, and to the survival techniques of black (and brown) folk who grapple with daily racism. Me'shell gives honest voice to that pain and anger, to the struggle not to succumb to bitterness. In conversation, as in her music, she has dual vision. On one hand, she knows that race is—as academics and media liberals drone—a "construct," a lie that has wreaked incalculable damage on humanity. Like most people, regardless of color, she wants to move past it.

But she also knows that the lie of race has spawned some bitter truths and painful realities. To merely acknowledge the "construct" and think that that is enough to counteract or dismantle the legacies of bigotry only compounds the problem. NdegéOcello's critics have harped on her scathing social indictments—in songs like "Soul on Ice" and "Deuteronomy: Niggerman"—without seeing that the world she's longing for is simply one of justice and equality. The distinction they've failed to make is that her politics are not a war on white folk, but a struggle against white supremacy and the way it continues to mutate and insinuate itself into the fabric of American life. One of her most resonant artistic riffs is on the connection between capitalism and white supremacy. A line from 1996's "Deuteronomy"—"My view of self was that of a divine ho/Like the ones portrayed on the white man colonized minded rap shows"—has only become more relevant, more painfully dead-on, in the past few years.

"It's hard being dark," NdegéOcello says. "I even get it from my mother. She tells me about my son, 'Oh, he's gotta stay out of the sun, he gets so dark.' I mean, my mother's very fair-skinned, and she's from the South. She can't help it, that's the way she was brought up. But it wrecked me as a child. I was always like, 'How come I wasn't light like my mother? How come I didn't get good hair?' And that's what 'Soul on Ice' is about. Everybody thinks that song is about me not liking white people. No, it's about me growing up feeling ashamed of the way I looked."

Federico Peña, her keyboardist and a close friend, offers a defense of NdegéOcello as he carefully dismantles the aura of angry, tortured artist that surrounds her. "I've known her since she was 15 or 16 in D.C.," he recalls, "and she's the same now as she was then. She's just like everybody else. She can get really depressed, really dark, but she also has these moments of just..." He pauses, searching for the right word. "She can get happy like no one you know," he finally smiles. "I think that a lot of her struggle comes from her quest to be accepted. I think there's a struggle within Me'Shell when she calls out these truths. I think that's why she touches a chord in people. In a way, she's a soldier for those truths that America doesn't want to take a look at.

"I'm sorry," he says, "I don't want to seem offensive. Because I didn't grow up here. I was born in Uruguay and grew up in Argentina. I had to learn about America when my family moved here when I was a boy. And what I've seen is that this is still such a fucked-up place. People honestly want to say that racism is a thing of the past, but it's not. It's like a ghost. Not everybody can see it, some people pretend they can't see it 'cause they don't want to be labeled crazy, but it's still very much here, wreaking havoc. I've traveled all around the world, and I'm still constantly astonished at the depth of racism in this country. And I think, historically, America has had a problem when black folks talk about the truths of [what's] happening [here]. They tend to label that black voice as angry, when it's a voice of truth. I think Me'Shell may have fallen prey to some of that."

As rap and R&B have devolved into the soundtrack for Wall Street and Madison Avenue, the aesthetic they've revived—especially in terms of female beauty and desirability—is a fucked-up brand of retro: It's all about light skin, good hair and Anglo features. With only a relative handful of artists working to the exception, the whole "I'm black and I'm proud" resistance movement once conveyed through the music and stage personas of people like Nina Simone, James Brown and Curtis Mayfield has been ground into dust.

"Have you ever seen the movie *Wattstax*?" asks NdegéOcello. "It's an incredible tribute to a black aesthetic that's all about Afros, kinky hair—a variety of skin tones and physical features. Darkness is celebrated just by being acknowledged. You watch this movie, and you're blown away by the consciousness that plays out in the way the people dress and talk and carry themselves. The way black people treat other black people, it's just love. What happened to us?" What indeed? Watching the movie is both exhilarating and heartbreaking. A cult documentary about the 1972 concert held at the L.A. Coliseum to commemorate the riots of '65, the film cuts back and forth among performance footage (Isaac Hayes, the Staples Singers, the Bar-Kays, Luther Ingram, Rufus Thomas, Jesse Jackson and more), talking heads of everyday black folk, and Richard Pryor as the narrative glue holding it all together. It's staggering to see how C-list divas from back in the day—women like Kim Weston and Carla Thomas, who were overshadowed by Aretha, Roberta and Mavis—could sing circles around most of today's A-level crooners. Pryor, in his first big-screen appearance and one of his best career performances, draws tears-on-the-cheek laughter from caustic observations on gender differences, police brutality and the resilience of Afro-Americans. Watching black folk dance in the stands, make flamboyant entrances and muse dryly on the nature of whiteness is to see blackness as a knowing performance. There's a lot of humor, but there's also affirmation of self, black fierceness giving itself props. The wild clothing and pimp strolls have been stripped, now, of all that subtext. It's been reduced to Beastie Boys video garb, kitschy costumes for white hipster parties, and mindless hip-hop celebrations of mackin'.

It's the last that most pains NdegéOcello. Speaking of the ways in which mainstream hip-hop has collapsed upon itself, she beomes especially animated and frustrated.

"It hurts me to my heart," she says. "I mean, there is some gangster rap or darker hip-hop that is absolutely relevant and needs to be said. But so much of it is just jumping on a bandwagon with nothing to say. You know, I'm a big Nas fan, so I went out and bought his last record [*I Am...*]. Now, the CD booklet opens with a sura from the Koran. But the actual record begins with a rant: 'Fuck all y'all faggot muthafuckas.' And it just killed me. I don't know what to do. Do I take my record back, you know? I mean, he talks [in interviews] about black upliftment and all the stuff he's read, and I'm like, 'Well, you callin' people faggots. Did you ever read James Baldwin, one of the great intellectual minds of our time, who was a gay man?' It's just really difficult for me to embrace and have an understanding of my brothers—and they are my brothers and I will love them till the day I die—but I just don't understand what they're doing." She shakes her head and sighs.

"You know," she revs up again, slightly changing course, "Mos Def and Talib Kweli are the freshest thing I've heard in a long time, but what the hell is RZA talking about? Who the hell is Bobby Digital? What is that? It just seems that, for the most part, you're either gangster mentality, Puffy mentality, or you're not at all. You don't exist.

"The really scary thing is that when I went to Africa, [I saw how] they think that Tupac Shakur—and I love Tupac to this day, he was my boy and I love him—but they think that's our new movement. They think gangsterism is the new black political movement and that it's what's saving black people. They've bought into the commercialism and the worst aspects of American culture. It's really hard when you go into these obscure little pockets, and they're embracing what shouldn't be embraced. It's scary."

At the exact moment that we enter Sante Kitchen on La Brea, the opening strains of Madonna's "Beautiful Stranger" blare over the sound system. NdegéOcello doesn't register the latest hit from her boss at Maverick Records. She hugs one of the waiters, who jokes about how often she comes in. "I'm only in here so much," she laughs, "because I've found out that I'm basically allergic to all four food groups. This is one of the only places I can eat where I will, like, survive the meal."

"That's Raju," she grins as she sits down. "He's worked at every restaurant I love in L.A." Raju comes and leans over the table, and the two chat a little more. This gives me a chance to glance at my notes about Bitter. It's a curve-ball departure for NdegéOcello. There are no funk workouts like "If That's Your Boyfriend (He Wasn't Last Night)," "Who Is He and What Is He to You" or "Step Into the Projects." Her voice is higher up in the mix, and her singing is richer, more textured and fluid. One of the album's real surprises, though, is NdegéOcello's bass playing. There's so little of it.

"Mmm-hmm," she nods later, spooning soup into her mouth. "That's why [the record's] so good. The songs dictated that. It was a matter of being true to what the songs were about, and they weren't about that."

Inspired in part by her painful breakup a few years ago with dancer Winifred Harris, this is an album pulled from the wreckage of a failed love affair. They're songs from the fetal position. Late night, stare at the ceiling, wonder if I should call songs. Too far gone to cry songs. Love hymns about closing your eyes and running on fumes of faith. Yet glimmers of hope twine into resilience: The album, finally, is a celebration of the ability to love at all, despite pain or grief, and in defiance of bitterness.

There are familiar NdegéOcello strokes: the terrifying father figure; a consuming fear of abandonment; loneliness so deep it feels like God calling you home; images of comforting angels. And there are wholly new aesthetic avenues explored: the use of steel guitar, the tripped-out industrial blues of "Wasted Time," the heightened folk influences. *Bitter's* two instrumental tracks, "Adam" and "Eve," purposefully carry the names of the most famous characters in perhaps the most famous myth of creation. It's a reminder that from the very beginning (though NdegéOcello clarifies that she doesn't believe Adam and Eve really are the beginning, they're just potent symbols), coupledom has been fraught with danger, with the devastation of deception and betrayal. "Loyalty" is sketched with lyric details ("His oversize Dickies cinched way up high / She lived in her books and fantasies...") that give it the power of a finely scribed short story. "Wasted Time," a duet with L.A. singer-songwriter (and, incidentally, Madonna's brother-in-law) Joe Henry, hijacks the ear with the hypnotic vibe conjured by the union of these two distinctive voices. Joan Armatrading's influence is all over the place. It's a lush, languid cover of Jimi Hendrix's "May This Be Love," though, that is *Bitter's* crowning glory. It's also NdegéOcello's favorite track on the album.

"My greatest influence is Jimi Hendrix," she reveals, "and if he's been reincarnated, or if he's looking down, sideways, or looking up, I just wanted to tell him that I love him and thank him for opening doors for me. I just wanted to make it beautiful for him."

She also wants it known that David Gamson, her best friend and producer on her first two albums, had started production work on this one when he was kicked off the project by powers at Maverick. "We handed them some stuff that didn't sound like Janet Jackson, and they didn't get it. I was sick of how they talked about him, how they treated him. I just couldn't see my friend treated like that. It was sort of a mutual decision. Then they named all these people I should work with—this guy who worked with the Beatles, then Daniel Lanois—but they did nothing to make it happen. I finally went to Craig [Street], 'cause I love his stuff, and they didn't say no. They gave us, like, a dollar to make the record. I'm really happy with it, though. And David actually did produce a lot of the vocals."

What ultimately makes *Bitter* such an ass-kicking, soul-stirring album, so radical, is that it's not trying to be. Not in superficial terms. In a culture gone mad for the faux rebellion and adolescent thrills of all things hardcore, it dares to be vulnerable and tender. But that's also part of what makes it another entry in the NdegéOcello diary of career struggles. There are no "singles" in the way they've come to be defined: hook-laden, singsong choruses and junior high poetry for verses. The understated arrangements guide attention to the lyrics and the emotion in NdegéOcello's voice—frayed and soothing, with a warm huskiness that slides from bruised to lustful with unnerving ease. It's exactly what a heartbreak album should be: simple. I ask what the company's reaction was when she turned it in.

"Well, I only made this record because I was contractually obligated," she admits. "And when I turned it in, I was literally told by the general manager, 'You're not going to sell a lot of records. If you really want to help us, you'll do a remix. Or maybe you could go write a song with a bigger name.' That was their vision. They were like, it's a beautiful record, but it's not gonna sell. I'm at a label where they obviously let me do what I do, but I just don't think they have any respect for what I do. You know, I had a really eye-opening conversation with Joan Osborne, who I think is so talented. I was telling her I handed in my record and they didn't like it, and she was like, 'I handed in my record and they told me to take it back.' I mean, I don't think anybody who works at *any* record company actually *likes* music anymore."

NdegéOcello is merely echoing the words of countless musicians who have gone before her and countless who will come after her. But I'm still struck by the note of bafflement beneath her frustration. Is she really surprised at the way she's been handled?

"You just think," she answers, "that if someone signs you, they get you. It's also a question of, what do you do when your art becomes your livelihood? See, I thought it would be a great thing that I could make music and make money. But it kinda warped my idea of my art. It's like, am I doing my art to make money, or do I just feel like if I didn't do my art I'd die? I try to take that [money] mind-set out. I'm not doing this for money. Maybe that's convoluted and delusional." She pauses. "I just go out and play music because I think there are people who want to hear what I do."

In a separate interview, Craig Street (who's also produced Cassandra Wilson, Holly Cole, k.d. lang) sounds more optimistic. "The fact is," he says, "that Maverick is putting the disc out. I believe they will get behind it. And hopefully somebody at Maverick will remember that when they signed Me'Shell, they signed her as a really intense, creative artist. Hopefully somebody at Maverick remembers that maybe it's not everyone's job to sell 30 million copies of a record, that some of the cachet of being a great record company is that you're able to balance those that sell 30 million against those that come out with great artistic statements."

He goes on to compare her to the Duke himself. "She's a phenomenal bandleader, in the style of Ellington, people who could do everything. They could write, play and perform. I've seen her on live gigs where, literally, things would be thrown together—musicians from all over the place who she would never have seen before—and she would literally go around, while still playing the song, and in a really natural, very easy kind of way, direct each musician into exactly the position she wanted them to have. I've seen her do that onstage a number of different times. It's an amazing thing to watch."

At the restaurant, sipping on an iced tea, NdegéOcello says, "They get upset [at Maverick] thinking I don't like them. That's not true at all. It's really not. They do what they do really well, but they're very pop-oriented. That's just not what I do. And it's hard to go to their office, and ain't no black people over there. So, I don't really expect them to understand me, you know? I mean, I'm on a label where Alanis sold 28 million copies of her first record for them. Candlebox sold 5 million. The Deftones went gold. I haven't even gone gold. And that made me feel like a failure. I just really wish that, if they don't know what to do with me, they'd let me go. Not that any other label would have a clue.

"It's very important," she adds, "that people know that [former Maverick partner] Freddie DeMann is the one who signed me. I love him. He may be a little difficult, or a little out of touch with music that's going on today, but I love him and am so incredibly thankful to him, because he really pushed to sign me. Everybody's always like, 'Oh, Madonna signed you,' or '[Maverick A&R honcho] Guy Oseary is this great genius.' No, it was Freddie who had the guts to sign me."

The exhaustion is clearly two-sided. In a faxed statement, Madonna writes: "Me'Shell is a musical genius and a brilliant lyricist, but she is also a tormented soul and a reluctant star. Her love of music is so pure, and she is very uneasy with the whole idea of promotion, marketing, and commercial success. It is a challenge to work with her, but also a great honor."

You don't need perfect pitch to hear the frustration, even impatience, in those words.

For all the prickliness of her career scenario, and the heartbreak that permeates the new album, NdegéOcello radiates bliss, serenity. On tour behind her last album, she was visibly shrouded in sadness. She spoke of changing her name - and leaving the business. Her conversation was peppered with words of weariness and disillusionment, and though she made it clear she wasn't suicidal, she also made it clear that she was "ready to go."

A lot of her current happiness can be attributed to Walker. Part of it is due to her move from L.A. "I loved my first three years here," she says. "My son went to a great school, and I did a lot of session work. I thought I could make it be what I wanted it to be. I guess I was a little delusional. I got really sick of it after a while. It's just not progressive." And she's clearly charged by her move north. "I really like it up there," she smiles. "It's quiet, has good food, has a cool music scene. And there's an activist culture. I just love the vibe of the people." But most of her newfound contentment is simply due to her rethinking of her place in pop culture, her hopes for her art, and her deflection of outside expectations.

"I stopped beating up on myself," she says. "I stopped asking myself why I didn't sell this number of records, why I don't have corporate sponsorship. I just don't buy into any of that anymore. Getting out of L.A. helped get me out of that mind-set. I just surround myself with people who have absolutely nothing to do with the music or movie business. I try to hang around writers, visual artists, conceptual artists—people who aren't concerned whether masses of people are going to accept their art.

"It's really important to me," NdegéOcello says passionately, "that I'm not only creating my own resistance movement, but showing celebration. It's a claiming of what is rightfully mine, my history, my heritage. I feel I owe this to people like Tom Wilson, a black man who produced the early Bob Dylan records but who no one knows about. He died in obscurity. It's about Richie Havens, who opened for one of the greatest musical experiences in our lifetime, Woodstock. It's about Joan Armatrading and Tracy Chapman, Lenny Kravitz and Ben Harper—people of color who resist these bullshit definitions of black life or black art. It's about not being defined by the color of your skin, and having people think that all you can do is shuck and jive. That's what I'm hoping comes across in my music, ultimately. That's what I'm striving for."

LA Weekly, September 10, 1999

do you know us?
ARMAND VAN HELDEN, MOS DEF:
A MASCULINE EQUATION

The cover art for Armand Van Helden's single "U Don't Know Me" makes for a powerful marriage of image and music. It's a reminder that album/CD/single packaging can carry a statement beyond simply "worship this pop star," that it can actually accent the message in the music. The artwork is a portrait that evokes the Statue of Liberty but with distinctly masculine, Negro features (broad nose, thick lips). His eyes are downcast. What makes the image especially potent, though, is its rendering of Lady Liberty's famous head ornament. Shadow and optical illusion create the effect of the crown having slipped, coming to rest on the brow. It's now a crown of thorns.

"U Don't Know Me," an angry, artfully raw House track that purposefully rekindles old-school disco flourishes (insistent strings and horns, even more insistent bass; slightly off-key but achingly heartfelt vocals), is an easy candidate for best-of-the-year status. With its pissed attitude and layers of infectious hooks, it's the dissected-wound-as-artistic-achievement that eludes the likes of Korn and the dazzlingly dull-witted Limp Bizkit. The song opens with sampled dialogue, wherein a male voice bitterly inquires, "What is my problem with man, you ask? No, I ask you, what was man's problem with *me*?" (When contacted, Van Helden's production office wouldn't positively identify the source, only admit that I was "on track" in recognizing it as being from a film.) The real achievement, though, is a bit of genre blending that's far more impressive than the currently celebrated union of rock 'n' roll and hip-hop. Van-Helden has once again found that under-mapped but deeply mined terrain where House faggots and hardcore b-boys speak the same language, strike the same poses and view the world through similarly dark-tinted glasses.

A rude boy who proclaims his heterosexuality in nearly every interview, Van Helden (an Air Force brat born to a Dutch-Indonesian father and a French-Lebanese mother) has always seemed profoundly uncomfortable with both the gay roots and faggot connotations of House, as well as his own natural affinity for the music. In the current issue of the British magazine *The Face*, he proclaims, "All we have in House is a bunch of bitch-ass, faggot-type personalities…" So it's laughably ironic that the best tracks on his most recent album, *2 Future 4 U*, are either incredibly gay in vibe ("U Don't Know Me," "Flowerz") or feature a female vocalist who comes off like a drag queen ("Entra Mi Casa").

It has to be unnerving for Van Helden to realize that the voice that most perfectly suits his grooves is that of the "punk"—even if it's one who refuses to be punked. Check out his early-'90s ghetto-fag anthem "Love Thang" (released under the moniker Banji Boys), a direct ancestor of "U Don't Know Me." The newer title, however, drips with freshly minted bitterness and earned rage. It's the sissy from the 'hood reading his oppressors within an exuberant musical setting. It's a reclaiming of the fury and resistance—the grown-up stuff, the subtextual political stuff hinged on issues of race, sexuality and underclass status—that were always the foundation of House but were largely shoved out once the music became the soundtrack for raves and the *nouveau*-hippie (i.e., white and hetero) children who swarmed them.

The track has been a huge hit in clubs that cater to *the children*. Van Helden's b-boy roots allow him to instinctively home in on the rougher elements of House music, and though he's too much a fan of mindless ruffneck posturing, he brings ethnicity, sexuality and humor back to the House genre. He also brings biting race-consciousness back to the grooves with a vigor that gleefully flies in the face of the Benetton bullshit that now passes for progressive cultural discourse.

2 Future 4 U is a flawed album (absolutely irresistible in parts, deadly dull in others) but its layered, often contradictory takes on sexuality, race and masculinity are what pull it into the conversation around hip-hop and rock 'n' roll, and what that merger really means. The divide between House and hip-hop is contrived, false. The two genres spring from the same cultural well, share a vocabulary of dance-floor movement (vogueing is the hardcore flipside to break-dancing), and are both voices of the culturally disenfranchised. Reflexive homophobia and ignorance have kept them apart, and that rift mirrors the larger, crippling schisms within the African-American community.

One of the reasons the hip-hop/rock marriage is so undeserving of praise is that it symbolizes the ill-advised consummation of the great, tense unspoken courtship in American culture—the one that is arguably at the core of so many of our ills. Hip-hop has finally cleared a space for little straight white boys and little straight black boys to come together and try on the trinkets of one another's masculinity. (This is far from a new phenomenon, of course, but today's market-prodded gray-boys make the White Negro of yesteryear seem like a suburban shut-in.) Black boys get to try on the fluidity of option, get to see what it's like to be mediocre and still be allowed to fall up in life, with the spotlight and ample financial compensation as their due. White boys get to pull on a maleness that is savage, inarguable. With the street/the ghetto as its kiln, this is a façade of insatiable sexuality and impenetrable cool. The ebony and the ivory of this equation come together around a notion of maleness that is determined by what they own, who they own, and vulgar displays of power. But it's the angry white boy glazed in hip-hop blackness that's being lauded in the media.

Not only is this character *not* a sign of progress, but it re-upholsters a definition of manhood that, while many weep for its demise, ought to be ripped to shreds. That definition, largely founded on fear, fantasy and myths, incubates homophobia and misogyny (and unexamined racism) as a form of self-preservation. It's telling that while rock critics praised the sight of 200,000 mainly young white men at Woodstock '99 chanting "My Nigga" along with rapper DMX as a harbinger of racial harmony (reclaim that birthright, yo), none thought 1) to question the fact that this newfound harmony centers on a controversial/commodified term of degradation for black folk or 2) to see the connection between this hip-hop-fueled white male exertion of power and the wide-scale rioting, looting and raping that marked the festival. Having worshipped their Negro patron saint *du jour*, DMX—a man whose intense anger is rooted in boundless self-pity (and there's the *real* point of connection)—and egged on by Limp Bizkit's Fred Durst, the crowd went primal because they *could*. They are the new men.

So where are the truly radical, artful treatises on race, masculinity and hip-hop culture? Mos Def's album *Black on Both Sides* is one example. It's the sound of an unapologetic race man making resistance art, a man who knows that racial harmony founded on consumption, conformity and the championing of black style over black life is a dead end for black and white folk alike. He also knows that it's no cure for one of white supremacy's most enduring legacies: the various strains of self-hatred running rampant in the black community that are manifest in so much modern rap music and hip-hop culture.

Having spent years as an iconic underground rapper (and as an actor with a fairly healthy resume, most recently appearing in the film *Where's Marlowe?*), Mos Def broke into the big time with last year's already-classic *Black Star*, with Talib Kweli. In many ways, *Black on Both Sides* is a continuation of that work. At its center is a paradoxical glow: Lyrics that could be read on the page as fiery prose poems, as sociological data or as heartfelt protest retain a pure musicality as they hit the ear. Po-faced critics whose appreciation of hip-hop is strictly neck-up will be as entranced as the brother who slides his headphones on in the dark and nods to the sounds of the words, the messages in the rhymes and the timbre of the rapper's voice.

Over a bed of jazz-derived grooves, Mos Def praises God and family while wrestling with the war of the sexes ("Ms. Fat Booty"); giving a sober reality check on his chosen genre's power and limitations in "Hip-Hop" ("Hip-hop will simply amaze you / Craze you, pay you / Do whatever you say do / But black, it can't save you"); penning a love letter to Brooklyn by pointedly hijacking "Under the Bridge," the Red Hot Chili Peppers' ode to L.A.; and re-teaming with Kweli on "Know That," a scalding bit of stream-of-consciousness philosophizing. But the albums highlights are "Mr. Nigga" and "Rock N Roll." In the latter, he parodies the rock/hip-hop hybrid, mercilessly disses Korn and Limp Bizkit—and Elvis and the Stones—and gives props to Bad Brains, Fishbone, Albert King and Hendrix, and traces all American music (hard rock, funk, hip-hop, etc.) to its origins in the slave shacks. On "Mr. Nigga," which features a turn by Q-Tip, the rapper pins pained observations on the seeming permanence of racism inside acrid humor ("Now, who is the cat at Armani buying wares / with the tourists who be asking him, "Do you work here?"), and you can't help but hear a weary heart beneath the flow of acid. What saves him is an intrinsic generosity of spirit that keeps his frustrations from spoiling into misanthropy.

Black on Both Sides—a critical favorite—has failed to make the crossover splash that was widely predicted (or, more accurately, hoped for) before its release and the reason my well lie in Mos Def's voice. His style, more often than not, veers closer to conversational than classically confrontational. There's a marked lack of bombast to his flow; it completely sidetracks the minstrelsy that has come to define rap as it takes up residence in the mainstream. (This deceptive cool/calm is something he manages to maintain even as he goes toe to toe with Busta Ryhmes on the incendiary "Do It Now.") While his voice isn't as quirky as, say, Slick Rick's, or as coolly idiosyncratic as Q-Tip's, it sticks out in ways that may not bode well for the trek from the underground to the mainstream. Its very lack of caricature may be Mos Def's biggest stumbling block.

African-American music—rap, House, techno, R&B—has suffered immeasurably from being yoked to the pandering, idiotic, media-constructed demographic known as youth culture, that over-hyped entity shaped and packaged by businessmen back in the '50s when they realized the deep pockets of disposable wealth that were owned by white American teens. The natural impulses to overthrow the old and celebrate the new, to rebel against parental and societal limitations, were long ago corralled into the impulse to shop, blindly consume, and forget history except as a costume. One effect of this massive dumbing down is that uninformed, uncommitted, unfocused rage is championed and celebrated, spun by PR machinery as substantive art or politics, which is where DMX, Limp Bizkit and the Woodstock '99 posse come in.

With rare exception, art and anger truly connected to history, activism and consciousness are marginalized, or dismissed all together. As American youth culture circles the globe, it often demolishes whatever is unique about the cultures it finds in its path, starting with those inside America. (Is there anything more depressing than MTV's show, *Global Groove*, where we get to watch participants in Hong Kong, Paris, Athens, Milan, New York, Atlanta, Philadelphia, etc., all wearing the same clothes, all dancing the same steps, all giving the same scripted shout-outs to the camera?) Mos Def's music swims against this tide. Ultimately, it connects with fans around the globe because in his call for black love, black unity and the preservation of black life—in the very specificity of his art—is a powerful respect for all humanity, in its many incarnations and flavors.

LA Weekly, December 10, 1999

howl
GHOST DOG

Forest Whitaker has a magnificent face: round, dark and full, with one eye sloping slightly downward. It's a face that, even at rest, is never really restful. I'd guess that it's rarely been truly seen. In *The Crying Game*, his cinematically revolutionary character Jody, an ordinary black man comfortable in his complex faggotry, was all but ignored in the media fawning over that simpering tragic mulatto at the film's center. Whitaker's physicality undoubtedly had a lot to do with his character being so slighted.

In *Ghost Dog*—a film laced with brilliantly knotted ideas on race, masculinity and cults of violence—writer/director Jim Jarmusch has Whitaker's weighted countenance pull double duty: As the title character, the actor functions as both the symbolic "black man," and as a painstakingly drawn individual. It's a testament to the depth of Whitaker's talent that he so nimbly pulls it off, crafting a haunting (and haunted) portrayal of black manhood.

The bare bones of the film's story are simple. Ghost Dog is a peerless assassin-for-hire who works exclusively for Louie (John Tormey), a low-level member of an aged, crumbling Mafia family based in New York. Heavily immersed in the philosophical tenets of Samurai culture, Ghost Dog has pledged unwavering loyalty to Louie, who saved his life years earlier. When a hit he's contracted for goes wrong, Mafia higher-ups want him killed, eventually pitting him in a life or death battle with his master.

Draped over those bones, though, are astute observations on the nature of masculinity, how it's honed and sustained through violence and death, how near-parallel rituals of bloodletting link men across various cultures and traditions— both real life and cinematic. And because this is a distinctly American film grappling with these issues, and the rare honest one, the black male is its locus: Invisible man and menace to society, the fount of and receptacle for sexual fears and anxiety, blindly worshipped and necessarily annihilated.

Jarmusch, who overhauled the Western by blasting apart genre conventions in the elegantly revisionist *Dead Man*, scores his point this time by making deep nods to gangster and gangsta flicks, to hip-hop (Wu Tang Clan's RZA provided the moody, beat-driven score) and Eastern philosophy—Ghost Dog's relentlessly quoted bible is *Hagakure: The Book of the Samurai*. Wonderfully utilized cartoon clips of Betty Boop, Woody Woodpecker, and Itchy and Scratchy from *The Simpsons* (among others) are strewn throughout the movie, both foreshadowing and commenting on the action. Those same clips also underscore the absurdist humor that's spread throughout the film: the old mob guy who loves classic hip-hop and quotes Flava Flav; the elderly Puerto Rican man who's building a ship on the roof of his apartment building with no way to get it down when he's done. Jarmusch's levity—and, even more, his skin tone—lets him get away with riffs that would probably find a black director massacred by critics, as when Ghost Dog's best friend, Raymond, a French-speaking ice cream vendor played by the beautiful Isaach De Bankolé, exclaims, "Vanilla is the most popular but chocolate is the best!" (Even if he employed an uncharacteristically light touch in the filming, Spike Lee would be crucified for simply penning such a line.) Or when Ghost Dog and Raymond speak wholly different languages, yet somehow are always in sync with each other, the inference being that shared race transcends different cultures, different native tongues—indeed, that race itself might be a bond of shared/similar experiences and perceptions. But the film presents this less as an essentialist's or nationalist's naïve manifesto than as a spiritual connection between the two friends.

What Jarmusch has done, in fact, is make the first fully realized hip-hop film, one where the filmmaking is as dizzyingly inspired and purposefully surreal—while keepin' it real—as the bravest, most pressing avenues of hip-hop culture, particularly rap music. He samples various film/music/literary genres and then juxtaposes his finds, having them double and triple back to comment on one another. In doing so, he's created a film that is both poem and polemic.

The pop-culture machinery has been working overtime for a long time now to make sure hip-hop culture is nothing more than the latest nigga-derived opiate for the masses, to defang its intrinsic blackness by paradoxically hawking caricatured Negro life. On the flip side of that coin, hack music scribes, social critics and artists breathlessly celebrate those *undaground* hip-hop gatherings where every race and dialect imaginable can be found, using them as proof of large-scale progress in race relations, as harbingers of a new day. It's bullshit, of course— Revlon in lieu of revolution, with the true goal being the maintenance of white folks' comfort zones. (Come on in, the shopping's fine.) It's also the willful turning of a blind eye to the hatred of black folk that continues to soak the fabric of this country. It's that hatred, the many layers of rage and frustration that it has spawned, and the various reactions and resistance to it, that are at the core of hip-hop.

In *Ghost Dog*, Jarmusch takes the off-kilter humor, the coolly measured visual and rhythmic style that he's perfected over the course of his career, and lines them up seamlessly against hip-hop mores, employing it in the service of thoughtful black representation. While the movie is filled with male collectives that enshrine masculine identity—the geriatric Mafia; a ghetto posse that rhymes in the park; a gang of racist white boys who beat the young Ghost Dog to a pulp in flashback; the spirit of Wu Tang that hangs lightly over the whole project—Ghost Dog himself is a loner, a man who has consciously embraced the paradox of his existence, the fact that he's both invisible and perceived as society's ultimate threat, and turned this paradox into a tool of survival. His worldly strength lies in his existential vulnerability, his willingness to engage death on every level while working from a moral code that's painfully aware of the beauty and harshness of life. He practices his rituals of manhood and spirituality in isolation, with no need for approval or validation. He has created his own definition of a man.

The film's settings (captured in gritty beauty by cinematographer Robby Mueller) are various environs in and around New York: dingy gangster hangouts, impoverished ghetto neighborhoods, moneyed suburbs. But its more crucial setting is simply the captured tenor of contemporary American life—that entangled realm of casual racism, violence and bloodied rites of passage. Throughout the film, characters speak longingly of the old days and the old ways, pointedly oblivious to the fact that it was precisely those "uncomplicated times" that lead to their complicated and empty, pain filled lives. While the movie is very much about male terrain—within and without—it also speaks to the toll all of this takes on women. The lone girl-child in the film is a precocious black pre-adolescent who's tackling W.E.B. Du Bois' *The Souls of Black Folk*. The daughter of the Mafia leader is a doped up, dazed young woman named Louise who sports a messy version of Louise Brooks' Pandora hairdo and carts around a tattered copy of *Rashomon*; when a hail of gunfire cleanses her world of almost all the men in it, she's almost instantly revitalized—clear-eyed, sober and coolly poised to take charge.

    Ghost Dog would be powerful in its own right, at almost any time on the American clock, but it's especially so right now. It's hard not to feel the press of Amadou Diallo's ghost as we watch an unarmed black man beaten by a gang of white men, as we watch black men cower in front of guns and hear the orders to kill any black man that looks like the one being hunted. Thankfully, Jarmusch pulls no punches. He doesn't worry about being polite or finessing the bigotry of his characters so that we know he's a good liberal. (He also offers no commentary on the fact that Ghost Dog calls Louie "master." The term is appropriately applied given Ghost Dog's immersion in Eastern culture and its disciplines, but it carries a loaded history when used by an American black man to address a white man. Jarmusch lets the audience work out that mind fuck on their own.) The lazily tossed, racist prejudice in the film is, at times, so raw that it actually engendered laughs of shocked recognition from me and the other black folk who attended a recent press screening. But it's the end of the film that breaks your heart. [SPOILER] As Ghost Dog and his old boss square off in the middle of a New York street, striking gunslinger poses, it hits you that Ghost Dog is doggedly following the rules of Samurai conduct not simply because he's a good student but because it has provided him with relief, with a way out from America and from a world of mindless cruelty and dulled consciousness. As he slowly walks toward the firing gun, his own weapon's chamber empty, you realize that Ghost Dog is not necessarily suicidal, but he is tired of *being*.

LA Weekly, March 17, 2000

naked
D'ANGELO

A few months before the release of his hit album, *Voodoo* (Virgin), D'Angelo appeared on the cover of New York's *Paper* magazine, sprawled on the floor, looking up at the camera from under sleepy lids, wearing what looked like a pair of glittery panties. His gym-overhauled body glistened against a glowing red backdrop. For fans still vibing off the reflective-ruffneck/thug-luvva persona that he'd come with on his '95 debut album, *Brown Sugar*, the reaction was simple enough: What the fuq? (*Paper's* fashion credits listed the psycho drawers as a "bathing suit by John Bartlett.")

It was a short while later that the *nekkid* video for "Untitled (How Does It Feel?)" made its splash on BET, and really set tongues wagging. With its extreme close-ups and teasing mid-shots (the camera cropping the singer's nude body so that the frame stopped just above his pubes, leading more than one desperado to go right up to the TV screen and peer down), the video was a brilliant marketing move. D'Angelo's long-awaited, much-delayed sophomore record was, according to some industry scuttlebutt, going to be a commercial and artistic dud. The less-than-lukewarm reaction to the CD's first video, "Left & Right" (featuring Redman & Method Man, hip-hop's sexiest and most ubiquitous couple), seemed to cement the whispers. The clip for "Untitled" quickly turned everything around.

In the weeks before the album dropped, the video stoked anticipation so much that *Voodoo* ended up debuting at No. 1 and is still resting comfortably in the Top 40, with almost double platinum sales to date. It didn't hurt that critics fell over themselves lavishing praise on the disc. But what's more interesting about the "Untitled" video is the questions it raises, especially when considered alongside the photo spread for *Paper*. Though the "artistic" impetus for the video was that it's meant to symbolize the rawness and honesty of the music, D'Angelo (or his handlers) was also clearly thinking about moving units when his new image was crafted: Sex sells.

Sexuality and black men is a topic strewn with land mines.

The fact that recent videos for almost every hip-hop/R&B male artist are filled with thong-clad white and mulatto girls bumping and grinding has been the subject of much debate and controversy within the African-American community, but there seems a real hesitancy to admit the complexity of issues subtextually dealt with in these clips, for to do so would open a Pandora's box of fears and taboos: miscegenation; intra-racial racism; internalized fear of both black male and female bodies; the exaggeration of heterosexual prowess in order to mask fears of appearing soft—i.e., faggot. (The irony is that current hip-hop and R&B imagery is a hotbed of homoerotic energy. The Ruff Ryders posse alone is a ghetto-fag fantasy writ large.)

"Identity" is the hottest commodity in the pop arts, but with both the natural and market-stoked confluence of cultures, the morphing of racial and cultural issues, and the ongoing anxiety over "authenticity," identity is now thrillingly/scarily fluid. The imagery in "Untitled" is notable for a number of reasons: the camera's loving caress of the black male body; the way D'Angelo's beauty is thrown into high relief (those lips, those abs); the unabashed tenderness of his pose—the absence of swagger, yet the essence of black maleness.

What's fascinating is that D'Angelo doesn't fully *own* it. He seems uncomfortable, both shy and a tad awkward in front of the video lens. Luckily, this tentativeness works well within the concept of the clip. And it makes you wonder, was this all his idea or someone else's? If it was his idea, or if he got on board with no arm-twisting, then his discomfort is even more interesting. What, if anything, was he trying to prove/convey/conquer beyond the charts?

D'Angelo's beefcake reincarnation becomes even more intriguing when juxtaposed against a similar—and seemingly failed—attempt by Q-Tip. Having achieved iconic status as one of hip-hop's intellectual and spiritual leaders in A Tribe Called Quest, Tip decided that he would *bling! bling!* for his solo outing, *Amplified* (Arista). It's a very good pop/hip-hop party album, one that doesn't sound quite like anything else out there right now. There's some real wit in the deceptively sparse production. But the album's fierce adherence to the ghetto-fabulous aesthetic in its lyrics has proved controversial. Longtime Tribe fans cried sellout and turned their back on the record. The videos, filled with scantily clad women, actually alienated a lot of headz, even though "Vivrant Thing" was a huge crossover hit. It's like the totality of Q-Tip's new music, videos and hunk posturing are a performance-art piece sans the wink and nudge that lets you know it's all actually trenchant commentary on the state of hip-hop. It's as though Tip, who spent years toiling on the alternative/"conscious" rap circuit, building up credibility but no *serious* ducats, decided he'd jump headfirst into the formula of contemporary hip-hop and finally get paid by pimping current trends, tweaking them with enough sonic twists to pull him ahead of the pack and buy him some leeway with his longtime fan base. So what went wrong?

There's a real playfulness in *Amplified*'s grooves. It's the giddiness of the saint pulling on the garb of the sinner, the giddiness of exploring possibilities. As disappointing as it is to hear him rhyme about standard-issue rap fare—Prada, banging bush and battling weak MCs—there's no denying the seductiveness of the tracks, the shine in his voice (one of the most seductive in hip-hop). But the balance of elements is off. Though he's clearly having a good time in the videos and on the CD, he's been awful in live performances (the Chris Rock show, the Grammys), detached from his own material and seemingly ill at ease. It's as though he's as suspicious of his new image as fans are. That makes the trappings—the fur coats, the video ho's—seem even more garish, even more fraudulent. He doesn't own them.

It's ironic: On the CD, Q-Tip's in complete command of this ghetto-fab party mode. He makes it seem completely natural. But he gives himself away when it comes time to hawk the stuff. Watching him in interviews is to see a man who's clearly going through some shit that's deeper and darker than the rhymes he spits on his latest record. (And tabloid reports of trouble on the set of his upcoming movie, along with his recent run-ins with the law, seem to bear that out.)

Like D'Angelo, Q-Tip was trying to fuck with his image, to dismantle the armor of his particular iconic status by coming out with music and a video that turned his artistic history on its head. He wanted to carve out wiggle room between the quotation marks, but got slammed instead.

D'Angelo's *Voodoo*, similarly, was meant to deflate, meet and exceed expectations all at once, but D'Angelo dived deeper into his shit to achieve that goal. D'Angelo's video discomfort reads as the tremble of someone who is literally and figuratively nude, who has stripped away the accoutrements that Q-Tip has pulled on. His unease, finally, comes across as an honesty that underscores his musical message, rather than negates it. Tellingly, his concerts in support of *Voodoo* have been nothing short of spectacular. His command of both his material and the stage bespeak a man who got the balance right, who can shirk the contrived image but stand confidently behind the content of his music.

Where *Voodoo* might initially seem rather slight, repeated listens reveal its heft, and the black pride at its core. Formless jams slowly take shape; distinct but subtle melodies rise from the morass of mumbled words and funk-based grooves. "Devil's Pie" explicitly decries the materialism and shallowness that Q-Tip is trying so hard to wallow in, while tracks like "One Mo'Gin," "The Root" and a cover of Roberta Flack's "Feel Like Makin' Love" are the sensuous workouts we used to routinely get from Prince. (D'Angelo has an obvious hard-on for the Purple One.) The craftsmanship of the album, from the production to the songwriting to the singing, mark D'Angelo as one of the very few chart-topping R&B acts clearly serious about the *music*.

You can hear in D'Angelo's voice that he's connected to something higher, something grander. He took an ice pick to his former persona in order to get closer to that thing, to bring fans along with him. The beefcake poses and soft-core video were his tools; ultimately, they didn't require him to fake himself out.

LA Weekly, April 7, 2000

jock rockin'
WELCOME TO THE MACHO HOUSE

There are some incredibly smart people making contemporary House music. Armand Van Helden isn't one of them. It's impossible to read an interview with him and not be blown away by the co-dependent relationship between his arrogance and the low-watt intellect of his public persona. What makes him fascinating as an artist is that his best work, the groove that hits you viscerally, dragging you onto the dance floor and daring you to leave, seems to spring unencumbered from his subconscious. That stuff is dazzling, it's frequently faggy, and it seems to unnerve him. His latest musical endeavor, *Killing Puritans*, comes from his hyped-up consciousness, from the front of his flamingly hetero brain. And with exception of only a handful of moments—most of which are more interesting in theory than in execution—it's a very bad album, both in its politics and its sound.

Killing Puritans is all over the place—heavy metal riffs, thudding hard House instrumentals, Van Helden's sneering taunts scorching across the grooves—but it's painfully contrived. The raw, dirty sound and feel of it are often assaultive, with no aim except to piss off old-school Househeads in clichéd, knuckleheaded metal fashion: It's Macho House. The album's pointed genre-hopping, contrary to its obvious intention, doesn't demonstrate breadth of vision or an organic, purposeful linking of wildly different types of music (the way, say, the late Larry Levan did when he'd throw left-of-center choices on his turntable) so much as come off like a bratty kid throwing his toys at you to try and draw blood.

To be fair, Van Helden does earn a few props. He's on the money in realizing that much of the wretchedness of modern dance fare is due to its pronounced lack of sexual heat. Blame a generation of DJs and producers who came of age in a time of AIDS-induced repression, in a culture that is paradoxically oversexed yet steeped in fear of sex. Blame a generation of dance-music fiends who can't envision their much-vaunted "positivity" encompassing the liberating roil of bodily fluids.

Whatever the cause, it's as though a "check your dick at the door" policy were in effect for almost anyone trying to construct a groove or dance to one. Armand is clearly tired of blue balls on the dance floor, and who can blame him? But his solution is pathetic: On tracks like "Koochy," the album's first single, he dips into played-out Luther Campbell territory for sexual healing: caricatured, pimped female sexuality as the solution, with the hip-hop ho pushing drag queens to the sidelines. It's already a big club hit.

Van Helden deserves credit for acknowledging the depth and harsh reality of racial divides within the culture, for not falling for the colorblind rhetoric that clubland's Benetton short-bus posse espouses even as they perpetuate age-old pop-culture racial hierarchies. Van Helden works hard to bring devalued, discarded blackness—black sounds, vibes and consciousness—back up in the modern House mix (next to his rock-star and thug posturing). The problem is that his notions of blackness, like his ideas on maleness and sexuality, are more often than not reactionary cartoons rooted in the bullshit chic of ghetto realness and hip-hop ghetto fabulousness. Check out his *bling-bling* b-boy photo spread in the current issue of *Urb* magazine, with video ho's lounging in headphones around him.

Van Helden's shaky credentials as a visionary spokesman for the House generation are revealed most clearly in a couple of quotes from that *Urb* interview. In one passage he says, "House is built on a vibe and an atmosphere, not built on a message or anything political." Later he states, "The thing that bothers me is that people have forgotten or refuse to acknowledge the history... They don't do the research, and the elders are just falling out of the loop and not giving back in any way... History is here to teach us, and if you don't let it then you're just going to... go through the same motions without evolving."

Taken together, the quotes reveal both his ignorance and hypocrisy. Many of the House elders he speaks of have been lost to AIDS or drugs; those that are left have been largely cast aside by the new dance culture whose exponents pride themselves on being beyond the grasp of corporate America and its manipulation, but in their self-chosen terminology—touting themselves as a "youth culture" movement—show how thoroughly they've been shaped and bought by the thing they rail against. That very terminology, "youth culture"—with its ageist dismissals and constant quest for the new at any cost—is what has squashed the intergenerational dynamics that were once found so easily in disco and House, and that once allowed for the kind of exchanges Van Helden says he longs for.

And the politics of House—like disco—may not have yelled out with the fury of punk or hip-hop (they exist beyond the narrowly conceived definitions of "political" that we've come to accept), but they were among the most potent and radical of any musical movement of this century. They celebrated sex and sexuality in all its manifestations; they removed the straight boy and the white boy from the position of cultural nexus, not to erase or deny him, but in pursuit of real equality for all, new terms of coexistence. But now the music and the culture have fallen victim to the ridiculous but reflexively enforced notion that the cultural spaces and subcultures carved out by sexual and racial minorities only evolve and make progress by the presence of whiteness and heterosexuality. New-school Householads have fallen before the beliefs that brutal macho energy is more daring and transgressive than that which is fluid and ambiguous. They believe that youthful exuberance and narcissism are enough to build and sustain culture. Van Helden benefits from and feeds these delusions more than he knows, and with his caveman music and politics he pisses all over House's truly revolutionary impulses.

For a more enlightening and entertaining take on dance music, its history and complex sexual and racial politics, pick up the new book *My Life and the Paradise Garage: Keep on Dancin'* by Mel Charen (as told to Gabriel Rotello). Cheren was co-founder of the influential disco label West End Records. His lover, Michael Brody, founded the Paradise Garage, forerunner of the multiracial boundary-smashing dance club philosophy of rave and electronic cultures. Initially, the book elicits groans as it recounts a personal narrative that has already wilted into cliché: A good Jewish boy struggles to emerge from under his mother's suffocating wing, giving furtive blow jobs to sailors as a teenager and feeling like the biggest freak on the planet. But it slowly evolves into a fascinating look at the inner workings of the music industry (Cheren's Rolodex of business peers and acquaintances reads like a Who's Who of the business), as well as a detailed overview of the gay rights movement and the birth and decline of disco, as well as a riveting account of the people and tales behind the Paradise Garage (including much space devoted to Larry Levan and Tom Moulton, a founding father of disco and a hugely influential presence in modern dance music). What's striking about this book is not the wealth of pop-culture history that is so richly laid out, not the gossip and name-dropping that fill the pages, and not even the painstaking remembrances of how the art of deejaying came to be, but the outlined utopian vision that dance music's early fans were so sure they were ushering into existence. Beneath the endless drug use and sexual musical chairs is a heartbreaking naïveté. Cheren and Brody actually thought they were going to integrate the races, break down the forces of homophobia, and bring about a consciousness full of love, brotherhood and endless possibility. For a brief moment, with the help of some classic music, and in a hallowed space, they did just that.

LA Weekly, August 4, 2000

sons and lovers
URBANIA AND *HUMAN RESOURCES*

U*rbania* begins inside the setup for an urban myth, kicked off with the question, "Heard any good stories lately?" The query is the modern-day equivalent of *Once upon a time...*, priming us for the dreamscape of flashbacks, flashes forward, memories and urban legends that writer-director Jon Shear carefully pulls together in what is, at its core, simply the story of what happens when everything dies but love. But it's not a simple story. Shear artfully fractures the narrative, filtering it through the cynical, paranoid and ruthless city streets of contemporary New York. He cleverly weaves it through familiar tales of poodles in microwaves and kidneys being stolen from unsuspecting victims, seizing the gasp-inducing power of these water-cooler shockers to illuminate another, more primal, kind of terror altogether. He also reminds us that every one of our lives—our misfortunes and misdeeds alike—are potentially the stuff of urban legend. It's a horrifying thought but also a perversely comforting one.

Charlie (Dan Futterman) wanders the streets of New York both day and night, obsessively leaving phone messages for a lover who never picks up and never returns the calls. As he sleepwalks through his office job, the inane chatter of co-workers filters into his head, underscoring his heartache. ("I love this city," laughs one. "Someone's always got it worse than you.") Flashes of tender lovemaking sessions, parties attended with the distant lover, and hand-holding walks all run through his head, sometimes playing out on the street right before him. But he's also haunted by apparitions, wounded men who approach him for help only to vanish when he reaches out to them. To ease his pain, he's found a new object of—what? Desire? It's not clear at first. But the rough trade that Charlie cruises all over the city, finally locating him in a bar a little too obviously called Karma, has a strange hold on him. It's obvious that the crude, dim-witted man is not really Charlie's type, but it also soon becomes clear that the stranger's palpably violent edge is the draw. Their consummation is a rug-pulling confounding of expectation.

Shear gives nothing away, telegraphs nothing in advance, and neither does Futterman. If the actor is at times a little too self-conscious in his physical mannerisms, he balances it by playing his emotional cards very shrewdly. Charlie is a gnarl of contradictory emotions, including numbness. Futterman fans them all with precision, making deft leaps from flirtatious to sneeringly sarcastic to deep, stunned remorse. He's matched by the film's purposefully tangential structure, where quick edits, skewed camera angles and abrupt but graceful shifts in tone and subplots mirror the character's shattered interior. It's a dazzlingly equitable marriage of form and content.

Urbania's supporting cast is also superb. Matt Keeslar, a gorgeous actor whose looks and genuine talent have often been the only redemptive elements in his films (*Splendor, Psycho Beach Party*), plays Chris—the lover made gold in Charlie's memory. He has the unenviable task of portraying perfection, and through a delicate balance of gentleness and fey sexiness, manages to pull it off beautifully. But it's Alan Cummings, as Charlie's friend Brett—an old-school queen who references classic Hollywood movies in soft camp tones—who all but steals the film. Disheveled, with the air of AIDS hanging heavily around him, Brett brings both comic relief and an unalloyed sadness to the film. Cummings has a tart chemistry with Futterman, and the two volley dialogue that's both darkly humorous ("I'm not going [back] to a therapist who survived Auschwitz," quips Charlie), and incredibly poignant. At one point, Brett quotes Glenda Jackson in *Sunday Bloody Sunday*, and, rather than the badge of hipness that such referencing now signals in films, the lifted lines strike a blue chord that serves to deepen the emotional current of the movie.

Shear and co-screenwriter Daniel Reitz have actually crafted a very straightforward tale about loss and regret. It's in the telling that they plumb the story's power. The twists and turns they employ as they rifle through big-city fears and folklore culminate in a wrenching emotional finale, but one that's foreshadowed early in the film when a minor character smilingly tells Charlie, "You're never given more than you can handle." To which he, also smiling, replies, "Bullshit."

The question of just how much we can handle is also at the

center of French writer-director Laurent Cantet's haunting *Human Resources*. The film—with its *Workers of the world unite!* theme—is so timely that it's a pity it wasn't playing here when protestors were trying to pull the Democratic Party off corporate America's teat a few weeks ago. But what makes this no-frills film—no flashy technique or notable camera tricks—so moving is that it keeps its scathing political commentary rooted in the struggle of everyday life. When Frank (Jalil Lespert) returns to his small French village from business school in Paris, he's employed at the local factory for a summer internship. His father works there, his older sister works there (as does a huge chunk of the local population), and Frank attended the company's summer camp as a boy. His trainee job is in Human Resources, which he tackles with the energy and optimism that only the truly naïve can muster.

Problems start for him almost immediately, but not just on the job. His education creates a rift between him and old friends, despite his attempts to play it down, and he's dismissed with the charge of being a snob. Efforts to improve factory work conditions are met with skepticism by the rank and file not only because he's working for management, but also because his education and new job have ostensibly catapulted him out of the working class in which he grew up. He has prospects, the luxury of dreaming. That makes him a suspect and leaves him stranded. It also creates a painful tension between him and his father, a man who has no fight left in him, if he ever had any at all, and who is such a famous toady that co-workers sneer at him. When Frank broaches the subject of workers' rights one night at home, his father flies into a rage, warning him not to get above his station.

Cantet focuses the bulk of his story on the father-son relationship. While there are some fantastic supporting characters (especially Danielle Melador's turn as Mrs. Arnoux, a tough-talking, cigarette-wielding union rep), the heart of the film and the crux of its unapologetically leftist political essay lie in the tension between the two men, symbolizing everything from the serrated lines between progress and tradition, the deceptive balm of capitalism versus the fizzy uncertainty of progressive politicking, and the primal battle of masculinity that is the seed of so much father/son conflict. As Frank grows more militant, joining in with the union workers, staging strikes and protests, his father feels both betrayed and furious. The irony is rich. The old man sacrificed much so that his boy would have a better life, could possibly be a powerful man. But when Frank eschews that status quo definition of success and works to truly improve the lives of others, not merely participate in a blatantly corrupt system, it's an affront to his father's dreams.

Human Resources was cast with non-professional actors (save Lespert) who were all plucked from unemployment lines and selected because their real-life jobs were aligned with the jobs their characters would have. You'd never know they weren't pros by the quality of work they do. There's an integrity to the performances that is unassailable. The film builds steadily to a showdown between father and son on the factory floor, with Frank blasting his father for infecting him with shame for who he is and where he comes from. "You gave me your shame," he shouts tearfully, "and I will have it inside me all my life." The devastation that then plays across the father's face is almost too painful to watch.

LA Weekly, September 15, 2000

i, too, sing hollywood
FOUR WOMEN ON RACE, ART AND MAKING MOVIES

Ten years ago, it would have been impossible to assemble a roundtable of black female directors, especially one in which each participant had a feature film under her belt. Almost all extant full-length films directed by black women—not just in the United States, but throughout the world—were made over the past decade. In 1991, Julie Dash became the first African-American woman to release a feature; her groundbreaking *Daughters of the Dust* remains a high-water mark in the canon of black film. Throughout the black film movement of the '90s, Dash remained the lone female director to be mentioned alongside such names as Spike Lee, the Hudlin brothers, Carl Franklin and John Singleton. Sadly, her inability to follow her debut feature with another big-screen effort would be shared by black female filmmakers to come, Cheryl Dunye (*Watermelon Woman*) and Darnell Martin (*I Like It Like That*) among them.

Dash helped open the door for black women directors, but they and their work remain subject to marketplace vagaries in ways black male directors and their work aren't. The summer box office success of films like *Scary Movie, Big Momma's House, Nutty Professor II: The Klumps* and *The Original Kings of Comedy* has renewed conversation around the state of black film—what it is, who makes it, who the audience is—but the conversation has largely centered on, and been uncritically celebratory of, a men's club. Although Chris Tucker, Eddie Murphy, Keenan Ivory Wayans and Martin Lawrence have gotten props for reviving, and perhaps transcending, black film, most of this praise ignores the movies helmed by women, which is to ignore some of the most challenging and innovative work being made.

To watch the films directed by black women in the last 10 years is to be reminded of the dazzling crop of black female writers in the '70s: Ntozake Shange, Toni Cade Bambara, Alice Walker, Toni Morrison. Like their literary forebearers, black women filmmakers broaden the parameters of both womanhood and blackness by giving us access to previously underrepresented territory. The *Weekly* recently sat down with four of these directors to get their takes on what it is to be black and women working in film. Participants included Kasi Lemmons, the director-writer of *Eve's Bayou*, who also directed the forthcoming *Caveman's Valentine*; Gina Prince-Bythewood, who wrote and directed *Love & Basketball*, and directed the upcoming HBO film *Disappearing Acts*; Zeinabu irene Davis, whose feature *Compensation* played at Sundance this year; and Cauleen Smith, whose feature *Drylongso* was at Sundance last year. Manohla Dargis, the *LA Weekly*'s film editor, also sat in.

How did you break into film?
Gina Prince-Bythewood: I went to UCLA to attend film school, but I didn't get in [the film program], so I had to petition them, which was basically writing a letter telling them why they had made a mistake. They let me in. In terms of getting into the business, the turning point was meeting Bill Cosby on the track at UCLA.

You literally met him on the track?
Prince-Bythewood: Yeah. I was running track at UCLA, and he came to the USC/UCLA meet. I asked the coach to introduce us, and for some reason we just hit it off. After that, every weekend I would train, then go to his house and watch football. His family was there, and it was very cool.
Kasi Lemmons: I was an actress for a long time. I did some off-Broadway, some cult films. I was feeling unfulfilled and went to the New School for Social Research film school to be a documentary filmmaker, and while there I made a docudrama. I ran into Bill Cosby at an audition and said, "I want you to see this film I made." And he said, "What I really need is a writer. Can you write a four-page scene?" He ended up hiring me to write a screenplay for him.

So it's all about Bill Cosby.
Cauleen Smith: Well, the Cosby connection ends here. My background is in experimental film, and there's pretty much one way you make those movies—apply for grants, wait for the

money, work two or three jobs, and spend all your money making films. I was in San Francisco doing video installations and performance art and got fed up waiting for money, so I decided to go back to school. I applied to UCLA grad school, got in, and at the same time received a grant from the Rockefeller Foundation—a $35,000 lump sum. This was in the early '90s, when there was all this hype about films costing $7,000 or $9,000, and I thought, "I can make three features now!" One of my friends, Salim Akil, and I wrote what ended up being *Drylongso* while I was in film school. Sundance took it, and I was launched into the industry.

Zeinabu irene Davis: I didn't get the baptismal water from Sundance. I'm originally from Philly and went to Brown to become a lawyer. While there, I landed an internship at public television in Rhode Island. Then I studied in Kenya, working with a writer there named Ngugi wa Thiong'o on a play of his—the English translation is *I Will Marry Whom I Want*. Most of the governments in Africa also run the school system, so as soon as there's any kind of unrest, the schools close. While we were making this production, the students were protesting for a second political party. It was a panic situation 'cause I was supposed to be trying to get these credits at Brown and it wasn't happening 'cause we didn't have school. Anyway, we hand-built the stadium for this production, and after the third performance the government bulldozed the theater. Ngugi wa Thiong'o had to go into hiding and, eventually, exile. I stayed in the country for a few more months, attending the school of hard knocks. Then I came back home and ended up going to UCLA Film School.

Who are some of your film heroes or influences?

Lemmons: Hitchcock, Bergman, Kurosawa. Spike Lee was the first African-American director I'd seen who was as cinematic, who was that into using the camera to tell a story. When I made my first short film, the young brothers were just coming up, and they really took me in. Reggie and Warrington Hudlin were running the Black Filmmakers Foundation, and they took my film to showcase. Every time I'd see Spike, he'd be, like, "When are you going to do your feature?" John Singleton, too.

Prince-Bythewood: You know, growing up, I wasn't really allowed to see anything but Disney movies. I couldn't see R-rated movies even when I was 17. I remember in film school, the film that influenced me the most was *The Graduate*. I just remember sitting in class being so blown away by the way it was made, by its use of music. *Now*, in terms of influence, it's [Martin] Scorsese and [Elia] Kazan. Just before I was about to shoot *Love & Basketball*, I started to panic. I knew I could direct actors, but the whole thing with the camera—I thought it wasn't going to be snazzy enough. So I rented a bunch of Kazan films and realized it's about the story. Then there's Scorsese. *GoodFellas* is just a perfect movie. I am so mesmerized by his work, by his choices and themes. Everything he makes is personal to him, and he keeps making things even if they don't make a ton of money.

Davis: I'm actually influenced by people in this room. I also have been very influenced by the filmmakers who came out of UCLA, which has a strong history of filmmakers of color—the African-American, Native American, Latino and Asian filmmakers who came out of UCLA in the '70s and early '80s. Charles Burnett and Julie Dash, in particular, helped me get through film school. Because I teach African cinema, I'm also very much into the work of African filmmakers, particularly more experimental people like Safi Faye, Ousmane Sembene and Djibril Diop Mambety.

Smith: One I might add is John Sayles. Not just his body of work, which is astounding, but the way he does business and goes about making films. I think, between him and Madonna, I've figured out how to work it. There are these great American independent filmmakers—including Sayles, Spike, Jim Jarmusch and Hal Hartley—who really fight to make their films the way they need to. I wish there was a way to cultivate a larger audience for the kind of work they do, but I'm not sure that can happen.

Lemmons: I go back and forth on whether that's important. Should we be John Sayles and say, "Okay, there's an audience for my movies, and I can reach them at a certain budget"? You know what I mean?

Smith: I do, except that I want to make science fiction. I need $50 million. I need it *now*.

Lemmons: I just did a movie that I needed $40 million for, for $13 million. It gets tiring working beneath the money that you need, letting the marketplace dictate what it's going to pay for a movie about, you know, a schizophrenic homeless black composer. [*Laughter.*] There's a budget cap on the subject matter, and it's not going to go above that, no matter who you have starring. That makes sense to me. I get it. But it's hard.

Smith: It's horribly frustrating that the kinds of movies we want to make, the kind of content that interests us, is something that the market tells us nobody wants to see. If you go see a black movie that makes $45 million and you hate it, you feel like "Am I crazy? Everybody else here is loving it."

I feel that way when I watch so much contemporary black film. It's pandering and sentimental or—in the case of the hip-hop–derived stuff—crude stereotypes presented as cultural truths. We talk a lot about the racism in Hollywood, but how complicit are black people in what Hollywood chooses to sell as black film?

Smith: I'll use hip-hop as an example. Now, I buy it. I love it. But it has become like one big minstrel show. There are all these incredibly gifted, intelligent black men who are selling a caricature of their own identities and experiences. They might as well be in black face, skipping around, *I'm a thug, I'm a thug, I'm a thug.* It's embarrassing. I listen to Dr. Dre, and in his music I hear a genius. In his lyrics I hear someone who's totally pandering to a very narrow idea of blackness. It's the same with film.

Prince-Bythewood: I agree, especially about Dre. I would've bought his record if it didn't have "bitch" all through it. The beats are good, but I was, like, fuck it.

It's interesting that you use hip-hop to critique those representations. To some extent that's what Spike Lee does in *Bamboozled.*

Davis: Then hopefully the film will generate dialogue.

Except that, in this town, there seems to be very little interest in Spike Lee. There was more buzz leading up to

Ladies Man **than for** *Bamboozled.*

Smith: Well, to play devil's advocate, Lee talks so much trash. I mean, if I were the person who put up $20 million for the man, and then he sat on *Nightline* and talked trash about me and my company, I wouldn't want to deal with him either. I know that's his persona, how he generates publicity, but it's got to rub people the wrong way. He talks *a lot* of trash.

A lot of white directors talk their share of trash.
Smith: Like who?
Lemmons: [Quentin] Tarantino.
Smith: I'm talking about a different thing. I'm talking about attacking the very people who got you in that seat by funding your movie. I don't see the white boys doing that at all. That's one game that they don't play.
Lemmons: No, that will come back to haunt you, certainly as an African-American woman. As soon as you get an agent, [the agent] warns you. I remember one time I was trying to sell *Eve's Bayou*, and I was talking to this executive. At a certain point, he said that there was a part of the script he didn't get. I did not suck my teeth or anything like that, but I did sit back and cross my arms. I got a lecture about it afterwards. I was told to never sit back and cross your arms, because now these people think you're a bitch. There's something about black women that frightens people. People are waiting for you to be kind of bitter. It's interesting, if what you say about Spike is true, because I don't know...
Smith: I was just wondering how he gets away with it.
Davis: It's a performance.
Lemmons: I wouldn't advise it for a woman.
[*The group breaks into a chorus of "No!"*]

Are there pressures on women to put on a different kind of performance?
Prince-Bythewood: Well, I started in TV, and I'm actually shocked that I stayed as long as I did, because every single one I was on—except *A Different World* and *South Central*—I was the only black writer. And I swear, it was months of fighting them trying to change my script, trying to

tell me this or that about black folks. It was ridiculous. I must have been annoying but I didn't care, because I was fighting for the integrity of my writing.

Smith: When I attended the Sundance directors' lab this summer, there was one young director who used expletives like adjectives and pronouns. I watched him, thinking, "There's no freaking way that if I came into an office and behaved like that that I would get a job. They'd call security on me." I mean, it's a construction and it works for him. I'm trying to figure out what construction will work for me. Haven't found it yet. Still broke, still ain't got a job.

Davis: My world is quite different, but people have the same kind of trepidation when they see you in the room. I made full professor this summer, and that makes me one of three black women teaching film in the country who are full professors. It's a constant struggle. You're usually the only black person, the only female, and to try to convince them that you are the right person to do X, Y and Z is still a struggle.

A lot of recent articles have suggested that we should retire the term "black film," that we're post-race.

[*The group scoffs.*]

Lemmons: I heard a white man who runs a studio putting a cap on black film and black audiences—what you can spend to make a black film and what our stars are able to make. We asked him what about Eddie Murphy? What about Oprah? And he said, "Those are no longer black people. Those are stars." I don't want to cross over and become just a filmmaker and not be counted in that census, you know? I want to be counted as a black person, as a black person who is successful. I feel very possessive about our actors. Eddie Murphy—yeah, he's internationally famous, but he's one of ours.

Prince-Bythewood: I consider myself a black filmmaker, and I say that because even though I want to do all kinds of genres—the next thing I'm doing is a thriller—I want black people in them. I mean, Carl Franklin, I love his career, I think it's amazing. It's just that at this point in my career, that's not what I want to do. There are so few films with black folk in them . . . if we're not doing it, who's going to?

Lemmons: I still think that if he directs *One True Thing*, he's still a black filmmaker who directed that movie. We can still claim him. [*Laughs.*] When Meryl [Streep] gets nominated for the Oscar, he's still one of ours.

Davis: I respect black filmmakers who say that they don't want to be labeled as black filmmakers. At least we've gotten to this point in world history where they can say that. That's fine. But that will never be fine for *me*. I'm still dealing with racism and sexism on a day-to-day basis. I'm not isolated from the world in which I live.

Smith: Yes, I'm a black filmmaker. Yes, I'm a woman filmmaker. And I don't really think too much about it. I think about it about as much as white folks think about what they're going to call themselves. I make movies about people that I'm interested in, just like they do. And, for the most part, those people are black. When I write a script, it's a given—unless I say otherwise—that they're black. Why would I sit around writing about white people? I can go see their stories any hour of the day. I go see every movie hoping to see a black woman who is intelligent, smart, strong, vulnerable and sexy. And those five things cannot ever be in one character if she has black skin. Never. I'm not interested in seeing any movie if it doesn't fulfill those requirements. I mean, there are a lot of black films made by brothers that I have to walk out of. I can't sit there and watch them do that to us.

You'd like to think that the rise of black talent in Hollywood would have signaled a shift in representation.

Lemmons: I absolutely think it will happen with more women. I find that women—as filmmakers and as people—are not interested in putting up with the status quo. Most of the women I know are aware of the deepness of women. There are many white male filmmakers who have captured women beautifully, and, of course, there are works of literature in which women have been beautifully realized by men. But in cinema we're just not seeing it, for some reason, in regard to black women. One of the things that motivated me to make *Eve's Bayou* the way I did was that I was sick of the image of the noble, slightly sweaty, angry black woman. I remember after I did

Eve's Bayou, someone said, "You were in Louisiana—why weren't those women sweating?" I said, "You know what? I've had enough sweaty people." I just didn't want to see any sweat. I wasn't feeling that. I was feeling this other thing that I experienced in my youth, looking at my family and my neighbors and the people that I knew—this beauty and glamour.

Smith: Even at the Sundance lab, I was advised that if the woman *had* to be black, then the male love interest should probably be white, because there was probably no other way I was going to get the money to make the film. That's why I'm interested in Gina's relationship with New Line.

Prince-Bythewood: The whole thing with *Love & Basketball* is that my budget would have been a lot lower if I hadn't got Omar Epps, because to them he was a star. It was, like, if you get a star in the male role, go ahead and cast the rest of the movie the way you want—because I wanted to cast an unknown for Monica [the lead female]. It wasn't like they gave me all this money based on the script. It was "Who's going to bring in the audience?"

Lemmons: The really interesting thing with *Eve's Bayou* is that studio people would ask me to put in white characters. I mean, even if they were negative white characters—just any white character. They would say, "Can't there be a racist?" And I just said, "This is *Eve's* bayou."

Going back to the Omar Epps thing, studios want to protect their investments by having names in the cast regardless of who's directing the movie. Did having Sam Jackson make a difference to *Eve's Bayou?*

Lemmons: Having Sam Jackson has made my career! [*Laughs.*] Thank God for Sam. When I was trying to make *Eve's Bayou,* the studios would say, "Oh we love it. It's a beautiful script. But you need to get a star. If you could get, say, Sam Jackson..." Sam's people read the script, and we attached him to the project. Then we went back to those same studio people and said, "We got Sam Jackson," and they were like "Oh. You got him. We didn't really mean that..." Even with Sam attached, in both these cases—it's not a piece of cake, because the subject matter is not mainstream.

Davis: Do you think if you'd been a white male director with Jackson attached you would have still had the same problems?

Lemmons: I can't even speculate. I was eight months pregnant with both my green lights. I went in thinking, "There's no way you're going to waddle in here and get the money to make this movie." So even though it was a hard road and we had three green lights on *Caveman's Valentine*—two of them fell through—I don't know. We were able to get the films made. I think there's a place for all of us as filmmakers, just as there's a place for all of them—from Sayles to Scorsese to [Joel] Schumacher. To me, Gina is the great white hope because she made something mainstream that everybody can feel. Everybody can feel *Love & Basketball*.

Davis: That's important. Gina's the first one to jump off on another feature film so quickly.

Prince-Bythewood: Can I be honest? I learned so much on *Disappearing Acts*, but the biggest thing I learned is that I want to write and direct my own things. I'm very proud of the result, but I don't want to be a director for hire. It's Terry [McMillan]'s vision, then Lisa Jones'—who wrote the script—then mine. It's not the same experience. I wish I had waited.

Lemmons: *Caveman's Valentine* was adapted by the novelist, but I worked on the script for three years. But I came out of that movie and said to my agent, "I'm going to write my next movie." If we let ourselves be directors for hire too easily, we're going to end up putting that same image out there that we're struggling against. Whereas if we write it, then at least we're going to control, to a certain extent, the female characters and the type of movie that it is.

Prince-Bythewood: I couldn't turn *Disappearing Acts* down, because it's always been one of my favorite books, but there was also a bit of panic: *I'm never going to work again.* Now I have the confidence that I can take a year-and-a-half off and write the next script, and someone's going to buy it. I have to keep telling myself that. There's a great amount of fear when you have your agent telling you that there's a six-month window of being hot. But if I want to stay special and have a voice, I have to write and direct it myself.

Kasi, you said that you think it's going to take

more women directors to change things. But do you think it's also going to take more women everywhere in the industry?

Lemmons: I feel strongly about women. Both of my movies have had an extraordinary number of women working on them. This last movie, all my keys were women—the DP, the producer, the editor, the production designer. On *Eve's Bayou* it was the same thing. I think that *that* is important for the industry. It's opening up. It's going to happen. It's inevitable. Even if they didn't want it to happen, it's going to happen. It's a wave that's been set into motion.

Smith: But on the level of studio producers and development execs, do you really think it matters if you're pitching to a woman or a man?

Prince-Bythewood: Oh, completely. For instance, Gale Ann Hurd. Look at the projects she's been involved with and the strong women in those movies. I know she had a hand in that. Women like that are who I gravitate toward, because they're up-front in saying, "We don't want to do the same crap." I'm not getting that from male execs. Only one actually—Tom Rothman at Fox, who's an amazing guy. But otherwise, the most exciting meetings have been with women who are saying, We're getting power, let's do something different.

Smith: I know a lot of great women working in the studios, I do. But overall, the product coming out of studios...

Prince-Bythewood: Oh, it's crap. Don't get me wrong; we're in trouble.

Lemmons: But I think the wave of filmmakers coming up is going to change the product so that it doesn't matter who the executive is. They're going to see that it's cool to green-light this movie, because *Love & Basketball* did make money, *Eve's Bayou* did make money...

Something we hear constantly is that in order for any film to be considered a good financial risk, it has to be viable in the international market, which black movies supposedly are not. How does that notion affect the way you conceive a movie, create it, pitch it?

Lemmons: God. How often have we heard that one? How

you pitch it is the big one. Definitely. I learned a lot when I was running around pitching *Eve's Bayou*, and they'd ask who I thought the audience for the film was. I'd say African-American college graduates, and the room would go dead. I learned to say, "Well, it's the *Waiting to Exhale* audience," and they'd go, ch-ching!

Prince-Bythewood: The word *universal* is very important.

Lemmons: Yes. You have to say to them, This is a movie for everybody; just like you related to the script, anybody can relate to the movie.

Smith: There was a luncheon during the Democratic Convention where a bunch of filmmakers sat down with editors from *Newsweek*, and there was an editor who was a Hong Kong correspondent who talked about how she was confused about why black filmmakers are told that our films are not commercially viable overseas. She'd just attended a black film festival in either Hong Kong or Singapore, and it was packed every night. And she said it wasn't the shoot-'em-up, hip-hop genre that was popular—it was the family movies, the character studies.

Prince-Bythewood: With *Love & Basketball*, after we had the first screening at Sundance, everyone was hyped. I remember the guy in charge of foreign distribution was like, This could definitely play overseas, because women's basketball is huge overseas. But during the conversation, he said I had to cut 20 minutes from the second half of the movie—because overseas audiences don't like long movies—and add more to the sex scenes. I'm like, *There is no more*. It's not like I trimmed it—there is no more. And then he was like, Well, we'll *try* to sell it. After that I got the same thing: It just doesn't sell overseas. I do not understand why someone in London wouldn't get it. Or Japan. Black culture is huge there. And that's why you start to think, honestly: Is it a conspiracy? Because it's not even like anyone is trying to change it.

Smith: I wish someone would just really look at the numbers.

Lemmons: You can actually get the information. I've been going to the Summit for several years now...

Could you explain what that is for the readers?

Lemmons: The Black Filmmakers Foundation started the Summit, and it's expanded beyond filmmakers. It's filmmakers, people in television, producers, executives—it's like the hundred hottest people. It feels like being in a room of the best and brightest that's out there. They bring in Internet people, black people that you don't even know about that are out there running corporations. They bring them down to the Summit [at a Southern California retreat], and one year we did a study on the international market and the list of black movie stars that sell foreign—which is incredibly large and which Hollywood overlooks. They overlook this information, which is factual. You can get a sheet, print it out and bring it into a meeting. Because I think it's a myth. I don't know why people wanna believe it.

Smith: I can think of a few reasons people wanna believe it.

What do you think the reasons are, Cauleen?

Smith: I think that the industry is forced in some way to make delineations about which project is going to get out and which project's going to stay put. And it's very easy—just as it's always been in this country—to determine who gets the privilege based on race, and that's what's happening in this case. The film industry, for some reason, is more interested in perpetuating that than making money, which is a mystery to me.

That flies in the face of all the pseudo-progressive rhetoric we hear now—that it's not about black or white, it's just about green.

Prince-Bythewood: It's not about green, because if that were the truth, black films would be marketed a lot differently. Both *Premiere* and *Entertainment Weekly* ran articles on how the state of black film has changed because *Scary Movie, Big Momma's House* and *Next Friday* all made a ton of money. But those are comedies. When a black *drama* makes that kind of money, things have changed. But more than that, when black dramas get the marketing dollars that *Scary Movie* and *Shaft* got, then you can truly say things have changed. Really, it's the same as it's always been. Comedy is so easy to cross over because...

Smith: White America has no problem with black people

being funny.

Lemmons: (*dryly*) They're not black people anymore when they're funny.

Prince-Bythewood: I do think white folks can go to a comedy that stars black comedians and identify, because funny is funny, but they don't think that they can go to a black drama and identify with the characters on the screen. That boggles my mind.

Another stumbling block for black film is the shoddiness with which it's reviewed. Even favorable reviews can be very shallow.

Smith: There's so little analysis of the films that we do. It's so hard to get someone to look at our work seriously. And it's really frustrating, because I know we all think a lot about everything in the frame. I'm just shocked at the lack of critical analysis.

Well, the critical establishment, like Hollywood, is very white, and that's a crucial element in understanding how they cover issues of race.

Smith: The film industry, in particular, because it's made up of people from all over the country, but they all move to the Westside and are scared to drive east of La Brea. They think they're going to get shot on the freeway. They don't know anything about how great it is to be here, how diverse it is.

How do you negotiate the fact that you live and work in a city and industry that both sell themselves as being liberal and progressive, but can be so racist and reactionary?

Lemmons: I feel that you have to patiently educate people, because they really don't know that they're being offensive. I mean, I've heard statements come out of people's mouth like, "You know, the *Waiting to Exhale* audience doesn't have the attention span for a long movie." And I was like, "What? Oh, excuse me, I drifted off." [*Laughter.*] I don't want to say it's not their fault, because that's not true, but they want to do the right thing, they just need educating. They need you to sit down and look them in the eye and say, "What you just said was offensive to me, and I'm going to tell you why." You know, patiently. And then the next day you get a bottle of wine and some flowers.

I wrote a script for Michelle Pfeiffer's company, and many people were fans of the script, but nobody knew that I was black. I went into a meeting at another studio, and somebody came in, sat next to the girl that gets coffee and said, I've got to tell you, I loved the script you wrote. And she was like, Well, thank you very much, but *that's* Kasi.

I had someone ask me once, how can you write a script for white actors? Well, black people know the shit out of white people. As a girlfriend of mine says in her book, "It's like I have one living in the back room." Because we have to live in the white world; we are forced into assimilation. White people don't have to know black people. They can live in a white world very, very easily. It's a completely different reality. And we have to say, Okay, let me clue you in, gently, gently, to the world as I know it, and also be sensitive to the fact that that's their reality.

Smith: Doesn't it drain you to accommodate that kind of privilege? It's like institutional racism that you have to accommodate and negotiate at every moment. I find it exhausting. Black people are used to handling it, but when you're dealing with people who are so congratulatory about their liberalness, that's actually when it's worse. I can deal with the average ignorant white person, but when someone's so proud of their buck-wild liberal antics, it drains me.

Lemmons: That's why you have to, like, go home and call your friends and say, "Do you know what this motherfucker looked me right in my face and said to me?" [*Laughter.*] I do think patience is the key. I think when you scream about it, sometimes they don't hear.

Smith: I don't think they ever hear it, because they don't have to.

How do you feel about the DGA stripping D.W. Griffith's name from one of its highest honors?

Prince-Bythewood: I'm so torn on this issue. My husband [screenwriter Reggie Bythewood] and I debate this a lot. It's like with Miles Davis. He's celebrated as one of the greatest artists of all time. But he beat women. I can recognize his brilliance, but something holds me back from celebrating him, which is the same with Griffith. I mean, I had to watch *The Birth of a Nation* in film class with people cracking up as if it were funny. So yes, what he did at that time was brilliant, but you cannot separate the racism from it.

Lemmons: Who was the woman that made all the propaganda films for Hitler?

Leni Riefenstahl.

Lemmons: It's a very similar situation to me. She had a certain artistic integrity in the film, but she was absolutely reprehensible in that she decided to propagandize. Miles Davis might have beat women, but that wasn't what his music was about, whereas with *The Birth of a Nation*, racism is what was being put forth.

Smith: Not only that, but the film had this incredible impact on our country and on us, in particular. And the truth of the matter is, Griffith stole all of his ideas from a bunch of Italian silent filmmakers who were 10 years before him. He literally stole entire set pieces. The man was not all that. And that's what really bothers me—on top of him being this insane, rabid racist.

Davis: I am happy that the DGA did change the name of the Griffith Award precisely because of the reasons Cauleen states. I actually think *Intolerance* is worth looking at, but *The Birth of a Nation* is so incredibly damaging to all of us as Americans. Why should we have this award that celebrates this man, particularly for this racist depiction that we still have to deal with? And the fact of the matter is that people protested against that film from day one. But that is not on record. That gets forgotten.

So does the fact that lynchings increased dramatically in cities where it was shown.

Smith: It was black people who were lynched, and it was white people who were doing the lynching, and it deeply saddens me that white people would be willing to celebrate this human being. If I were white and in the industry, and this was the icon of the industry that I love, I'd be mortified.

Lemmons: I think the film should be taught as a history lesson; that's its real value. We should not forget that there were people out there who made this kind of film and that it influenced a nation. People should see where we came from, who this person was and how art can influence society and be used as an instrument of incredible pain, suffering and evil.

Davis: But a lot of times what happens when you see it at film school is that most of the film professors who show that film do not deal with the racist imagery.

Or they excuse it.

Prince-Bythewood: Thank God we all agree about *The Birth of a Nation*, but how do you all feel about the fact that Tarantino is so celebrated for *Pulp Fiction*?

Lemmons: It's complicated, because I don't think Tarantino is bringing down our race. I think he's stuck in a pattern of something that he thinks black people might sound like. But he does manage to have fairly interesting themes and characters. I mean, let's just acknowledge, first of all, that he's in a completely different league, you know.

Davis: And it's a different historical period, thank God. You don't have African Americans or any people of color being lynched as a direct consequence of his films.

Prince-Bythewood: But he does have a white character saying *nigger* a thousand times, and it's supposed to be funny. Suddenly, there's a whole bunch of young white kids thinking that shit is cool.

Lemmons: Obviously I support freedom of speech, and I think that he makes interesting films. I also think that he lives in a box. I guess the story is that he heard that in prison or something like that, and that's what he thinks black people talk like.

Smith: Oh, please. He was in jail for a parking ticket at most.

Lemmons: It's his shtick. It's what he does to attract attention.

Smith: I think a huge part of his popularity is based on that monologue; it was a cathartic moment for a lot of young white males. And I think that's why *Jackie Brown* didn't do well—because it was a very complicated rendering of a black woman, and they just wanted to hear another monologue like where he stood at that sink and said *nigger, nigger, nigger* with glee. He validated white people's desire to have entitlement to say that word. People who are used to feeling entitled to anything they want—that's one thing they're not entitled to do, and Quentin made it okay.

He restored that birthright.
Lemmons: The funniest thing to me about Quentin doing it is that it doesn't roll off his tongue. He puts himself in a movie and he says it awkwardly. I thought that was interesting.

How do you feel about him, Gina, since you brought him up?
Prince-Bythewood: You know, *Pulp Fiction* comes on cable a thousand times a day, and I can't even watch it for five minutes without getting pissed off about it. I just hate how people, as a whole, are able to separate content from form. I just think it's wrong. And I have the same problem with black filmmakers using *nigger* all through their stuff. When my husband was working on *Get on the Bus*, he had to tell the actors that he consciously wrote the script without that word so they shouldn't ad lib it. I said up-front to my actors: You don't see it written here, that means it's not in the movie. So it does drive me crazy when I hear it in movies and then hear the argument that, you know, we're just keeping it real.

What would you like black film—or film in general—to say that it's not saying now?
Lemmons: I would like to see movies where the black female characters act like real women, the women that I know, the women in this room—our mothers, our sisters, our friends. A well-portrayed, well-rounded female character with depth.
Davis: It seems so little to ask for, doesn't it?
Prince-Bythewood: You know, I struggle with myself. Sometimes I think that I'm not saying enough in my work. During *Love & Basketball*, I panicked because I was like, I'm not saying anything. This is just a love story, and at the end of the day, that's not changing anything. But now I think about all the little girls that came up to me after the film was released. Just seeing yourself reflected positively onscreen can do so much for somebody. Why can't we just have that more?
Davis: I think if I could see any change in black film, I

would like us as filmmakers to stay in the vanguard but to also expand our vision so that we include more of who we are as international peoples. I'm dying to see some black Caribbean folk in some movies. I really wish we could be more inclusive in that regard. I just think those stories would really knock everybody out of the water.

Smith: I'm really interested in the way that black women are rendered in the media. Part of the reason that I'm a filmmaker is that I have to change this myself. I've just lost patience with the world at large about the way that we're rendered. This is like a mission with me; I just can't rest until this is done.

Lemmons: When I look at my nieces and nephews and the effect that Brandy playing Cinderella had on them, it's a beautiful thing. Because all of a sudden, Cinderella has this whole other meaning for them; they're able to see themselves in Cinderella. We can't underestimate the importance of putting black faces in classic roles, in everyday dramas and love stories.

Prince-Bythewood: And not even just positive images—truthful images. There's nothing wrong with black characters with flaws. Just make them interesting and real and true.

LA Weekly, October 20, 2000

god made them phunky
OUTKAST: ART, ARTIFICE, BOOTY AND THE BEAT

The video for Outkast's hit single, "B.O.B. (Bombs Over Baghdad)," opens with Dre (a.k.a. Andre 3000), currently hip-hop's most doggedly nonconformist—therefore unlikeliest and most potent—sex symbol, lying sprawled on a bed, torso rippling and shirtless, his processed 'do falling just above his shoulders, polyester pimp pants hugging his slim hips. As the track's ferocious beats kick in, Dre takes off running through a housing project, jumping over concrete fences, tumbling down a hill. But these projects are absolutely surreal: The colors are so bright they pop off the screen; the grass is thick and lush—hell, there is grass (albeit purple). This ghetto compound is shot and framed to resemble a gorgeous resort; there's none of the broken glass, barking pit bulls or glaring ruffnecks that have collapsed inner-city life to video clichés.

But the point of the video isn't to fetishize or candy-coat poverty or despair. The video's message is more pleasantly perverse than that: Everyday black people populate this cartoon-overhauled reality; *they* are what is being celebrated. As Dre flees the 'hood, he runs through a polished housing tract, his ghetto peeps right behind him—their slumadelic pied piper. When Dre's first verse ends, Outkast's other-half, Big Boi, along with Outkast protégée, Slimm Calhoun, and members of Goodie Mob, steer us toward a more traditional b-boy fantasy: bouncing pimp-mobile, blaring car-speakers and a few James Bond-style stunts.

The seamless stitch of artsy aesthetics and playa poses—each element drawn in race consciousness, simmered in (under) class-consciousness—is what makes Outkast hip-hop's great black hope, not an inconsequential thing to be in this MTV/TRL era of shuck & jive Negroes and cultural appropriation. From their very first album, 1994's *Southernplayalisticadillacmuzik*, the duo have done a nimble balancing act, complementing one another while creating a union by which they celebrate 360 degrees of black maleness. Big Boi is the *erryday* homeboy, brain on information overload, clad in style and sensibility that is pure street. Affectation is Dre's natural stance, though he's grown and evolved into it. Check the duo's early videos; Dre was just an around-the-way dude draped in rap's status quo gear, only hinting at his next-plane aesthetic.

Dre uses artifice (oversized blonde wigs, outlandish stage costumes) to divine truth, effortlessly spinning off on some "next" shit. He's almost scary in his gloriousness, in his awareness of it. He's the one we watch with baited breath. His organic but hyperstylized "otherness" makes him sexy and deeply sexual, with a blazing intelligence and not so quiet rage spiking his rhymes. He's the point of connection for many Outkast fans because he's the one walking a tightrope, making him a rarity in rap music in that he lays hold to both the pop charts and that which jazzes *undaground* heads.

But America is especially cruel to her Negro eccentrics, with black folk often leading the charge, fueled by timidity and what-will-massa-think conservatism. (Hip-hop, by the way, hasn't done that much to cure the syndrome of Negro Reflexive Cowardice.) We watch Dre in awe and nervousness. Big Boi is the stable compound, the familiar. Dre is the unpredictable one that renders the composition volatile, keeping all eyes on him.

Greg Tate recently wrote that "American racial identity is less a thing to be contemplated than performed—not to mention paraded, primped, politicked, and prostituted, as loudly and wrongly as possible in civic space." That's a statement gnarled in meaning, but what it's saying, in small part, is that blackness has been reduced to a metaphor for someone else's angst, alienation or crappy day at school or work. And Negroes in the rap game are cashing in by playing dumb and dumber with disheartening glee, flattening out their own reality in order to be bought. Outkast, though, know how to play with surfaces and humor while keeping their artistic fingers dug deep in the blood, sweat and shit of modern day blackness. They pump the metaphor back up to real-life dimensions, finessing stereotypes and unmasking truths. So, the duo's "country" accents are proudly flung, complete with regional slang and pronunciation, but serving poetry and Negrocentric politics that shatter preconceptions of the hick or Bama. The divide between 'hood rat and intellectual is proved to be contrived and bridgeable—as is the split between Negro Bohemian and ghetto denizen. *Stankonia* (LaFace/Arista), the latest opus by the Atlanta-based duo, is not just a rap album; it's a genuine hip-hop artifact. That means it's music, philosophy and unbound sexual heat—vision and politics wrought in human terms. It's also funky as hell, full of blazing guitar licks, electro burps and assaultive beats. The collection re-contextualizes far-flung culture shards, reminding us of their blackness (a nod to Hendrix here, a stroke of Detroit techno there) and connecting them to one another. (In terms of production and musical roots, "B.O.B." is simply booty music on steroids, which is also why it's the frontrunner candidate for single of the year.)

But despite having made a record that's incredibly nuanced in its unabashed reclaiming of rap music and hip-hop culture, Dre and Big Boi pointedly avoid self-righteous posturing. They're not willing to toss any black folk overboard as their art ascends. On the track, "Gasoline Dreams," Dre raps, *"All my heroes did dope / every nigga 'round me playin' married or payin' child support..."* And from "Humble Mumble," he drops, *"I met a critic, I made her shit her draws / She said she thought hip-hop was only guns and alcohol / I said "Oh hell naw!" but yeah it's that too / You can't discriminate because you done read a book or two..."* At the same time, the team calls out mindless ballers and shot-callers. On "Red Velvet," Big Boi intones, *"Ball if you want to, but do it with some class, G... Prioritize and tell these other niggaz how you / Brought your kid some tennis shoes / Let these brothers know that your mama got her house too... Do this here and keep that bullshit out our ear..."*

George Clintonesque in their sci-fi street funk (and in Dre's sartorial choices), Bill Clintonesque in their unbridled libido, and armed with their own sharp eyes and gifts for cerebral but accessible lyrics, Outkast flip from sensitive male ("Ms. Jackson," "Toilet Tisha") to wounded soldier to unrepentant dog at the drop of a dime—and sometimes in the same song. The greatness, for example, of "Ms. Jackson" is that this ode to baby-mamas *mamas* incisively and honestly owns up to the male-inflicted pain that's at the base of so much feminine rage—and then, without diluting that point, gives voice to the indignities heaped upon men (especially fathers) when relationships go bad. The gendered perspectives conflict but don't necessarily contradict, meaning no one emerges as pure hero or bad guy, and the knot of human relationships is essayed with an insight rare in modern pop music.

It's in the duo's voices and deliveries, though, that *Stankonia* (like their previous three albums) really takes off—the way they can each swivel their flow to sidestep a beat, pause, and then drop a rhyme square in the pocket. Funk has taken up residence in their Southern drawls, with vowels pulled and stretched like soft taffy, for both humorous and poignant effect. The playfulness of their R&B falsetto (*"I'm sorry, Ms. Jackson / I am for reeeeaaaaalllll…"*) is both send-up *of* and tribute *to* old-school soul jams. Rap music in the last few years, and with admitted exceptions, has contracted like a dick caught in an arctic wind. It's become small and embarrassing, a too-often impotent tool of show. Outkast has brought back the heat with genuine artistry.

The "B.O.B." video concludes in a cool fantasy realm of church and juke-joint, where big-tittied video hoochies bump and grind to the beat-driven, lifted voices of gospel choir matrons, all while cornrowed Black frat brothers execute step routines with blinding precision. Dre (now clad in a turban and genie gear) and Big Boi have landed here not just as an escape from the 'hood, but to demonstrate that those who live in urban confines also have dreams and fantasies, vibrant inner lives. This video ghetto is not just a place of pathology and psychosis, but a place that functions as ground zero for a lot of people's reality—and for a creativity that can be as transcendent, beautiful and resilient as it is stark.

LA Weekly, November 24, 2000

before night falls

In his memoir *Before Night Falls*, Reinaldo Arenas writes that he grew up "surrounded by trees, animals, apparitions, and people indifferent toward me. My existence was not even justified." It's not a statement of self-pity. In the lines that follow, the late gay Cuban writer makes it clear that the combination of the familial shrug, his own imagination and the unqualified embrace of nature (the farm animals that he played with, the trees that whispered their secrets to him) granted him a profound freedom. It's what turned him into a sensualist whose rage at political oppression (in Cuba, in the world) was both intellectual and spiritual, whose awe at rainstorms, great literature and male beauty flowed poetically through him. His was a slyly off-hand humor that did more than just deliver a punch line; it encapsulated a pungent point. In one passage, he tells of the sundry livestock who bore the brunt of male libido on his family's farm. Of a rooster who died after one such encounter, Arenas writes, it "died of shame from getting fucked."

With the filmed adaptation of the book, '80s art-star-turned-director Julian Schnabel captures the spirit of Arenas' words and life with surprising skill and unexpected artfulness. While the film is kept somewhat at a cool distance due to the thickly accented voice-over by leading man Javier Bardem (there are moments when it's impossible to decipher what he's saying), Bardem's flawless performance and Schnabel's sigh-inducing visuals are hypnotic, conveying the essence of its subject's voice and contoured perspective. Little in Schnabel's 1996 feature debut, *Basquiat*, gave proof that he had any real facility for filmmaking, and only the ever reliable Jeffrey Wright in the title role made the film worth seeing.

In *Before Night Falls*, though, the director gracefully fuses performance, politics and style into a film that's social commentary, coming-of-age tale and a glimpse into the psyche of the artist, all in one. Epic in scope and ambition, tracing Arenas' journey from unwanted bastard to political prisoner to American exile, the film maintains a lush sense of intimacy throughout. Credit for that goes largely to Bardem, whose liquid eyes are almost lethal in their emotional precision. He gives a delicate performance, one in which his sissy-sway stops short of caricature, conveying strength and vulnerability, wit and self-aware humor. His Arenas is fiercely intelligent, highly cerebral, but never loses sight of the fact that he *lives* in his body.

Schnabel fills the screen with breath-taking images—raindrops sliding off leaves, a billowing hot-air balloon. One scene in particular is among the best in film this year. The young Arenas is driven to a nightclub by his new beau (we see the trip in languid slow motion), who promptly abandons the writer to dance with a woman. There's no dialogue, only sparse, evocative music that has an undertow of sadness, bottomless longing. Elegantly dressed people dance and laugh on the crowded floor while Arenas watches wistfully, as another handsome young man approaches him for a dance. Desire is palpable. It's a perfect moment, a captured memory—an elegy to not only a time gone by, but to the beauty and possibilities that would soon be vanquished and that are short-lived anyway, even in the best of circumstances. In the joy and heat of the exchanges—the lust, looming erasure and whisper of melancholy behind the smiles—Schnabel has captured that which is both fleeting and eternal, the human life force in all its transcendent fragility.

LA Weekly, December 22, 2000

bonus disc

*Since I wrote this story in 2000 and watched it fall through the cracks at the **LA Weekly**, never getting published, a lot has changed on the cultural horizon. The "DL" phenomenon blew up and was exploited by both the media (mainstream and gay) and by Negro huckster J.L. King with dazzling stupidity. Black gay/queer/same-gender-loving identity crashed onto the mainstream in ways controversial, triumphant and horribly fucked up. And the rapper Common had an evolution of consciousness and art (Check his track, "Between Me, You & Liberation," on his much-maligned **Electric Circus** CD) that happily renders some of the comments and lyrics cited in this piece outdated.*

— EH, July 2005

punks jump up to get theirs
HOMO-HOP: A MUSICAL ODYSSEY

TRACK 1 (INTRO): SHAKE YA ASS

Saturday night parking for Rimshot, a downtown Oakland dance club that caters to "the children"—legendary and otherwise—is almost impossible to find; there's nothing closer than three dark city blocks away. As you finally enter the club, the ridiculous (a House remix of Destiny's Child's "Bills, Bills, Bills") is slowly giving way to the sublime: Barbara Tucker's anthemic "I Get Lifted"—a rush of keyboards, horns and Southern Baptist vocals. The place is packed, from the small sitting area just past the entrance, to the stairs leading down to the cramped dance floor. The deejay is on an OG House trip, following Tucker with River Ocean's "Love and Happiness," then spinning into Cevin Fisher's "Women Beat Their Men." The vibe in this melanin-ruled space (mainly Afro, plenty Latino, a sprinkling of Asian and white) is lovely: lots of smiles, a contagious playfulness. Liquid-bodied ruffnecks and their boys ring grinning dykes and their sweethearts. People are dancing with partners, yet no one seems bound by coupledom; everyone is dancing with everyone else.

A cute young homo Latino, tragically dressed in white Capri pants and a blue wife-beater, loosens his pants and lets them fall halfway off his ass. He's wearing pink briefs. As the music progresses, his pants fall lower and lower and he—without drawing overt attention to the act—slowly pulls the underwear into the crack of his ass, improvising a thong. He giggles as he dances with his mighty bodied fag-hag who smacks his butt and grinds into him whenever he turns his back to her.

The deejay throws on Whitney Houston's "Fine" and the harder-edged R&B is jarring at first—there's no graceful way to mix out of the classic House grooves into the nouveau funk of Houston's DJ Quik-produced track. But that was only a clumsy segue. What follows next is the hip-hop set: Black Rob, Ja Rule, Dr. Dre, Trick Daddy, Juvenile. Swizz Beatz is predictably over-represented. There's a palpable shift in the club's energy: Chests are puffed out. Jaws are squared. Smiles are either hardened at the edges or quickly tucked away. The fine young Latino no longer looks like a gay boy tripping on possibility; he sucks in his cheeks and hardens his eyes as he lets his pants fall well below his butt and does the booty-clap. Now he has the cold, mirthless sexuality of your everyday video ho.

A few brothers who'd been scowling and holding up the walls during the House set make their way to the floor: *Homo thugz inna hizzouse.* But my eyes are drawn to a stunning woman who—depending on which shaft of light she's standing in, depending on how the shadows fall across her face – looks like either Lisa Bonet or a Slim-fasted Faith Evans. She dances by herself, arms extended above her head, eyes closed, hips swaying. I can't stop staring at her. Hours later, when leaving with Tim'm (spoken word artist, rapper, scholar/activist, and my guide for the evening) I make a confession.

"I think I'm now a true head," I joke.

"Oh, yeah? Why is that," he asks.

"Because," I reply, "out of all the bodies in that place, I fell in love with the light-skin'ded girl with good hair."

He laughs.

TRACK 2: BACK DAT THANG UP

It was four years ago that fear was given form. *One Nut*, a previously little-known hip-hop publication, published the article, "Confessions of a Gay Rapper," and set off a firestorm that is still crackling throughout the hip-hop community. An unintentionally humorous coming-out tale, it's a poorly written piece whose impact has far outstripped its rote and flimsy insights. Sample:

"Yo, a nut is a nut." He laughs to himself. "You know when you are on lockdown, it is alright to have a sissy suck your dick... Yo, you may even fuck them, but when your ass is free and everything is supposed to be lovely, you are not wit that kind of shit. But yo, that shit is like crack. One good whiff and your ass is whipped. You see, only a brother can satisfy your need. Yo, I believe that a man is made for a woman and a woman is made for a man, but only a man knows what a man needs and feels. Only a man can satisfy another man."

It reads as though a straining-to-be-'hood Jackie Collins smoked a rock, fired up the word processor and riffed on *Black Inches'* fiction section, all while listening to a Def Jam compilation. The speaker pockmarks his confession with exculpatory/excusatory loopholes around his own pleasure and nature, rocking the soft beat of self-pity while reflexively, and at his own expense, extolling a hetero status quo.

Melodramatic—*"I have promised to carry [the secret of his identity] to my grave,"* writes the author—and cliché-ridden, the interview keeps you riveted by mining the titillation of untrammeled territory. But it's the details, especially as they mount, that slowly convince you the story just might be true. It's also the details ("He removes his sunglasses, showing his light-colored eyes for the first time,") that briefly made life a PR hell for a certain old-school hip-hop hero with light-colored eyes. In the end, the fact that "the gay rapper" is quoted speaking in such hoary cliché is what lends credence to the story. Almost everyone nowadays speaks about the world and themselves as though reciting from a hackneyed movie script or formulaic pop song. Popular cadence is lifted from sitcoms; pre-fabricated catch phrases are cut & pasted from TV commercials and slipped into everyday conversation. And in rap, where *"keeping it real"* has come to mean, *"I'm ready for my close-up,"* personal truths are increasingly packaged in choreographed poses and sampled epiphanies. Ironically, it's the very triteness of both revelation and presentation that give the *One Nut* piece whatever air of truthfulness it might possess.

The fallout from the article has been incalculable. For

months after the article appeared, urban radio talk shows blazed with the question, who was the gay rapper? The desperation with which some folks clung to the belief that there was just the *one* is both pathetic and very funny. Every other record that dropped seemed to have one rapper blasting another by outing him as the gay rapper. Magazines and newspapers ranging from the *Source* to *Mother Jones* to the *Village Voice* either did articles on this lone rapping faggot who'd captured the imagination of heads, or ran pieces on the heretofore unknown demographic of queer hip-hop fans. Most of those stories were penned either by black boys who proclaimed their hetero status at every turn, letting readers know that they'd finished the assignment with their booty hole intact, *yo*, or by white boys smart enough not to wave a sexuality badge, but incapable of avoiding predictable and useless liberal pieties.

Few of the brave documentarians rolled up their sleeves to tackle the complexity of issues at hand. Gay hip-hop fans—or the notion of a gay rapper—were treated like freakish occurrences, rooted in some laughable strain of delusion or self-hatred. (And even if that were the case, it's not as though those qualities are wholly foreign to the American psyche.) The prevailing sentiment was that hip-hop was some citadel of heterosexuality being stormed by faggots and dykes.

In truth, the reality of gays and lesbians in hip-hop before the "revelation" of the gay rapper is much like the reality of queers in America before the Mattachine Society was formed, before the Stonewall uprising boosted mainstream visibility: They've always been there; they were among the architects of the culture. They were some of the movement's first constituents.

This is not a radical notion, but common sense. There is a strong thread of homo/lesbo/queer presence and contribution to every cultural rebirth and reinvention of American Negro creativity, from the literary bloom of the Harlem Renaissance (Langston Hughes, Countee Cullen, Wallace Thurman, Alain Locke, Angelina Weld Grimke, Bruce Nugent, A'Lelia Walker), to blues (Ethel Waters, Alberta Hunter, Ma Rainey, Bessie Smith, Gladys Bentley), jazz (Andy Bey, Billie Holiday, Bud Powell, Billy Strayhorn), rock 'n' roll (Little Richard), disco, techno and House. And hip-hop.

As much as it shapes, hip-hop also reflects and refracts; the culture is not some alien nation where values or prejudices fall out of the sky void of larger cultural or political context, absent historical precedent or large-scale social conditioning. Nothing happens in hip-hop—not reheated gangsterism, blistering homophobia or scalding misogyny—that hasn't already been furiously stoked on the larger cultural and political landscapes of America. One of the most potent elements in hip-hop music is its sooth-telling reflex. In the progressive lyrics and overall politics of "conscious rappers," as well as through the gangsta/thug/hardcore reportage of 'hood attitudes/practices/beliefs, rap music (through pointed effort and unconscious revelation alike) blasts away the lies about equality and justice that America tells the world and itself *about* itself. It lays bare the racism, misogyny and homophobia that are hardwired in this country's DNA. In doing so, it proves itself perhaps the most American of this country's folk musics. The low-nigger-on-the-totem-pole status of *in-the-life* hip-hop artists and fans strikes an especially familiar chord. Hip-hop started, in part, as a refuge of the "other," as a place where the underdog or outsider could find and hone a voice, and possibly accrue status. It quickly turned into a space fiercely policed to keep the "other" out or on brutal lockdown, all while still giving lip service to freedom. What could possibly be more American than that?

TRACK 3:
AND I ASK MYSELF, HOW DID YOU GET HERE?

I'm in Oakland to attend the Black Gay Letters and Arts Movement (B/GLAM) festival, the centerpiece of which is a spoken-word and music performance in celebration of the re-issue of *Ceremonies*, the late Essex Hemphill's groundbreaking book of prose and poetry, and to meet with Deep/Dick Collective (D/DC), an Oakland-based crew of openly gay/bisexual hip-hop and spoken-word artists. The two cultural founts overlap—D/DC will be performing at the B/GLAM festival—but they also spring from a single source. At heart, both are about race and power, about black male sexuality and self-determination. They're both anchored in ever-pressing questions about Afro-Am masculinity—what constitutes it, who owns it, and why white boys are sliding on its signifiers and profiting from them while so many black men continue to be herded, housed and marked for assorted deaths. Those queries are filtered through two of contemporary pop culture's most over-commodified identity markers: hip-hop and homosexuality. In Reese's Cup conjoining, homo-hop.

TRACK 4: SWEET DADDY, BREAK IT ON DOWN

Homo Heights is the nickname of the spot where Tim'm (a.k.a., 25percenter; real name: Timothy Terell West) and I are sitting, looking out onto Lake Merritt from beneath the shade of a crooked tree. "This is where the brothers used to cruise real heavily," he smiles. "The whole area is just a large black gay community." Looking around, though, what mostly catches the eye are white folks climbing out of SUVs, wrestling with baby strollers. "Yeah," laughs Tim'm when that's pointed out. "That's the *new* Oakland. There's a lot of tension right now because all these people are coming over from San Francisco 'cause there's no place left to live over there—especially no place that's affordable. They realized that these beautiful old Victorians and all this amazing architecture were over here, and that it was really affordable. Unfortunately, they brought that San Francisco arrogance with them. No one's dealing with the fact that people are being displaced, that rents are rising to the point that people who already live here can't afford it. But that's progress, right?"

Tim'm, 28, is a third-year Ph.D. student in the Modern Thought and Literature program at Stanford; he also works with racially diverse queer youth around issues of AIDS and HIV for SMAAC (Sexual Minority Alliance of Alameda County). Born in Cincinnati, raised in Arkansas, and having lived for a while in New York, he's a child of hip-hop. His encyclopedic knowledge of both the music and the culture is rooted in activism, progressive gender politics, and a fierce race consciousness. Along with Pointfivefag (Juba Kalamka), Lightskindid (Phillip Atiba Goff), G-Minus (Ralowe Trinitoluene Ampu), Louie Butler, and Byron Mason, he's a member of the Deep/Dick Collective—D/DC. What started out as a tongue-in-cheek dig at spoken-word pretension has become a viable entity unto itself.

"Initially," says Tim'm, "it was a joke because we'd been to too many spoken-word/hip-hop shows where you had punanny poets and pussy-poet collectives, you know? There's just a kind of clichédness about it—the women in these scenes with their baby dreads, writing their angry black woman poems. We were like, 'Hey, fuck the pussy-poet collectives, we're gonna be the deep dick collective!' And actually we changed it from Deep *Dick* Collective—because there the focus is on the deep dick—to the *Deep* Dick Collective, D-slash-DC, where the focus is on the depth of what we're saying. But we have a sense of humor about it. Occasionally we say that D/DC stands for Decolonizing Dark Cities, or other political riffs that we can think of."

Background check: Tim'm was the lead singer/MC for the funk outfit, Freekanos, which played around San Francisco in '98 and '99. Pointfivefag, while attending Chicago State University as an art education major, performed with the regionally popular group, Raw Material, before joining the boho hip-hop outfit, He Who Walks Three Ways. That group recorded two locally distributed EPs before disbanding.

And Tim'm says of G-Minus, the newest member of the collective, "This boy is *tight*. He thinks he sounds like a sissy, though. He's always like, 'Is my voice too punked out?' He and I have these long conversations about X-Clan and Poor Righteous Teachers. He grew up in the same era that Pointfivefag and I did, where we were embracing hip-hop and its more Afrocentric, nationalistic lyrics, but seeing that we, as queer men, were consistently being bashed and cast out. But that's the inspiration for what we're doing—socially conscious black hip-hop."

He elaborates on that last point. "America is increasingly becoming this place where its almost like you're backwards if you aren't open to everything being multicultural," he says wearily.

What Tim'm means by multiculturalism in this observation isn't the organic fusion of differing peoples and cultures that mark the way most of us live. He means the ham-fisted "multiculturalism" practiced by media (mainstream and so-called alternative), big business, politicians and arts institutions. That particular multiculturalism keeps whiteness at the center; it flattens other cultures and experiences into baubles to be draped around white shoulders, to accessorize whiteness. It's a cultural front that, beneath the veneer of progressiveness, vigorously maintains white privilege and power. It's also a way to, under cover of colorblindness, belittle or dismiss conversations and actions that have as their focus Black love and self-preservation, black folk healing and taking care of self without the fruit of those exchanges being harvested to feed white (or other) folk.

"I'm all for the multicultural spaces," he continues, "but I also need spaces where I can just talk to my people. There are things I would say there that I wouldn't say in a multicultural space. I'm someone who believes in exclusive spaces. There are things that I'm not going to say if white people are present. I'm just not. And these are things that I want to say to my people, that I need to say to my people." He goes silent for a beat.

"It's very important to us that we identify as black queers," he continues. "In the hip-hop world, there's real resistance to hearing those voices. In the Bay area, specifically, the black hip-hop and spoken-word crowd is much more comfortable with a white gay spoken-word artist or white gay hip-hop artist because it's still something that's other-than-them. I've had a much more difficult time asserting my voice in that space as a gay man, to not just be perceived as a straight guy who's open-minded and doing gay stuff. But what do I do? Do I make my material so much more blatantly gay? In my everyday life, I don't talk about gay, gay, gay all the time.

"The interesting thing for me is, I have this body and I have this [deep] voice and Black people in hip-hop want to read it as the average [read: heterosexual] black hip-hop body. They want to read it as, *'Oh, he's a positive black man. He spits rhymes about Mumia. He's down for the cause.'* But somehow that can't also occupy a space that is same-gender loving and critiquing misogyny. At this point in hip-hop, you *have* to qualify. You *have* to say, I'm a gay man. Otherwise if you speak with the voice you normally speak with—in hip-hop, where gayness cannot exist in a black, male, masculine body—people won't even get it."

He pauses thoughtfully. "Juba and I just got really frustrated trying to assert a queer voice in hip-hop and having people, after shows, come up to us and say, 'Wow, that was really liberal.' Fuck that. It ain't liberal, it's my fucking life. I'm not some straight guy who's trying to be edgy 'cause he moved to the Bay area."

Of course, for many gay hip-hop fans and closeted artists, that presumed heterosexuality is the ultimate compliment. It's the proof that all flaws—any hint of the sissy—have been erased: *Banjee realness.* To be real is to be nigga or thug—polar opposites of the punk or faggot for those still snagged on binary maleness. (*You can get with this or you can get with that...*) But it's far too simplistic to say that this over-prized, caricatured masculinity is a hip-hop thing, or even a black thing. In truth, all hip-hop has done is amplify that which already existed. The swaggering, femme-free male is a classic *American* fetish. Gay b-boys are only "acting" the hardcore part to the extent that their straight counterparts are: It's become the overriding model for us all. As Tim'm points out, "This hypermasculinity amongst straights *and* gays now is pure performance."

It's interesting that while the media has repeatedly gone out of their way to emphasize that a whole generation of [presumably straight] white boys has grown up with hip-hop as their primary cultural language—therefore it's only natural that the b-boy stance would be theirs to claim—that same media expresses shock and condescending bafflement that black and Latino queer youth would have any connection to the culture and music whatsoever. But this is a generation of people of color who breathed in hip-hop with their first breath. For many, consciousness of hip-hop culture, their immersion in it, pre-dates any real knowledge of a racial or sexual self. Hip-hop is often the gateway to the assorted selves housed within. For better or worse, it plays a large role in dictating how those selves will be shaped.

Young faggots and dykes of color lay claim to the culture in the same ways and for the same reasons that their hetero counterparts (of all races) do: It's their cultural birthright. It speaks from and to their reality—they walk the same streets as their hetero brethren, come up through the same schools, warily eye the same racist cops, step gingerly through the same minefields of poverty and struggle, are targeted for the same prisons, watch the same Saturday morning cartoons and eat too much of the same shitty fast food.

The ignorance of mainstream media, the refusal of its ofay gatekeepers and their jigaboo lapdogs, to grasp this simple and obvious fact, is not surprising. For all the close reads given to rap narratives, for all the sociological analysis applied to the lyrics, and despite (or, more likely, because of) the deep commodification of 'hood reality, the nuances and intricacies of Negro life are still not acknowledged. The many manifestations of it go ignored. The media don't even take the lives of heterosexual Negroes and Latinos seriously; it's a joke to expect more for faggots and dykes of color.

More twisted, if no less predictable, is how so many black and brown hetero rappers and rap fans who speak of the unifying and communal qualities of hip-hop will rush to jump on some rapping white boy's jock (*yassum*) or speak of the brotherhood extended to rappers and rap fans around the globe, all while dissing the colored sissy at their side.

TRACK 5: HARVEST FOR THE WORLD

Since its birth, hip-hop has evolved and captured the globe. It's become a common global language, an American Negro-rooted worldwide youth culture that voices political dissent and simmering cultural revolutions. But much of it also acts as a stealth bomb whose active ingredients are unbridled capitalism, the celebration of mindless consumerism and the reassuring brace of dated gender and sexual models. The false stability of rigid and retro gender/sexuality roles that so much (certainly not all) hip-hop provides is a desperately held anchor in a world of rapidly blurring racial/ethnic identities and morphing sexual mores.

But it's not only the big-money exports of pop and gangsta rap that can be oppressive in their uniformity. Check many *undaground* or alternative hip-hop spaces, and you'll see the same gender divides and manners of physical carriage found in mainstream outlets. That last item—the physicality—is especially noteworthy; it's the uniform's foundation.

It's not just the swagger of the b-boy stride or the droop of his baggy pants. It's the way fingers are locked and splayed before they jab the air, the way shoulders are squared as they move through the crowd. It's the way performers, with one flailing arm as oar, glide across a stage, either surrounded by an army of robotic and joyless dancers or backed only by a deejay. It's the pimp walk/gangsta lean that is the default setting for the way niggas, wiggas and latter-day CEOs move. Check the percussive hand movements of MCs as they emphasize a lyric's dopest point, simultaneously raising a knee, hunching their backs, and contracting their bodies to the beat. Tellingly, these 'hood-honed mannerisms also make up the movement vocabulary of every *angry-white-boy* fronted hip-hop/rock outfit—as well as the Disney-spawned boy-bands. Peep the music videos or performance footage of hip-hop and pop artists from Cuba to Russia, Japan to France, and it's all eerily the same.

Contrary to the hype, this is not a victory. It's scary as hell. It's stylized conformity draped in urban American garb, clad in hypermasculine signifiers, macho vibes and street cred emblems so as to appear beyond the maw of the machine. In truth, it now is the machine.

Rewind: The term "playing dress up" brings to mind little girls sporting their mother's clothes and high heels, but men play dress up throughout their lives. And the peacock that is the American black male—ranging from the conked elegance of Duke Ellington to the processed '70s pimp, to the Adidas-then-Timbs-then-Adidas again gear of the b-boy—is without peer when it comes to sartorial grace and influence. Negroes love to play dress up, and their moves are clocked and mimicked by watchers around the globe. The performative aspect of blackness is part of the gift that rap (like jazz, R&B and funk before it) bestows on the world. And there is a knowingness to the performance. Negroes are not without awareness that we are on stage 24/7, that we're expected to deliver across the footlights, to the back of the room, to the very last row. But the force of that performance can also abolish nuance and detail. At home and abroad. While hip-hop culture absorbs assorted influences and molds itself around the cultures where it lands, it also often sets down a template that can obliterate the beauty and ages-old configurations and definitions of masculinity (homo and hetero) that existed before its arrival.

Play: So what we're seeing now is a worldwide youth market shaped, bundled and handed over to pop culture barons and multi-national corporations. Even when it's the anti-bling strain of rap that takes root, progressive and radical politics of resistance and revolution are often bundled in cookie-cutter (and therefore conservative) dress, mannerisms, cadence and attitudes on gender and sexuality. Whether it's Afro-American nationalists railing against this country's ingrained white supremacy, black Cubans giving voice to the unacknowledged power of white skin privilege in Cuba, or disaffected Russian youth protesting the dearth of opportunity in contemporary Russia, local messages of distress are diminished when the messenger unwittingly or uncritically pumps the same heterosexist/misogynistic/consumerist toxins that lie at the root of much of the world's dysfunction.

TRACK 6:
FOR THE LOVE OF MONEY (I'LL BEE DAT)

What's even more depressing than the sight of Tommy Wear blanketing the world (is there much on the planet that's uglier?) is the way so much contemporary rap conflates life-or-death political inequity and social injustice with the desire to wear designer gear, party with old-money bluebloods in the Hamptons, or bathe in Cristal. Genuine need and market-stoked wants have been fused. A handful of rappers' newfound ability to shop without end is heralded as radical social change, as the whole point of centuries worth of social struggle. Even those still oppressed based on gender, sexual orientation, race or class are conned into believing this, to the point that many participate in their own silencing because there's no profit potential, no strobe-light validation, in serious voicing of their real-life issues. When the late Audre Lorde warned that the master's house can never be dismantled by using the master's tools, could she have envisioned a time when there wouldn't even be a desire to dismantle that house—that, in fact, we would master the tools only to turn them on ourselves in order to protect that same house?

It's not difficult to figure out the prerequisite for being a player on the cultural field whose maintenance crew is currently found in rap lyrics and videos, enshrined in the pages of glossy hip-hop periodicals. The rule for being seen or acknowledged at all is to uphold hetero/macho/consumerist standards. Faggotry or androgyny (even the suggestion of them) opens a Pandora's box of possibilities that are not so easily boxed or sold, and that may even expose the lie of accepted—and steadily selling—"truths." What's happened for a lot of young black and Latino faggots, especially those who identify as heads, is the forging of the DL/down-low identity, one where you secretly get your freak on and nobody ever thinks you're anything but straight. You still register on the cultural radar because all "mistakes" have been erased. It helps to be somebody's baby-daddy, to have a revolving cast of (biologically female) bitches on your arm.

Flyers for Blatino sex parties, floating orgies geared toward the young gay ruffneck/*cholo*/*boricua* crowd, warn that no sissies or femmes will be allowed. The same language is found on many web sites and chat rooms that cater to black or Latino queer communities. Very important to note, however, is that this language also mirrors ads for hyper-exclusive parties and hookups in white gay environs. The sentiment is pervasive across cultural, social and racial divides: If you must, you can be secretly "freaky"—just not a fag, not a sissy.

There's a crucial distinction to be made between those who are simply low-key but honest about their sexuality and those who resort to debilitating psychological contortion in order to distance themselves from any whisper of faggotry. There are countless reasons—political, cultural and even intellectual—that a gay/queer/SGL man or a lesbian might choose not to identify with what passes for modern queer culture or community, and they're not all rooted in self-hatred or denial. On the other hand, the harsh sexual policing of self and others is so reflexive, so ingrained in hip-hop culture, that in many quarters options aren't even considered; they're not conceivable except as a joke. The consequences of that myopia can be life-threatening.

"I think," says Tim'm, "that on the other side of this new hardcore homo-thug thing is a lot of risky sexual behavior. It's about experience, not identity, so you experience gay sex but you're not talking about gay identity. When I came out, there was Essex [Hemphill] to read, [the late filmmaker] Marlon Riggs to look at. There were all these things telling me that it's not just about sex. I think the reason those brothers started speaking up is because of the toll AIDS was taking on the community. But it's really sad now. So many of my kids are turning up HIV-positive. The statistics on new infections are really scary. And part of it has to do with the fact that there is no conversation, now, about what it means to be an African-American gay male. It's more about an aesthetic, now."

That triumph of that materialistic-hetero-thug aesthetic over substantive conversations about sexual identity means that the likely audience for D/DC won't even be the folks they're trying hardest to reach.

"I would love an all-black hip-hop context," says Tim'm. "But there's a lot of self-hate among black gay people, especially the younger generation. They'd rather go to a club and listen to Puff Daddy say somebody is '[as] pussy as RuPaul.' That's always upsetting to me. I think our stuff is going to be received more in the progressive straight black hip-hop crowd and in the progressive white gay scene than in the black gay scene. That really saddens me and it's troubling. It says a lot about the state of our community. You have a lot of black gays who are comfortable with this silence around our lives; it's our new identity."

TRACK 7:
MISS THING, THERE IS NO GUEST LIST TONIGHT

When it does what it should, when it truly honors its roots, hip-hop opens the door for listeners to access every avenue of themselves, to speak their innermost thoughts, beliefs and perceptions into reality. That's where the joy is, in that expression. The point of this article is not to suggest that rap and hip-hop are joyless realms for sheep-like gay or straight folk. The culture has too many tentacles for that to be true. There are countless spots of intervention—De La's discography, an old Pharcyde track—that are sheer bliss: when sly subversion and skilled storytelling meet in rhymes that speak to blackness that is not yet commodified or stunted, when political acts are about subverting rather than reinforcing the status quo. There are even moments when the sissy triumphs.

"Back when I was in New York," says Tim'm, "the club Suspect opened. *Suspect*," he repeats incredulously. "What does that name tell you? Anyway, people were pulling me to go. Everyone was like, 'Oh, he does hip-hop; he's a hip-hop boy. Yo, come to our down-low club.' And I was like, I'll come but I'm not into this down-low stuff. When I got there, there was a band of queens sitting outside the club because they couldn't get in; the people managing the door weren't letting people in who seemed hyperfeminine.

"Well, a couple of weeks later, the queens figured the shit out. They put on some fucking Timbalands, rolled up one of their pants legs, lowered their voices and got in the club. And then people were wondering, how did these queens get in here? Well, the bitches do what they have to do at the door, and they work it! They came into the club and started vogueing!" He cracks up. "I think that's just a perfect story. It speaks to the power of a queen. I love my black queens."

You have that in common with Common, I tell him, and he laughs again. "Yes," he chuckles, "I have that in common with Common."

TRACK 8: MY EMANCIPATION DON'T FIT YOUR EQUATION (THE ET TU, NIGGA? MIX)

Common is one of hip-hop's black saviors: A fantastic lyricist and MC, he's charismatic and conscious. He has faith in Allah, much love for black people, and is in the game to drop knowledge. He respects black women. He refers to them as queens. With his strong religious and political convictions, he's a rapper whose name is uttered with reverence by "real heads." But he was caught up in a minor controversy following the release of his album, *Like Water for Chocolate*, last year. It's a near-brilliant album that's marred by homophobia which Common and his defenders claim isn't really there, and that shows just how circumscribed hip-hop's forward motion can be.

But the lyrics—and the way they're spit—tell a different story. He disses "sophisticated sissies [who] strut like this is *Beat Street* in backpacks," on the cut, "Coldblooded." The track "Nag Champa" contains the lines, "You couldn't hang if you was a poster/ Posin' like a bitch for exposure / It's rumors of gay MCs, just don't come around me wit it / You still rockin hickies, don't let me find out he did it." The album's most debated couplet, though, is found on the track, "Dooinit," where Common says to an unnamed rapper, "Niggas hate you, they ain't paying you no attention / In a circle of faggots, your name is mentioned." On the Okayplayer web site, Internet communal home of Common, the Roots and D'Angelo, Common was recently asked by a sycophantic writer, *'So, are you a big fat homophobe like some people say?'* (Oh, the irony: You can see the writer's own knee pads being strapped on in the softball phrasing of the question.) Common responds, "I'm not here to judge. It's not my place to judge people. But I do feel like it's my human choice to say the type of people I want around me. We all choose the type of people we want to surround ourselves with. If I have to deal with a homosexual on a business level, of course I'm not going to disrespect him or nothing like that. I just don't understand it. I'm not a gay hater like some people on the boards think… You gotta hit people where it hurts and it ain't cool to be a faggot where I'm from."

Any effeminate black boy, gay or straight, who grew up in a circle of disapproving males (daddy, uncles, cousins… niggas-on-the-block) and who hears the venom with which Common spits the words sissies/bitch/faggot in his rhymes recognizes the scald in the delivery. Males who flow outside the hard lines of conventional, if not caricatured, hetero poses risk being called out, exiled from community. While the rapper's defenders dismiss the baiting rhymes as generic battle fare, the contempt in the dismissal is clearly rooted in a disgust that goes beyond the mere wackness of another rapper's skills, something made apparent by the number of times the slur of the feminine is leveled. And Common's true feelings are crystal clear in his Okayplayer response. The charge of homophobia, like that of racist, is incredibly easy for guilty parties to squirm out of nowadays. If a cross isn't burned or a body beaten beyond recognition, they feel you have no case. What's most telling is Common's admission that on a bed of potential currency, he'll begrudge the homo some respect. That's the kind of facile *tolerance* that leads idiots to chant, "Bigotry I$ dead. It's all about green, not gay (or black)." Capitalism rocks, ya'll.

"What's interesting about Common," says Tim'm, "is his whole black nationalist thing—*I'm the new righteous brother showing people how to live*. He says he's not homophobic, but that stuff serves a very specific function. I'm like, okay, Common, you write some of your rhymes. Your whole album isn't freestyle. If you're free-styling, there's a space where you might slip and say something that's colloquial. But if you're *writing* a rhyme and in that space you say, 'In a circle of faggots your name is mentioned,' that means something. It serves some specific purpose.

"People talk about how gayness isn't present in hip-hop. It's present all over hip-hop. It's present in its absence and in its abjection. When the butt of the joke is the bitch nigger or the pussy nigger—all these references that are about reclamation of a masculine black identity—gayness is present in that. If people in hip-hop were secure in their heterosexuality, none of this would be an issue."

And Common is far from the only "conscious" head chilling the hearts of politically aware gay boys who are struggling to be honest about who they are in the cypher. Talib Kweli injected many vibe-crushing rhymes on *Black Star*, his classic 1999 collaboration with Mos Def. But Tim'm digs even further below the pop radar for examples of cultural redlining.

"You find these people that have tight flows," he sighs, "they're rhyming about interesting stuff, it's politically charged and it's on point, but then they have one or two lines that are just like, why did you have to do that shit? Like Del and Souls of Mischief, Casual and Peplove—they're all a part of Hieroglyphics—we dig them; I dig them a lot. But there are still those threads of homophobia in their stuff. Like Jeru for example. I love Jeru tha Damaja—*love* him. I just think he's like, *Boom!* But he *goes* there and it's just like [Tim'm pauses thoughtfully] *wow*. Does it add anything to your rhyme? What does it add? That's what I wanna ask him."

He smiles. "Now, any hip-hop artist choosing a name like Del the Funky Homosapien—it just sort of sets up this..."

He stops to collect the right words and, having found them, continues. "One, the fact that *homo* is even in the title, and two, that a lot of people don't know what homosapien is..." He breaks into laughter. "It's like setting himself up. And then he's also this funky, bohemian, Bay Area hip-hop boy—that's where I think a lot of his homophobia comes from. When you look at these figures in hip-hop who, for all looks and purposes, based on their style or whatever, might be thought to be gay—Andre from Outkast, Common, DJ Quik—their thing is, *I have to be all the more obvious about my disdain or dislike of homosexuals because I don't want nobody thinking I'm gay*."

TRACK 9:
FRIENDS... HOW MANY OF US HAVE THEM?

We hop on a train to San Francisco to meet Juba/ Pointfivefag for lunch. When we arrive at the art gallery where he works, he's busy so we hang back and check out the merchandise. A woman who works in the space comes over to chat, explaining that they've had great success renting art to prospective buyers. I ask if many people actually end up buying the stuff they rent.

"Oh, yes," she replies. "Sometimes you just have to live with a piece for a while before you know if you like it." Tim'm and I exchange looks. When she leaves to help a customer, he turns to me, repeating *sotto voce* with a grin, "Sometimes you just have to live with a piece for a while to know if you like it. *That is so true.*"

Finally Juba—a dark-skinned brother with long dreads—comes over. The divorced father of a 6-year-old, a columnist for *Anything That Moves*, a magazine geared to bisexuals, and a hip-hop devotee, he often finishes a thought before he finishes his sentence—dashes and ellipses are a staple of his speaking style. "Aw, man," he says in mock dismay after glimpsing my notepad. "You're not gonna say that I work in an *art gallery* right in the heart of *San Francisco*, are you? There goes all my hip-hop cred."

"Nigger, there goes all your *black* cred," quips Tim'm before turning back to me. "Nigger is a word I use a lot," he offers. "I've completely taken that term, and its sorta like, your nigger is [he growls playfully] *your nigger*," he laughs. "And it becomes, for me, this sort of ultimate term of endearment, affection, desire, love, sex, whatever. I do it so much that now people are reluctant to just come up to me and say, 'Whassup, my nigga?' They're like, 'Oh but *you* use the word *that* way!'"

Over lunch at a local diner, I ask them the most pressing question regarding gays and lesbians in hip-hop: Why do dykes make the best *I-Wanna-Fuck-a-Ruffneck* songs? They look shocked for a minute, then break into hysterics.

"I never thought about that before," says Juba. "I think a lot of it has to do with the same thing I see, culturally, when I see dykes playing basketball, going up against the guys. They don't have that same inculcated fear of maleness, of male-bonding rituals. They don't have the precept of *pretending* in order to get a man. They don't have to pretend that they're soft, that they're weak. You can be a dyke and be like 'Yeah, fuck me and I'll fuck you back.' So, it's not an issue for them the way it is for a straight woman who's trying to get married, trying to have a baby. For straight women, it's like, *'To keep him in this place, I can't threaten his manhood.'* I think that probably has a lot to do with it."

While waiting for our food, we make small talk that settles on the deep reserves of queer art and imagery in hip-hop that has gone unacknowledged, unexamined.

"If you're familiar with Jean-Michel Basquiat," says Juba, "if you know anything about who he was hanging with or what his life was like, it was decidedly queer. Same with Keith Haring. These are seminal figures, our graffiti foundation. So much of early hip-hop, if you look at its aesthetic and what it was taken from... Because of the punk scene that was developing in New York, you sort of had this cross hybridization. If you look at styles—look at Grandmaster Flash when they first came out: They looked like the Village People. They had spikes; they were wearing furs and leather, and of course no one associated [gayness] with them because black buff male bodies don't—or didn't—get conflated with gayness or with queerness, so people just couldn't attach that to [their image].

"If you go back to '80, '81, '82, that whole hip-hop aesthetic is Village People, it's the New York Dolls. And that's not considered quote/end-quote, *black.* That's Foxy, Queen and David Bowie. You could talk about how it's all in the tradition of Parliament and George Clinton, how it's an offshoot of that stuff—but then you'd have to talk about how queer *that* whole scene is. But the more commercially viable hip-hop became, then that aesthetic started to slide out of favor. What you started to have was the Rakims."

I suggest that some classic Afro-American paradoxes were at work, there, that as rap grew beyond its origins, and as black men in hip-hop starting receiving attention and validation from white folk (i.e., the mainstream), they had to put forth an image of hardness that wasn't only intended to reflect the harsh realities they were speaking about, but to also mask the craving for that very validation. It had to conform to taut (but stylish) lines of undiluted, unassailable maleness in order to be "universal" in its marketability, to appeal to both black and white folks' fetishes and limited notions of authentic black American manhood. It had to actually *contain* the volatile and expansive "product" of black life, art and imagination, offering reassurance that something of the status quo was being maintained even as it was challenged. It was also meant to broadcast that, this time, brothers wouldn't be ripped off or played—i.e., punked.

One of the most crucial dynamics at work in hip-hop is the interplay between the mythic black man and the mythic white man; they wrestle daily in the "realness" of hip-hop. So much of what modern rap presents as black reality is simply an unconscious/uncritical pandering to white expectation, a fulfillment of someone else's blueprint, someone else's fears and desires. Especially where fear and desire merge. What's become clear in the last few years—especially with the steady profits of gangsta rap and rapping Negro materialists—is that much of the modern rap rule book is lifted straight from plantation manuals: the Negro longing to bond with massa; the overdrive fetishization of the female mulatto; the return of both the violent, oversexed Mandingo (a.k.a., thug, nigga, pimp, gangsta) and the voracious black ho; the belief that blackness—*realness*—is defined by both a foundation of material lack and a deep lust for status-quo symbols. And by negation of select "others." But one of the strongest legacies is a fear that has not often been voiced.

We know that female slaves were raped, that they had no agency over their own bodies. Their sexualities were at the mercy of white dick. Much of the black American hetero male's adherence to rigid gender roles, to the notion that they must police and protect the realm of black sexuality, is rooted in long simmered anger and frustration at not being able to protect black women. But another source of that rage is the fact that black men, too, were at the mercy of white dick, with no agency over their own bodies, unable to protect themselves. Castration fears and anxieties are acknowledged realities and legacies of life under slavery for black men. But there is no male equivalent of Hottentot Venus to act as locus for the anxiety around the whisper or possibility of black male ass, mouth and dick being seized and pimped—punked. But that whisper, at least in subtext, is part of what fuels so many of the racial/sexual fears that exist not only between black and white men, but also between black men and black women, between black men period—gay or straight. That's why the black male body and his sexuality must be guarded so fiercely, to squelch both whisper and possibility. That (in part) is why heterosexuality is the only acceptable model of black sexuality for the gatekeepers of the race. Ironically, the policing is largely based on models of dominance and power that were forged on those same plantations that haunt modern black life.

In both the often stated fears of yet another white co-option of black art, and in the idiot's mantra that white boys in hip-hop equals the triumph of a color-blind America or (in true cracka supremacist postulating) the *evolution* of the art, few seem willing to address the possibility that what many white boys are actually connecting with in the music has less to do with rainbow coalitions and widened views of the world than with the status-quo obsessions (sexual, political and material) that are tucked in the seams of much mainstream contemporary rap. Dig beneath the *phat beats* and ghetto-fab rhymes of the music, and what you'll uncover are massa-scribed mandates on ownership and oppression, skin-tone hierarchy and assorted forms of sexual paranoia. White boys—ironically, through hip-hop—are simply receiving their forefathers' most fucked-up notions of privilege and world-order, but with the added bonus of nigger-chic—an evergreen commodity that's exploded in value even as the real worth of nigger lives plummets. What many black boys—gay and straight—are doing now is simply staking their claim to that same perverse birthright; wasn't massa their "daddy," too?

"People can deal with multi-racial presentations," says Tim'm, "but patriarchy needs to stay in place and so does gender clarity, for lack of a better word. We need to know that a man is a man and a woman is a woman. And we've reached this place where white people can occupy this black and brown male-constructed space of masculinity, and where homophobia and misogyny are what is seen as subversive. I also think that white people set the foundation for a kind of nuclear-family/head-of-household/virile masculinity that black men—in their obsession with emasculation—have become obsessed with and adopt. We're saying we don't want to be like white people, but that's all we want to be, just like white people.

"I think there's a way in which you have 1) a model of virile black masculinity, 2) this notion of the emasculated black male, and 3) this reclamation of a masculine identity that becomes hypermasculinity—it outdoes the first masculinity, it outdoes white male masculinity, which automatically gets read as gay and weak. So, the ultimate masculinity is the black masculinity, but then you have the full circle thing of the white boy coming and re-occupying the space of that hypermasculinity. My problem with all that is 1) Why do we accept our status as emasculated black men? Is it just because women occupy a certain place in our families? Why can't that just be our thing, instead of this comparative thing of 'That's what **they're** doing, so that's what we want. We feel oppressed so therefore we need to emulate that behavior.' Again, it's always full circle, and the circle ends where it begins. Whiteness is occupying the power at the beginning and it's going to occupy the power at the end—even if you have had certain interventions along the way."

So, what do you think about Eminem, I ask. He flips the question back to me.

I tell him that I think Eminem's rage is older than he is and will be around as long as straight white boys are conditioned from birth with a sense of skin-based entitlement and then react with misplaced fury at being treated like niggers—even as they lay claim to being "niggas." It's the breathless reception of Eminem (and what he's giving voice to) as some sort of newfangled creature that is so laughable. How can the fact that such hostile, damaged creatures are trolling through America be news to anyone with functioning brains, eyes or ears? He's undoubtedly talented but what's most interesting about him is the way he's coalesced the culture's reactionary undercurrent and the bullshit rhetoric of "anti-PC" champions into a hip, slickly produced commodity. That this straight white boy can, even as part of a jokey shtick, target the usual suspects (women and gays) to settle his psychic scores rather than give any inkling that he knows who the truly oppressive powers are, and the fact that the media and music industry can be so squarely in his back pocket, just shows how intellectually bankrupt all parties are.

As the poster boy for angry, disenfranchised white boys, he's pointedly distanced himself from the "N-word," saying he would never use it. That decision may be rooted in genuine respect for black folk and black struggle. It may simply be the tack of acquiescence before full-scale appropriation. Or it may be that he, unlike so many of his champions, knows just how much he owes to white skin privilege, regardless of his skills as a rapper.

His use of and approach to queerness compared to his take on race is one of the most interesting things about him. Lots of his fans, gay and straight, point out that he's pro gay marriage in the single "The Real Slim Shady," and that he even says "...I like gay men," in the song "Criminal." At the same time, however, he's reflexively contemptuous and dismissive of "fags." *Don't ask; don't tell. Don't flame.* It's the same distinction that keeps popping up throughout the cultural strata—among DL hip-hop heads, within the larger [white] queer community, in mainstream discourse. Eminem reflects a schism that shows a cultural determination to hold on to a social hierarchy that fears the feminine and hates and mocks any suggestion of it in men— even as his own presence in hip-hop is used by his supporters as a sign of positive social change.

Bumper-sticker feminism trills that pussy rules the world. That's barely a half-truth. It's fear of pussy that rules the world: Fear of not getting it, fear of (and resentment at) being at its mercy, fear and distrust of any male who doesn't *feen* for it. And—biggest one of all—fear of being called it. Fear of pussy is one of rap's primary hinges; it's what made Eminem a star.

"Eminem has the right to say whatever he wants to say," says Tim'm. "I'm not down for censorship. There's some stuff that

D/DC does that a lot of people are not gonna like. We're very comfortable having certain kinds of sexual references in our material that will probably make some people uncomfortable. We're not PC rappers. So I'm very conscious about saying we can't just shut that person down.

"I just think that rather than censoring him, the gay and lesbian community—and those people in hip-hop who don't support what his lyrics stand for—should boycott his shit. I don't buy his albums. I think he's a very talented MC. I wouldn't battle him. Not right now. Gimme another year and I might get onstage and battle his ass, but he's skilled. It's just a shame that all of that skill gets used for what it does. I mean, that's what he's known for now—a gay-bashing white boy. It pisses me off that *that's* what he's taken from rap, that *that's* what he uses to define himself as *real*. And he's too skilled for that.

"But," continues Tim'm, "part of me looks at it like, as a white MC in hip-hop, does he have to do something that far-out? Because no other white MC has been as respected in the hip-hop community as Eminem. I could throw out some names from the old school, but for the most part no white boy has come close to getting the respect he has. And maybe that requires him to be so on the edge of things. In some ways, his misogynistic acts and homophobia 'race' him. They give him some sort of ethnic identity and make him something other than white. Because gayness is so often associated with..." he pauses.

"I mean, *look at him*," laughs Tim'm. "He looks like a little rave queen. I'm like, *c'mon now*. So, I think there's some anxiety around his presentation. I think that provocative edge is a way for Eminem to position himself as an outsider—*I am whatever you think I am*. He's made himself into the ultimate rebel-victim. And he's put the straight white boy back in the center of the conversation."

Time is running out on Juba's lunch hour and as we settle up the bill, Juba offers a knock-out observation.

"The gay b-boy is the new church sissy," he says firmly. "He's the Y2K church sissy."

"See," agrees Tim'm, "you *can* be a gay hip-hop artist—just do *straight* rhymes. What gay rappers consistently hear is, 'We don't care if you're gay. We just don't want to hear you talk about it. Don't talk about sex and don't be political.'"

"Go back to that *Village Voice* piece," says Juba. [He's referring to writer Guy Trebay's article, "Homo Thugz Blow Up the Spot," which was about gay hip-hop clubs in New York; the article ran last year and had come up earlier in our conversation.] "It was all about the kids saying, 'Here's a space for us, where we can be with each other... and just *be*.' As much as *being* is possible in a place where you still have to hide—and they're still hiding basically."

"What's interesting," says Tim'm, "is right before I left New York I started doing a lot of poetry readings, and people were like, 'Why have you been holding back all your stuff?' But something didn't feel right about it there. While there was an acknowledgment of gay hip-hop culture, everything was that same old, 'Yeah, you can be gay in the 'hood, just don't be a faggot'—like that quote in the *Voice*. And that's problematic for me. Why aren't we having a conversation about how that statement is really problematic? Why can't you be a faggot in the 'hood? What's wrong with a faggot in the 'hood? Does that person deserve to be beaten down or denigrated just because they're effeminate or whatever?"

"That quote spoke volumes to me," adds Juba. "It was the same thing that has existed in the black community for years in the church—with the sissy behind the organ, the sissy directing the choir, the sissy in the pulpit. It's like, you can be here, be a sissy and flourish on the organ, but don't come in here with your lover, don't come up here and ask for communion, don't come to the church social. Don't let me know that it's something *real*. The same thing is happening in hip-hop. The crux of hip-hop is *keep it real*. But it's not about keeping it real. It's about *keep it where we can handle it*."

TRACK 10: INTERLUDINAL SKIT

I'm sitting in a small rib joint, going over my notes. It's lunchtime and two sistas are sitting across the aisle from my table, fucking up some swine. They're dressed in conservative office attire but have the no-nonsense air and energy of women from the 'hood. We all turn our heads to look out the window as a flash of color goes by. It's a black teenager, about 16 or 17, running and laughing to catch up to someone up the block. All his clothing—a baseball jersey flapping open, a white T-shirt beneath it, baggy jeans—is several sizes too big for him. He swims in his gear. As he runs, he holds tight to the waist of his pants, which are sagging low. His boxer-clad ass is all out. Immersed as I am in this story, starting to see homo signifiers at every turn, I smile and say to myself, "What a cute baby faggot," as the kid runs by. The sistas see something else.

"Now, I wanna know," says Sista # 1, "who was the first woman who told a man, 'Ooh, baby, you know what's sexy? When yo' pants hanging all off yo' ass.'"

"I don't know," responds Sista # 2, "but we need to find that heffa and handle her. 'Cause this shit has gotten outta hand. Look at him! Can't even run for stopping to pull his pants up. That's a goddamn shame."

I chuckle as the women's dialogue jolts me out of my brand new conditioning to see faggotry at every turn, in every 'hood rat signifier. It makes me laugh to be reminded of the obvious— we all process shit from where we live, applying our biases and realities to the workings of the larger world. I happily surrender my preconceptions and don't trip on the open-ended possibilities of sexualities all around me. I wonder if the two women across from me could do the same.

TRACK 11: HOL' UP, WAIT A MINNIT / TIME TO PUT SOME TROOF INNIT...

As is true with any notion of iconic purity, an opposing icon of degradation is needed. Entire cultures and religions are built on that precept. So is the marketplace. The thug/ruffneck is a cultural (and marketing) phenomenon spun from legacies of shame and bigotry; in order to survive, to prove its value and purity, it needs something to stand against. The punk/faggot (compromised maleness) and the ho/bitch (degraded femininity) serve that function. But ironies abound. Two emcees battling it out on a stage or on record, if they're any good at all, will actually mirror the back and forth between queens reading one another. To wit: When Cannibus dissed LL Cool J—using the slur of the feminine, of course—by saying, "99% of your fans wear high heels," LL shot back with "99% of your fans don't exist." How can you not hear the "snap" at the end of that?

As icon, though, the ruffneck is simply a reheated staple of gay culture. He's the piece formerly known as *trade*: Shirtless and sculpted, scowling and clutching his dick—a come-on tucked inside the menace (or vice versa). The promise of a brutal fuck/the threat of a slit throat. Machismo that offers obliteration, sexual high (or both) to all who come in contact with it. When you look at DMX, Ja Rule or even D'Angelo (just for starters), what you see is old-school-meets-new-school Mandingos, sold in a package of ghetto danger and fabulousness. Hardcore rap fans (and gatekeepers like Common) are not clueless to the homoeroticism at play in the images. After D'Angelo and Q-Tip struck beefcake poses for their respective cover stories in *Vibe* magazine last year, the letters-to-the-editor page was flooded with hostile reactions from male readers who were offended that "bitch niggas" were given that space.

"I think that what you saw in the letters pages," says Juba, "was a reaction based on the idea that to be sexual, to be sexually male within hetero culture, is to be in a position to objectify female bodies. It's okay for women to show skin. In the reverse, as a male, you immediately become object to whoever is the viewer by wearing a wife-beater, by showing skin, by being shirtless. Now, within this hip-hop/hetero paradigm, a woman is not powerful enough to sexualize you. Who's looking at you that has the power to do that? Another man. And that was the male readers' discomfort. That was their problem."

That these black men voluntarily positioned themselves as bitches?

"Exactly."

TRACK 12: YA'LL GON' MAKE ME LOSE MY MIND

Marvin K. White (poet, AIDS activist, one-time member of legendary performance art troupe, Pomo Afro Homos) and I are sitting in a small Oakland diner having a breakfast of grits, eggs and homemade biscuits. We're talking about the state of Negro life—art, politics and faggotry—and he's bummed about most of it. When we talk specifically about gayness & hip-hop, and about the high rise of the D-Low, he sighs deeply. In the larger picture, he sees a clear connection between the general coarseness and meanness of the times we live in and the art and music that is being consumed by both same-gender-loving/gay/queer rap fans and their hetero counterparts. He gives an example.

"At Cables," he says, "which was the only black gay bar in Oakland a couple of years ago, there were a couple of songs that the kids would just go *up* over every time they came on. One was called 'Beat That Bitch With a Bat,' and the other was 'Bitch Better Have My Money.' The kids would just go off, and I was mortified. I don't care if they were singing along and it meant nothing to them, or if everyone knew what they were singing along to but was just like, *'That's what you do,'* that stuff seeps in if you say it long enough and hear it often enough. I *know* it does."

I agree but tell him that there's no way he's going to get a lot of the younger generation to see his point. He and I are both in our early thirties; we came of age and consciousness in a different era. We've been able to see and feel the shift in cultural tenor, in the way that people treat themselves and one another. We can see the role that popular culture plays in all of that, noting the differences in the ways popular music once fed black culture and life, versus what it offers now. For many kids born into this coarse climate, the idea that the music shapes attitudes and beliefs, and not merely reflects them, is laughed at and dismissed. To them, that notion is a scare tactic of the clueless.

In that shift, though, there have been losses that range from subtle to profound, and the effect that hip-hop has had on black gay culture is complicated and somewhat painful. It has deepened wounds inflicted by AIDS, diminishing traditions and dismissing elders who have no desire to *bling! bling!* What once seemed a godsend for black and Latino queer youth—a way for them to possibly mold and shape themselves without having to leave "home," sashaying over the rainbow into the racism and erasure of the Eurocentric "queer community"—has instead codified self-destructiveness and self-denial, for many. While there is a fair amount of playfulness, of knowing theatricality, in pulling on thug drag (for straights and gays alike), there are also high costs for those who adhere to the persona without pressing tongue in cheek, for those who live or fuck deep inside thug outlines in order to escape themselves or society's preconceptions of who they might be. Crucially, the emotional lure of the ruffneck for gay boys is one that hasn't really been dissected before. Marvin gives it a shot.

"Let me just preface all of this by saying I like gay boys," he smiles. "I like going to gay places and meeting gay folks. I don't want to bring you home and then have to figure it out. I don't wanna wrestle you for it, I don't wanna get you drunk for it, and I don't wanna talk about girlfriends for it," he laughs. "I just wanted to say that *first*.

"Now, if we talk about the whole of black culture, I think a lot of us who came from black families and black neighborhoods have been attracted to the boys who tormented us either physically or sexually because we couldn't have them. I'm often attracted to men who look like the boys I grew up with. But the level to which we see that now—it's about *protection*. And we've gotten this thing now where some *woman's* man is the ultimate prize; it's just weird to me.

"This whole DL culture thing—you know, boys who don't go to the gay clubs. But they *do* belong to a club: The club of people who circle the block all the time but don't go in. Their reasoning is, *I'm not gay 'cause I'm not going in. I just pick up the boys on the street.* It's like how wolves hunt sheep. You work in tandem and kind of get one off to the side and then you can pick them off; that's how the boys in the cars work. And there's something in that anonymous situation..." He pauses. "People aren't even looking back or feeling to see if their partner has a condom on. It's like AIDS can't be transmitted because no one is watching you have sex."

It's that protection you were speaking of, I tell him. It's the belief that the unassailable, cross-culturally over-fetishized "heterosexuality" of the boy you're fucking (or who's fucking you), can heal you, hold you, make you whole. It's the belief that said straightness is both pure and "purifying," able to redress the crisscrossing wounds of racism and homophobia, able to vaccinate against the countless ways those bugaboos of bigotry mutate and manifest at "home" as social norms and deeply acclimated [self] hatred. Those beliefs are a sugar pill, of course, but no less psychologically powerful for being that. And if you've swallowed the line that your life has no value, you don't even recognize the unsafe act as risk. It seems like salvation.

We eat in silence for a minute before Marvin says thoughtfully, "*Venus* magazine did an article a while ago on this guy who has this salon in Harlem. He was decked out in this Hermes-print, unbuttoned shirt and just lounging; it was really beautiful. He said that he missed the days when boys wore blouses. All that's gone now. AIDS really has decimated that segment of our community. Those were the people who didn't leave our neighborhood. Those were the drag queens who lived at the bottom of the hill, and that everybody knew about. They were the ones that your mama sat up with, talked with. And for those of us who lived in apartments and projects, they were the first ones ready to fight when shit happened, when the men came around and were fucking up your mama or your aunt. Those were the ones who stepped in. And they're gone.

"They were the transmitters between what our mamas know and what we should know as gay men. That's where we learned what was going on, and that part of the culture is gone. I think AIDS has a lot to do with that leap to this hypermasculinity, because we needed to show that we weren't all sick. We've always had this element of folks who didn't want to be associated with the feminine. That's cool. But I haven't seen so much erasure of our culture before. I've never seen it the way it is now."

He falls silent before laughing dryly, "And you can't clock people now. Gaydar is just of no use anymore."

TRACK 13: BROWN SKIN LADY

Katey Red has been proclaimed "The Gay Rapper" by both *The New York Times* and *XXL* magazine. A New Orleans-based transvestite who wants tits but not a full-on sex change, Ms. Red has released an album—*Y2 Katey: Millennium Sissy*—whose radical elements shrivel beneath the retrograde politics at work in both the music and her image. (It doesn't help that Katey sounds like a broke-down Trina backed by uninspired Bounce grooves.) There's no denying that props have to be given to any open transvestite who steps into the rap game. That takes big-ass ovaries and shoves a jeweled fist in the faces of all who would banish the sissy from hip-hop.

Katey's ghetto-stunted take on sexuality and life in general (she's about blunts, '40s, designer gear and strip-joints) may actually serve to demystify her for less progressive rap fans (*She ain't dat different from us, G!*), but she—like hip-hop's thugs and pimps—embraces and hawks dumbed down totems of black realness in order to get paid, to be seen in the marketplace. It's a bleak but proven formula: Adhere to lowest-common-denominator ideals and blow the fuck up.

Even more complicated is the reality that while Katey is inarguably brave for stepping into the rap arena as a transvestite, it's actually easier for hetero heads (and the media) to envision a cross-dressing sassy queen as "the gay rapper," than for them to think it might be the b-boy next door. While her mere presence *is* a startling statement, the mediocrity of her lyrics, banality of her politics and shakiness of her flow ensure she's more novelty act than artistic force to be reckoned with, someone who will truly fuck with—as opposed to ultimately confirming—stereotypes. She shakes up boundaries and borders but when the dust settles, not much has really been challenged.

TRACK 14: OUTRO: I AM I BE

"It might blow up, but it won't go pop," raps Tim'm along with De La Soul's "Patti Dooke," from their *Buhloone Mindstate* CD. "I love that line," he grins. "And that's my favorite CD." We're listening to the De La disc as we drive to a benefit concert for Mumia Abu Jamal that's being co-sponsored by Tony Toni Tone and will feature performances by such Bay Area musical heavyweights as Dwayne Wiggins, Martin Luther and Ledisi. The Roots are also scheduled to perform. Alice Walker is the featured speaker.

As we walk into the auditorium, a banner reading "Critical Resistance: Beyond the Prison Industrial Complex" hangs over the stage. As the crowd slowly mills in, Mumia's voice booms into the auditorium over the speakers. It's the track "Rap Thing," from his CD *All Things Censored*. Christina Vasquez Gutierrez, of Mobilization to Free Mumia Abu Jamal, comes onstage and gives a brilliant, vintage Bay Area anti-capitalist, pro-love, anti-racist, celebration-of-life speech: "I tremble when I hear that famous people are needed to agitate on behalf of Mumia, that famous people are needed to bring about change. That idea perpetuates [our] capitalistic and celebrity-addled culture. The struggle to free Mumia is a struggle against racism, capitalism and imperialism. Stop falling for the line that the fight is between young and old, whites and people of color..." The crowd goes wild.

Gutierrez leaves the stage and there's a lull as the stage crew sets up for Martin Luther. I spot Me'shell NdegéOcello and her girlfriend Rebecca Walker in the audience and go up to say hello. Me'shell gives me a hug; she's so tiny, so incredibly delicate that even giving her a gentle hug engenders the fear that you'll crush her. "What are you doing up here?" she asks.

"I'm doing a piece on gay rappers."

She widens her eyes and grabs my arm in playfully exaggerated excitement. "Who? Where are they?" she laughs. "And have you heard of this rapper in New Orleans who dresses all in drag and his flow is supposed to be the dopest, tightest flow but no one will sign him 'cause they're all afraid to be associated with him? I forget his name but he's supposed to be dope."

"I suspect that's this rapper named Katey Red," I tell her. "And he-she is kinda weak."

"For real?"

"Yeah."

The musical acts start to do their sets and most are hampered by really shitty sound. Martin Luther performs "Mamas, Don't Let Your Babies Grow Up to be Gangstas." Ledisi, a phenomenal singer, earns a rapturous ovation for her too brief set. DMX's "Party Up" and the last Meth and Redman single play over the sound system just before the Roots come on. They're amazing but the crowd is only lukewarm, not really getting into the experimentation that Black Thought, Questlove and Co. are ladling out. A highlight of their set is a frenzied country-music bit where Black Thought and another guy onstage square dance to a furiously escalating tempo, grinning exuberantly the entire time.

Next, Alice Walker, regal and charismatic, comes onstage and the crowd falls to a hush. Her words are so powerful that I only intermittently remember to jot them down. She speaks of her days as a civil rights activist in the '60s and compares that political climate to the present, citing "the painful déjà vu of losing black men... If we lose [Mumia], we lose something of ourselves that is very precious. Young, brilliant, important black men are assassinated in every generation. This [benefit] is not about creating and elevating pop stars. It's not about wanting to participate in the culture of celebrity. It's not—or is not only—about laying claim to the latest proof of the vitality and centrality of blackness in American culture. It's about life... If there is someone in your family who is in need, abandon judgment and commit yourself to helping." After asking us all to wear white the next day "because it has so often been the symbol of our despair," she concludes by gently admonishing the audience to not, in our anger, "become the thing they think you are. Don't give them that power."

On the ride back with Tim'm to drop me off at my hotel, Ms. Walker's words resonate deeply. They insinuate themselves in this story on gay rappers and gay fans of rap music, and how the larger politics, histories and cultural biases that both bracket and gird hip-hop culture so often work to erode the culture's restorative and liberating qualities for its queer audience: *Young, brilliant, important black men are assassinated in every generation.* Those assassinations aren't just carried out against acknowledged, high-profile political and cultural leaders. And they're not just committed by CIA/FBI/COINTELPRO agents. The assassins are ministers, political leaders, entertainers, blood and kin. The targets are brothers, sisters, sons, daughters, cousins, nieces and nephews. And often, the slaughtered continue to walk around, to live and breathe in close proximity to their assailants. It's only their minds that have been mangled, their hearts and spirits that have been murdered. As I walk back to my hotel room, my mind wanders to the totality of the answer Juba had given me in response to a question I'd asked him:

"That [*Village Voice*] quote that said that in hip-hop you can be gay but you can't be a faggot spoke volumes to me. It was the same thing that has existed in the black community for years, in the church with the sissy behind the organ, the sissy directing the choir and the sissy in the pulpit. It's like, you can have that stereotypical effeminacy but don't let me know that you suck dick. Don't let me be real with it. You can be here and be a sissy and flourish on the organ but don't come in here with your lover, don't come up here and ask for communion, don't come here and ask for a commitment ceremony, don't come to the church social... and don't come to my house. Don't let me know that it's something that's *real*.

"That's the same thing that's happening in hip-hop. It's like they're saying, *Be gay. We can't deny that queer people exist because we're inundated with it in the media. It's not something we can pretend away. We got [gay] cousins. We can't pretend you don't exist anymore. But don't be **gay**.* And gays in hip-hop are complicit with that when their actions say, *I cannot allow that to enter my mind by being active, by being sexual, by being open, by saying this is my partner, this is who I love.* It's like this guy who posted on the Okayplayer site saying, "I'm not a homophobe. I don't mind gay rappers. I just don't want to hear about what you do in bed."

"Now, what would hip-hop be if you forced every rapper to stop talking about how many girls he fucked? How many records would there be left? How many records would be on the radio? There wouldn't be many.

"And for me personally, what happened on the board when somebody said, '*Why do you have to say [your rhymes so explicitly] like that?*' My answer was: Because you asked me why I have to say it like that. Because you had an issue. Because you told me you had an issue with me saying it like that but you wouldn't dialogue with me about **why** you had an issue with me saying it like that. You didn't say you disagreed with it; you said you disagreed with me opening my mouth. And that's what I really have a problem with. It's not about you liking it or not because that's not why I'm saying it—for you to like it. For the most part I know you don't like it. I know you ain't with it. That's not something that's even important to me. But what bothers me is the idea that there's no space for conversation, that there's this attempt to shut people up. And the irony of that is that it's happening in a culture, hip-hop specifically, which allegedly prides itself on freedom of expression. The crux of hip-hop is *keep it real*. But it's not about keeping it real. It's about keep it where we can handle it."

Previously unpublished. The interviews in this article were conducted between June 6-10, 2000. The Bringing Mumia Home Benefit Concert took place Saturday, June 10.

Outro

Writing this book—compiling and fine-tuning old pieces, working on the new—was an exciting, exhilarating and angst-filled process. I think most (not all, but most) critics and academics who release such compilations/anthologies of their work do so to stake out territory, to assert their credentials and mark themselves as authorities on their subject. It's a foundation to stand on for future job possibilities, for building or cementing career status. Criticism for me has always been rooted in the very personal impulse, and the art I have been most viscerally drawn to (and which has inspired what I think is my strongest writing) has been that which wrestled with the questions that have plagued me since adolescence, having to do with issues of race and class and sexuality, having to do with the ways that pop culture reflects and shapes the realities and dreams of the audience, but also how people construct themselves from the cultural artifacts they are sold (movies, music, TV, radio, music videos.) I'm just trying to figure shit out for self, then share whatever I deduct just in case it might be of interest or value to someone else.

Volume One of *Blood Beats* and the upcoming second volume are not necessarily about me staking claim to future position as critic. These books come at a time when I am at a crossroads in my life, more in love with writing than ever but far less enamored of criticism and all the bullshit that surrounds it—the hardship of trying to earn a living while doing it, the cheap-whore poses (perfumed with both street slang and the chatter of academia) you have to or are expected to adopt in the writing, the expectation that you would and should ingratiate yourself in a machine that you should be taking to task—it's an age-old, tired lament and I ain't figured out how to best it.

These books are about providing clarity for me, so I can figure out if I am going to continue on this path or make a hard left and open some other door to some other life. Pure selfishness. But I do hope, and believe, that there is something of value beyond my melodramatic personal narrative—bringing a different voice and perspective to the table. Not definitive because I don't believe in "definitive" takes on art. But maybe some angles other than familiar ones. The filter of questions around race, sexuality, class, gender and the making of art... that filter being something than white/het'tro/male. A critical center that is melanin-based/pro-woman/pro-faggot & dyke/unabashedly-leftist/accessible, presented with the certainty that it is as valid and valuable as the still too white, still too male, still too hetero *status quo* setting for the critical voice.

That's all.

For Sakia Gunn and Rashawn Brazell

coming attractions
BLOOD BEATS: VOL. 2:

Same Old, Same Old: Black (and White) at the Movies
Stronger Than Pride: Sade's *Lover's Rock*
The Godmother of the French New Wave: Agnes Varda
Fuck, Die: *Baise-Moi*—Porno Art from France
Film Director Raoul Peck
Freddie Gets Fingered: Notes on the Prinze of Hollywood
Supa Sista: Ursula Rucker
Ja Rule, Krayzie Bone: Inside the New Sensitive Thug
Q-Tip: *Kamaal the Abstract*
Meeting Ledisi on a Wednesday: The Best Soul Singer in
America Breaks It Down
For Colored Girls: Kim Hill's Real Hip-Hop
The Cockettes: Living at the End of Imagination
Lauryn Hill *Unplugged*: She Makes the Songs Cry
Eminem's Imitation of Life
Antwone Fisher: Bonds Beyond Blood
R. Kelly: Tossed Salad, Tossed Cookies
Assholios and Goddesses: *Raising Victor Vargas* and *Lilya 4-Ever*
Whale Rider: Forefather Envy
Luther Vandross: *Dance with My Father*
From Capoeira to Catfights: *Madame Sata*
Worldwide Underground Sonic Jihad: Erykah Badu and Paris
Young Soul Rebels: Negro/Queer Experimental Filmmakers
PSTOLA: Packin' Heat
Fear of a Black Titty: Treating Janet Like You Don't Love Her
What Lies Beneath: Carl Hancock Rux
White Man's Burden: Eminem's *Encore*
David LaChappelle and *Rize*
Get Your Streak On: Missy Elliot's *Cookbook*
Meshell 2005
Kanye West: Up From the Middle Class
Mary J. Blige: *The Breakthrough*
Fugees Reunion: Hollywood & Vine

About the Author

Ernest Hardy writes about film and music from his home base of Los Angeles. His criticism has appeared in the *LA Weekly*, the *LA Times*, *Vibe*, *The New York Times*, *Rolling Stone*, the *Source*, *Millennium Film Journal*, *Flaunt*, *Request*, *Minneapolis City Pages*, and the reference books *1,001 Movies You Must See Before You Die* and *Classic Material: The Hip-Hop Album Guide*, among others. He's written liner notes for *Chuck D Presents: Louder Than a Bomb*, the box set *Say It Loud: A Celebration of Black Music in America*, *Curtis Mayfield: Gospel*, and the box set *Superstars of Seventies Soul*. A Sundance Fellow and a member of LAFCA (Los Angeles Film Critics Association), he's sat as a juror for the Sundance Film Festival, the San Francisco International Film Festival, the Palm Springs International Short Film Festival and Los Angeles Outfest. He's also co-programmed the FUSION Film Festival in Los Angeles. *Blood Beats: Vol. 1*, Hardy's first book, is a collection of his writing from 1996 to 2001.

Other titles from RedBone Press include:

does your mama know? An Anthology of Black Lesbian Coming Out Stories, ed. by Lisa C. Moore (ISBN 0-9656659-0-9) / $19.95

the bull-jean stories, by Sharon Bridgforth (ISBN 0-9656659-1-7) / $12.00

the bull-jean stories (Audio CD), by Sharon Bridgforth (ISBN 0-9656659-2-5) / $12.99

last rights, by Marvin K. White (ISBN 0-9656659-4-1) / $14.00

nothin' ugly fly, by Marvin K. White (ISBN 0-9656659-5-X) / $14.00

love conjure/blues, by Sharon Bridgforth (ISBN 0-9656659-6-8) / $14.00

Where the Apple Falls, by Samiya Bashir (ISBN 0-9656659-7-6) / $14.00

Spirited: Affirming the Soul and Black Gay/Lesbian Identity, edited by G. Winston James and Lisa C. Moore (ISBN 0-9656659-3-3) / $16.95

You can buy RedBone Press titles at your local independent bookseller, or order them directly from the publisher (RedBone Press, P.O. Box 15571, Washington, DC 20003).

Please include $2.50 shipping for the first book and $1.00 for each additional book.